Premodern Trade in World History

Trade and commerce are among the oldest, most pervasive, and most important of human activities, serving as engines for change in many other human endeavors.

This far-reaching study examines the key theme of trading in world history, from the earliest signs of trade until the long-distance trade systems such as the famous Silk Road were firmly established.

Topics covered include:

- products that were traded and why;
- the relationship between political authorities and trade;
- the rise and fall of Bronze Age commerce;
- the development of a maritime system centered on the Indian Ocean stretching from the Mediterranean to the South China Sea;
- the integration of China into the world system and the creation of the Silk Road;
- the transition to a modern commercial system.

Complete with maps for clear visual illustration, this vital contribution to the study of World History brings the story of trade in the premodern period vividly to life.

Richard L. Smith is Professor of History and Williams Distinguished Teaching Professor in the Humanities at Ferrum College, USA. His research interests are in North and West Africa and world history. He is the author of *Ahmad al-Mansur: Islamic Visionary* (2006) as well as numerous articles and book reviews in scholarly publications.

Themes in World History
Series Editor: Peter N. Stearns

The *Themes in World History* series offers focused treatment of a range of human experiences and institutions in the world history context. The purpose is to provide serious, if brief, discussions of important topics as additions to textbook coverage and document collections. The treatments will allow students to probe particular facets of the human story in greater depth than textbook coverage allows, and to gain a fuller sense of historians' analytical methods and debates in the process. Each topic is handled over time – allowing discussions of changes and continuities. Each topic is assessed in terms of a range of different societies and religions – allowing comparisons of relevant similarities and differences. Each book in the series helps readers deal with world history in action, evaluating global contexts as they work through some of the key components of human society and human life.

Gender in World History
Peter N. Stearns

Consumerism in World History
The Global Transformation of Desire
Peter N. Stearns

Warfare in World History
Michael S. Neiberg

Disease and Medicine in World History
Sheldon Watts

Western Civilization in World History
Peter N. Stearns

The Indian Ocean in World History
Milo Kearney

Asian Democracy in World History
Alan T. Wood

Revolutions in World History
Michael D. Richards

Migration in World History
Patrick Manning

Sports in World History
David G. McComb

The United States in World History
Edward J. Davies, II

Food in World History
Jeffrey M. Pilcher

Childhood in World History
Peter N. Stearns

Religion in World History
John Super and Briane Turley

Poverty in World History
Steven M. Beaudoin

Premodern Travel in World History
Steven S. Gosch and Peter N. Stearns

Premodern Trade in World History
Richard L. Smith

Premodern Trade in World History

Richard L. Smith

LONDON AND NEW YORK

First published 2009
by Routledge
2 Park Square, Milton Park, Abingdon, Oxon OX14 4RN

Simultaneously published in the USA and Canada
by Routledge
711 Third Avenue, New York, NY 10016

Routledge is an imprint of the Taylor & Francis Group, an informa business

© 2009 Richard L. Smith

Typeset in Garamond and Gill Sans by
Taylor & Francis Books

All rights reserved. No part of this book may be reprinted or reproduced or utilized in any form or by any electronic, mechanical, or other means, now known or hereafter invented, including photocopying and recording, or in any information storage or retrieval system, without permission in writing from the publishers.

British Library Cataloguing in Publication Data
A catalogue record for this book is available from the British Library

Library of Congress Cataloging in Publication Data
Smith, Richard L. (Richard Lee), 1945-
    Premodern trade in world history / Richard Smith.
        p. cm. – (Themes in world history)
    Includes bibliographical references.
    1. Commerce–History. 2. International trade–History. I. Title.
    HF352.S65 2008
    382.09–dc22   2008003200

ISBN 978-0-415-42476-9 (hbk)
ISBN 978-0-415-42477-6 (pbk)
ISBN 978-0-203-89352-4 (ebk)

For Kathleen Charpentier Smith
My wife and partner in work and life

Contents

Preface		viii
Acknowledgments		xi
1	Some introductory musings	1
2	In the beginning	13
3	The first link	24
4	Land of gold	40
5	Into the Aegean and out of the Bronze Age	54
6	Of purple men and oil merchants	63
7	Shifting cores and peripheries in the Imperial West	75
8	When India was the center of the world	84
9	Following the *Periplus*	99
10	The all-water route	110
11	From the Jade Road to the Silk Road	121
12	The last link	130
	Epilogue	137
	Select bibliography	144
	Index	150

Preface

Teachers of survey courses in world history have become increasingly aware of the need for suitable supplemental reading material on matters to which textbooks, under the command "to keep it short and sweet," can give only brief treatment. In most general texts, economic history is allotted short shrift when compared with political, military, and diplomatic concerns, and often even topics drawn from social, cultural, and intellectual history fare better. In a chapter about this particular state or culture or that particular time period, it is not unusual to find trade and commerce covered in a paragraph or at best a half page. Yet trade and commerce are among the oldest, most pervasive, and most important of human activities, serving as engines for change in many other human endeavors.

Recently the editors of several series designed for the supplemental readings market have made attempts to address this situation, and a number of useful books have become available. In general, they focus on trade in a particular commodity or related set of commodities, or a specific trade zone or system, or the interrelationship between trade and culture. They are intended to be case studies from which students draw larger conclusions. This book represents an attempt to go beyond the case study by providing a more general overview of the development of long-distance trade from its beginnings in the prehistoric period to the emergence of a system linking Afro–Eurasia in the first millennium CE.

Trade, like art and religion, appears to be characteristic of our species. Signs of trade in the form of seashell necklaces 100 miles from the sea appear very early in the archaeological record of *Homo sapiens*. The invention of the sled followed later by the wheel and sail provided the means for the movement of increasingly larger quantities of goods. The spread of agriculture, resulting in a huge growth of population, increasing social complexity, and the introduction of new products, caused trade to grow exponentially.

The organization of long-distance trade began to take shape in the early river valley societies that developed along the Tigris–Euphrates, Nile, and Indus. The great empires that succeeded them created trade zones for overland and riverain traffic. Powerful states became dependent on income from taxing trade and in return provided protection and built roads. At the same time maritime commerce brought shiploads of goods by wind and current across huge bodies of water such as the Mediterranean Sea and Indian Ocean. Long-distance systems merged into a system of systems tying parts into a single whole so goods could flow over land and sea from the Atlantic to the Pacific and the Siberian tundra to Madagascar and New Guinea. Overland its backbone was the so-called Silk Road, actually a complex of roads that reached its mature form in the early centuries of the first millennium CE. At sea a great maritime route linking the Mediterranean, Red Sea, Indian Ocean, and South China Sea coalesced at about the same time.

In its plan this book offers a blend of chronological and geographical organization with topical, thematic, and conceptual elements embedded within. Its principal focus is on the emergence of a great exchange system ultimately spanning parts of three continents, a process that took several thousand years. The themes that emerge from this study center on a series of interrelated questions. First, who did the trading, and what motivated them to do so? Second, what goods were traded and why, meaning what was the purpose for exchanging these particular goods? Third, how was the trade conducted, meaning how were goods transported, and what methodology did people employ in the act of exchange? And finally, what were the long-term consequences of this activity, particularly as they related to political matters (since there are excellent studies available on the cultural impact)? Too often in general surveys the political tail wags the economic dog, but not in this book.

Several points of clarification may be in order. First, the focus of this book is on long-distance trade, what in a modern sense may be thought of as foreign or international trade except that in the premodern context long-distance trade was possible within the Roman or Chinese empires while trade between independent Sumerian city states may have been foreign or international but was hardly long distance. Terminology can be a sticky point on other matters as in, for example, the use of words like trade, commerce, exchange, traffic, business, barter, and market or, in another example, goods, commodities, merchandise, wares, products, items, articles, and vendibles. Sometimes such words are interchangeable, and sometimes they refer to something very specific. In choosing words I have tried to be precise without being fussy, generally deferring to common usage with help from Webster's Third International when necessary. In place names I provide the name as it was in the period under consideration with the modern name, if available, in parentheses.

In matters of time this topic allows for a relatively loose framework, which is why I often refer to millennia or centuries rather than attempt more precise dates. I have used the somewhat awkward term of "premodern" (for lack of a substitute) to designate that period of human history extending from earliest times to the beginning of our era, marked off by the fundamental changes that occurred between the sixteenth and eighteenth centuries. Since this book concerns the development of the premodern system of long-distance trade, which was largely in place by the early centuries of the first millennium CE, only a brief synopsis is provided on the final millennium or so before the onset of the modern period.

Finally, at the conclusion of each of the first five chapters, I have added a section entitled "A closer look." This was inspired by the use of sidebars in textbooks and includes in-depth examinations of related material best highlighted by being set aside.

Acknowledgments

I would like to thank Peggie Barker and Cheryl Hundley of Stanley Library at Ferrum College for the cheery year-in-and-year-out assistance they provide in getting research materials to me and also John Bruton and Leslie Lambert of the Ferrum College administration for their support. I would also like to thank the anonymous staff in the interlibrary loan section of Aldermann Library at the University of Virginia for sharing their largesse so generously. I appreciate the suggestions made at the outset of this project by Professors Stephen S. Gosch of the University of Wisconsin-Eau Claire, Jerry Bentley of the University of Hawai'i, and Patrick O'Brien of the London School of Economics. To my mentor, Peter N. Stearns, I say once again, thank you for your direction, your wisdom, and above all your friendship.

Chapter 1

Some introductory musings

On the business of business

Exchange is a form of interchange between individuals or groups. It is the act of giving and taking one thing for another: goods, services, or some intangible item must change hands. Exchange is the engine that drives the circulation of commodities, items that flow through the economic system until they are consumed. And exchange involves reciprocity. Although goods circulate as the result of predatory activities such as brigandage, plundering, robbery, and piracy, these cannot be considered as exchange. Throughout history humans have engaged in a variety of consensual exchanges, two of the most important forms being gift-giving and trade. Whatever is being exchanged must have some utility, functional or social, in order to have a value assigned to it. That said, exchange can involve useful products such as metals and grains or products having only ceremonial, symbolic, or prestige value.

One of the oldest and most universal forms of consensual exchange is gift-giving, which originated as an aspect of intra-family and clan relations. In this, exchange was motivated more by social than economic factors: the goal was to maximize social contacts rather than reap material benefits. The giver of a gift gained esteem according to the perceived value of the gift. Thus it was not the possession of wealth that conferred prestige and power but the giving of wealth; it was truly better to give than receive. In tribal societies a common venue for ceremonial gift-giving was the feast where guests ate their fill and went home with presents as well. However, gift-giving was not simply a matter of gaining prestige through generosity, and usually the item was not a present in the sense that the giver expected nothing in return. Gift-giving established an obligation that led to counter gift-giving or the fulfillment of some duty, which in turn required a new round of transactions that theoretically was never-ending. Gift exchange often was used to forge links between groups or states. Among states in the ancient world, rulers often exchanged gifts and referred to each other as "brother," symbolizing their friendly relations. For centuries this served as the most important mechanism for transferring goods among certain states.

A gift could be repaid in many ways. If it was given from a superior to a subordinate, the return was usually in the form of service since a subordinate could not be expected to return an equivalent or more valuable item to a superior. Gift-giving usually involved delayed reciprocity: counter-gifts were not required immediately. Nevertheless, some reciprocity was expected sooner or later, and failure to repay within a reasonable time was taken as a sign of hostility. Among equals, a counter-gift that was worth less was a sign of weakness deserving of contempt. Far from being motivated by disinterested magnanimity, gift-giving could be as calculated and self-serving as profit-based trade.

The development of commercial trade based on market principles out of earlier forms of exchange was a cumulative process, not an accidental discovery or calculated invention that can be traced to a specific series of events. Like gift-giving, commercial trade was a consensual act. The object of commercial trade was to create wealth by generating profit. Trade operated through the "market," a process, which should be distinguished from the "marketplace," a location. The market was driven by profits or value maximization and controlled by a supply and demand mechanism in which commodities moved according to price. Trade required entrepreneurial behavior and was characterized by investment and risk-taking. Since the purpose of trade was to maximize returns in order to enrich oneself, economic considerations dominated social and political considerations. In gift-giving the social relationship was the crucial factor whereas in commercial trade the desire for the commodity itself motivated the transaction. No social bond was created as a result of the exchange. Trade was negotiated and funneled through intermediaries, who could be strangers, and the return was immediate rather than delayed. Furthermore, trade was a discrete transaction separate from any previous or subsequent acts between the parties and terminable at the end of the transaction. It was not part of a continuing process unless the parties agreed for it to be, and then it continued only as a "business relationship."

Gift-giving and trade were never exclusive to each other. Societies bound together through ceremonial exchange could simultaneously engage in commercial trade. And if gift-giving evolved earlier than trading for profit, the competition between the two did not remain steady over the centuries. In the modern world a residue of gift-giving can still be seen in such practices as birthday and holiday presents, but long ago exchange became dominated by commercial trade as gifts gave way to commodities.

In long-distance trade a society, at least in classical economic theory, concentrated on goods it could produce more efficiently than other societies either because it had better access to raw materials, superior technology, cheaper labor, or some other advantage. Trade was based on the cost of production in one place versus the cost of production in another with transportation expense added. In many instances the presence or absence of specific natural resources, such as metal, was the most important factor in determining imports and exports. As a society with a desirable commodity became part of an integrated network in which other societies with other commodities were doing the same, all parties should have reaped advantages. And as commercial networks expanded, competition increased, requiring more efficiency, which often meant increased specialization.

New goods that came in through exchange were often transformed from desirables into necessities. Demand could expand to cover an almost infinite range of commodities, but supply was usually limited and not very flexible. As an item came to dominate the production of a society's economy, that society came to depend more and more on trade. Thus, a larger and more varied economy had less need to trade with outsiders than a smaller economy. A place that had a lot of copper, olive oil, or horses but little else, or whose people were especially adept at producing beautiful jewelry or potent medicines and were capable of making more than they needed, was more likely to engage in trade than a place that had all of the above.

Natural resources were not always the most important factor. A place that had plenty of skilled labor but little in the way of natural resources was more likely to produce a labor-intensive product more efficiently and thus more cheaply than an area that had lots of minerals, forests, or fertile land but a smaller, more scattered, or less skilled work force. However, an export market was not likely to be based on an unskilled labor force: in the premodern world, unskilled labor was everywhere. Some qualitative difference had to be evident to induce customers to pay for an import. From earliest times the ancient Greeks exported olive oil and wine, products that were carried in pottery. By the classical period, the ceramics being produced by craftsmen in cities such as Athens were so beautiful that they became items for export themselves.

Demand endowed a commodity with value, which was assigned through the process of exchange. The value differed for each side: it was this judgment that made the exchange desirable. The value may have been based on the usefulness of the commodity, some social meaning that was attached to it, or some aesthetic property associated with it. In basic barter, to gain a desired commodity, a trader had to sacrifice something that he believed was of less value than the item he was getting. The key to this process was that each side had to be convinced that it was getting more for less. Looking at the transaction from the outside, however, an observer ought to conclude that these commodities had an equivalent value.

The long-distance trader made his profit by taking advantage of the different values accorded to commodities from area to area. He bought an item in one place and sold it in another where he knew the price was higher. He subtracted his costs, and the result was his profit. In theory, no one was the loser: bargains were made only when both sides could realize a profit. The exploitation, and there was plenty of it, took place on the production rather than the exchange level. Losses to the trader were mostly the result of misfortune – the death of pack animals, the sinking of a ship, spoiled or plundered cargo – or misinformation, such as bringing a shipment of goods to a place where the price turned out to be less than expected. A trader who ended up with a caravan of dates, hides, textiles, or tin in a place where the price was insufficient to cover his costs was not long for the business.

All trade situations eventually changed: either improved, deteriorated, or just went in new directions. A huge number of variables impacted on trade, including changing tastes, fashions, and consumption patterns; traditions and taboos; political and social upheavals; and war, to name a few. Nevertheless, even when most of the variables appear to have been similar, people often responded to them very differently.

On theories of trade

In recent years the study of the exchange and circulation of goods has been dominated by two controversies. The first centers on a theory referred to as "Substantivism" advocated by a group of scholars led by Karl Polanyi. This in effect elevates the old gift-giving versus profit-seeking discussion to the level of a theoretical controversy. Substantivism attacks what is referred to as "Formalism," which maintains that the way in which modern capitalist economies work – that is, through a market system – is the normal, standard way all economies have worked; it is a universal paradigm.

The Substantivists claim that the use of supply and demand to establish price did not appear until the fourth century BCE (in Greece) and that the mature market-driven profit-seeking system of price-fixing markets was not firmly established until the industrial revolution of the eighteenth and nineteenth centuries CE. They believe that people in earlier societies had non-market economies in which the exchange of goods was essentially a social act. The goal of exchange was to engender social relations, to form contacts, and to gain prestige as well as to acquire desired goods but not to make a profit from the sale of one's own goods. Supply and demand played no role in setting price. Thus the study of trade is useful primarily to determine social and political patterns. In place of entrepreneurs haggling in a free market, Polanyi saw what he called administered or treaty trade organized between governments. The traders were not private businessmen but government officials, and the prices and quantities of goods to be traded were fixed through treaties negotiated beforehand that remained in effect for long periods of time.

In recent years much new textual and archaeological material has been amassed that was not available to Polanyi, who wrote in the 1950s, or his followers, whose heyday extended across the two decades that followed. This new material shows that the Substantivists greatly overstated the role of the state and understated the importance of private entrepreneurship in premodern trade. Markets in which prices were set by supply and demand and evidence of private capital accumulation, investment, and risk-taking appear between the late-fourth and mid-third millennium BCE. So do indications that merchants were motivated by the desire to make a profit. And to confuse matters, private and state capital were often found within the same economy.

The second controversy involving long-distance trade centers on the ideas of Immanuel Wallerstein and is known as World Systems Theory. World systems were trading networks that spanned separate communities meshing them economically into a single whole. The driving force of such a system was the accumulation of capital, which was market-oriented, profit-induced, and structured to transfer surpluses unequally through the core–periphery concept. World markets create interregional and international divisions of labor in which the peripheral areas supply the core area with resources, in particular raw materials, which are undervalued, in return for manufactured goods, which are overvalued, ensuring the accumulation of capital at the core at the expense of the periphery. Thus cores exploit peripheries, rich states exploit poor states, and technologically advanced societies exploit technologically underdeveloped societies. The net beneficiaries are the ruling or elite classes of the cores, although they make sure the elite classes of the peripheries also benefit, guaranteeing their support in perpetuating the system.

Wallerstein believed that such a world system emerged in the sixteenth century CE and is a unique characteristic of modern capitalism. Others, however, have decided to use his model for understanding trade in much earlier periods. For them, modern capitalism is nothing more than the most recent incarnation of a system that extends in various manifestations far back in time. They see core–periphery structures as inherently unstable: cores could grow, shrink, and disintegrate. If a core grew enough, its periphery could become part of the core. New peripheries could be added to a core, and established peripheries could drop out. Peripheries in time could develop their own peripheries. If a system shifted enough, a periphery could become a core, often as the result of technology transfer, and a core could likewise become a periphery. Skeptics of a strict interpretation of world systems theory see the various permutations going farther. In some places, they maintain, cores and peripheries didn't exist, and in other places there was a multitude of cores. Nor did the component parts always function according to the model. For example, cores didn't always dominate their peripheries, peripheries were not always dependent on their cores, and finished products sometimes flowed from peripheries to core rather than vice versa.

Cores, peripheries, and the systems they were embedded in did not have to be synonymous with political entities. Cores and peripheries could exist together in the same state as, for example, in the Roman or Chinese empires, or a core could constitute a region of independent states as in ancient Sumer or Greece that exploited an area not under its direct political control. World economies were generally larger than the political entities that were contained within them.

Not everyone has joined the world systems bandwagon. Wallerstein himself continued to deny that his model could be projected back in time, maintaining that there is a fundamental difference between the modern capitalist world system and all preceding systems. Thus the controversy over world systems became an extension of the older Substantivism–Formalism debate, with Wallerstein joining the followers of Polanyi in insisting that modern capitalism is distinct from all earlier systems and their adversaries seeing continuity from ancient (or even prehistoric) to modern times. Those critical of extending the theory backwards point to the level of technology and the transportation and communication systems as being too underdeveloped to allow for any real economic unity across large geographical areas for any significant length of time. What, they ask, qualifies a commercial network in the Bronze Age, for example, as being a "world system" in any meaningful way rather than seeing it as nothing more than a series of interconnected local trading systems? They wonder aloud why the word "world" is used. The terminology ends up being grander than the historical phenomenon it describes. World systems theorists respond by claiming that a world system when applied to premodern history doesn't have to span the globe, nor does it require direct contact among all its participants. Instead it refers to a trading network extending beyond a physically delimited zone that is so integrated through exchange and trade that it forms a single commercial whole. Thus there can be simultaneous regional world systems, each in a sense comprising its own "world." Some casual observers see the whole matter as degenerating into a question of semantics.

For historians who see the development of world systems as extending back into the ancient world, the land of Mesopotamia and the larger region of Southwest Asia play a crucial role. Mesopotamia served as the oldest core, to be followed in time by Egypt, India, and China. Eventually world systems grew together while simultaneously expanding outward, encompassing new peripheries. Westward this process extended to the Mediterranean basin and later Europe; southward it traveled up the Nile into the African interior and down the Red Sea and Persian Gulf into the Indian ocean and across to Southeast Asia; northward and eastward it moved into Central Asia and beyond to Siberia and Mongolia. Dating this process becomes a matter of determining when separate systems were integrated enough to become a single system. The final product was an interacting Afro–Eurasian exchange zone from Atlantic to Pacific held together by interconnecting sinews of land and sea routes through which increasing quantities of raw materials, finished products, luxury items, and in some places basic consumer goods flowed.

So what can we learn from such controversies? First, as is typical of theoretical disputes in history and anthropology, both sides are right, and both sides are wrong. Carefully devised abstractions can obscure reality as easily as elucidate it. Strict theoretical positions may be interesting intellectual constructs to those smitten by the logic or beauty of an idea, but too often they don't fit the empirical evidence and thus don't help if our goal in studying history is to try to determine what really happened in the past. Second, models don't have to be universally applicable or completely right (no matter what their advocates say) to be useful when trying to determine general trends or in examining history in a conceptual way. Anyone studying the history of trade can learn much from the ideas of Polanyi and Wallerstein or for that matter from earlier theorists such as Marx and Adam Smith, keeping in mind that history is always sloppier than theorists would like it to be; that's why it's not a science.

No doubt, there were different kinds of exchange networks working in different ways, each with its own particular set of quirks. However, in the larger picture, over the course of millennia, commodities increasingly flowed ever farther afield. Slowly but irreversibly, as different ecological niches were absorbed and smaller trading systems became intermeshed, an interdependent Afro–Eurasian trade zone emerged, spatially connected even if its internal dynamics were not always structurally uniform. This system would continue, with many starts and stops, until the onset of the modern era.

A closer look: how we know

Reconstructing a picture of long-distance trade in the premodern world is done through a combination of ways. The two most important sources of information are archaeology and written material. Archaeology must begin with common sense. If we know that a certain people used a substantial amount of bronze but did not have local access to copper and tin deposits, we must question how this society got its bronze. Where did the raw materials come from? If we are able to discount warfare and plunder, what was exchanged in return?

Archaeology can indicate the movement of goods and sometimes provide enough information to make estimates of the quantity and frequency involved. Archaeological evidence is a good place to start looking for patterns since long-distance trade that is historically important should show consistency. In their excavations, archaeologists look for indicators of trade. Pottery from the Ubaid culture of Mesopotamia (5300–4000 BCE) has been found scattered across northern Syria up into Anatolia (Turkey) to areas where metal deposits were abundant. This likely signifies a trade route. Seals made from stone or metal to indicate ownership and the presence of lead weights and scale pans used for measurements are indicators of trade even when the products they were used for are long gone.

Important sites for archaeological excavations begin with tombs and hoards. Tombs often contain grave goods intended to accompany their inhabitants into the next world whereas hoards usually consist of valuable gold and silver objects, including coins. Another type of deposit consists of votive offerings left in a sacred place associated with gods or ancestral spirits. Often this was a particular spot in a river, marsh, or other body of water. Goods found in tombs, hoards, and votive deposits are indirect indicators of trade if it can be determined that they were not made locally.

A new field of archaeology that has proved fruitful although challenging and expensive is maritime or nautical archaeology. Shipwrecks are little time capsules, like grave sites except that the goods found in graves were deliberately placed there. Occasionally underwater work allows for spectacular discoveries as, for example, the Uluburun shipwreck (discussed in Chapter 5).

Sunken wooden ships deteriorate as do much of their cargoes but not clay-based ceramics. Pottery remains can help archaeologists deal with two central issues, dating and sourcing, the first a general matter in archaeological studies, the second more specifically related to questions involving trade.

Pottery is useful for the archaeologist because it was easily broken. When that happened, there was usually no reason to clean up the mess, so the shards were left where they fell. The material itself was virtually indestructible and could not be reused. Different places made pottery in their own ways, and styles and decorative fashions changed over time. Also various types of clay contained elements from different places, all of which give archaeologists a good idea as to when and where a piece originated.

Unfortunately, archaeology can be of little help with organic commodities referred to as "archaeologically invisible." These include foods – grains, spices, condiments, beverages, preserved fish, and vegetable oils – and such products as papyrus, skins, unguents, medicines, cosmetics, salt, timber, exotic woods, and many more as well as slaves. Textiles tend to disintegrate, but spindle whorls do not. Raw materials such as metals and glass leave few traces once they are converted into finished products. And if metals don't rot and can't be digested, most corrode, and all can be melted down, which is frequently the fate of anything made of gold or silver. Once metal is alloyed or remelted, chemical analysis cannot be used for sourcing. We must operate under the realization that archaeological evidence is usually patchy, circumstantial, and ambiguous, and conclusions drawn from it are speculative and can be overturned from new data uncovered on the next big dig. Archaeologists deal in probabilities; they are usually cautious in drawing conclusions and rarely make definitive statements. As a result, the literature on long-distance trade is punctuated with sentences that begin with "it is likely," and the word "might" is used a lot.

Along with archaeological evidence, the other major source of information on premodern long-distance trade is written accounts. Of course, the huge bulk of everything written on trade and every other topic in the past has been lost, and much material modern scholars would be ecstatic to find never existed because it was not considered important enough to record. If archaeological evidence comes with no intrinsic meaning and must be interpreted, some forms of written evidence come already interpreted and can be biased or even intentionally falsified, although this is usually more the case for political than economic history. An archaeological find represents a concrete fact, words written down by an ancient author not necessarily so. On the positive side, written sources often provide a context for understanding and interpreting artifacts. The actual process of exchange cannot be detected archaeologically; written sources can tell us how trade was carried on not just what was traded.

Written sources can be divided into two categories: documents, which can be administrative, economic, or legal in nature; and narrative, which may include travel accounts and works of history, geography, natural science, religion, and literature. Documents found together in stockpiles are usually referred to as archives. They can come from government administrative units, temples, commercial entities, families, and private individuals. Archival sources have distinct limitations since whoever was responsible for producing a document was under no compunction to provide a complete picture of the commercial system it represented. Rarely are state and public administrative records, for example, helpful in understanding such matters as how markets worked. Nevertheless, documentary evidence can provide an immense amount of information, the equivalent of an intact shipwreck or unplundered tomb.

Using documentary evidence is largely the realm of specialists. Access to materials is usually limited, and possessing the necessary linguistic skills can be challenging. Many narrative accounts, on the other hand, are readily available in translation, including some firsthand travelers' accounts. The most important source for Indian Ocean trade in the early first millennium CE, for example, is the *Periplus Maris Erythraei* written by an anonymous author, probably a Greek-Egyptian trader. The *Periplus* is intended to be a practical guide for shippers and merchants sailing from Egypt through the Red Sea and either down the East African coast or across the ocean to India. It includes some sailing information but is mostly about trade, including what was bought and sold in each port, taxes and duties, and the disposition of local authorities.

The *Periplus Maris Erythraei* is an exceptional source but not unique. A genre of accounts known as the periplus tradition (from *periploi*: circumnavigation) developed from reports by merchants and sailors describing foreign places. However, there are dangers in dealing with travelers' accounts. Along with their own firsthand observations travelers brought back hearsay, and often it is not clear exactly what the writer actually saw and what he only heard about. Accounts could include real or imaginary journeys and often contained flights of fantasy. The most insidious use of bad information came from sources that intentionally disseminated false material. Such commercial dirty tricks usually originated with middlemen intent on discouraging interlopers by conjuring up monsters, freaks, evildoers, bad weather, impassable geographical features, and other creative devices. Sometimes this worked, and sometimes it didn't. When the Roman naturalist Pliny the Elder was told a fantastic story about the source of cinnamon, he sneered: "these tales have been invented by natives to raise the price of their commodities," and he was right. Nevertheless, Pliny's work – like that of other ancient writers – contains its fair share of humbuggery. Once in writing, inaccurate information could be copied from book to book, often over a period of centuries, until it was considered to be fact.

Probably the best known traveler of the ancient Mediterranean world was Herodotus, the only literary source of any importance for the classical Greek period as, for the most part, the Greeks didn't consider commerce as worthy of writing about. For Herodotus and other writers it was all a matter of choosing good informants or, too often, using whoever was available. Herodotus made sincere if not always successful attempts to obtain good information and frequently advises his readers "this is what I've been told about such-and-such by so-and-so," with the implication that you can take it or leave it.

Herodotus was more than just a traveler. Much of the information in his work came from other sources, which qualifies him in part as a second type of narrative author, the scholar. The most useful writers of the Roman period often traveled quite a bit, but essentially they were scholars. A good example is the Greek author Strabo, whose life straddled the first centuries BCE and CE. He journeyed around the eastern Mediterranean gathering information in many places, including Rome and Alexandria, the latter containing the world's most complete library. The result was the *Geography*, the best of all ancient geographical accounts providing information on the world as known by the educated classes of the Roman Empire. Strabo used many sources, and it is through him and a few others that parts of lost works have survived.

Sometimes earlier sources were used indirectly through an intermediary as in the case of Strabo borrowing from Artemidorus (now lost), who in turn borrowed from a second century BCE writer named Agatharchides. He wrote three works, a history of Europe and a history of Asia, both of which are lost, and a book on the Erythreaean Sea (the Red Sea and western side of the Indian Ocean), which a modern scholar, Stanley M. Burstein, has cleverly reconstructed in part by putting fragments of it together from three later sources, including Strabo. Agatharchides got much of his information from reports made by official missions of exploration and trade sent out by Alexander the Great and the kings of the Ptolemaic dynasty in Egypt, which Agatharchides had access to because he was an assistant to a counselor of one of the Ptolemaic kings.

Strabo's work, so crucial to our understanding of the ancient world, is fortunate to have survived intact given that an enormous proportion of what was written did not. Complementing (and sometimes contradicting) Strabo is the even larger work of an author known today as Pliny the Elder, who lived a generation after Strabo. His great work, the *Natural History*, remains a virtual encyclopedia of human knowledge for its time, ranging in topics from cosmology, astronomy, and meteorology to famous wine drinkers and the bad breath of animals. Parts of it are extremely useful as, for example, a large section dedicated to the olive and its oil, one of the engines of commerce in the ancient Mediterranean.

The generation after Pliny saw the last ancient source to provide a substantial body of information for use today. Claudius Ptolemy (85–165 CE) was from the scientific school of geography (Strabo represents the descriptive or human school), a scholar more interested in mathematics and map coordinates than economics and culture. He worked out of the library in Alexandria, and much of his information was obtained third hand. Unfortunately, Ptolemy's opus as it passed down through the centuries has been worked and reworked by later scholars incorporating new data in an attempt to update and keep him current, which is why there are multiple versions today, none of which can be determined definitively as being the most authoritative.

The people who lived in the Mediterranean basin were not the only ones to write accounts and keep records that can be useful today. On the other side of Eurasia, the Chinese were developing their own genre of narrative in the form of official dynastic histories. In the Han dynasty (202 BCE–220 CE) the state began employing historians to compile official histories from archival sources that continued under later dynasties. Chinese historiography had several practical goals, the most important of which was to serve as reference material for use by government ministers in making decisions. Histories often incorporated texts or summaries of documents, official reports, statistics provided by various offices in the bureaucracy, and records from embassies and accounts of travelers, which now serve as a major source of information on areas such as Southeast Asia.

Authors of dynastic histories were essentially compilers, although sometimes they showed a distinct critical element as well. The best of them was also the earliest. Sima Qian (145–86 BCE) came from a family that had served for generations as Grand Astrologers. His father, Sima Tan, had started writing a general history of China but apparently did not get very far, so on his deathbed he charged his son with the task of finishing it. This took Sima Qian most of the rest of his life. The result was the *Shiji* (*Historical Records*), a sweeping tour de force from the mythical beginnings of the Chinese people down to his own day, which if completely translated into English would likely amount to several thousand pages. The *Shiji* set the pattern for all future government-sponsored dynastic histories. Of these, one is particularly useful in examining the opening of Chinese trade with the west. The *Han Shu* (*History of the Former Han*) by Ban Gu (32–92 CE) covers the events of the first half of the Han dynasty (202 BCE–9 CE). It is instructive to note that

Ban Gu died in prison, and Sima Qian was castrated (for something he said rather than wrote), which has led to the observation that historians in China were in a risky business. Parts of the *Han Shu* are so similar to the *Shiji* as to indicate wholesale plagiarism, and for a long time it was assumed that Ban Gu had simply lifted relevant sections from Sima Qian. However, some modern scholars now believe that parts of one or the other manuscript were lost and eventually reconstructed using the surviving manuscript many centuries later. The question of which manuscript survived and was copied has not been resolved to everyone's satisfaction.

Both the *Shiji* and the *Han Shu* include discussions of commercial relations with trading partners. Historical annals, however, whether Chinese or otherwise, have not proved to be great storehouses of material about trade. They are more interested in political and military ventures, the great acts of the high and the mighty, not the common behavior of ordinary people engaged in such mundane matters as how merchants reached a price, or where they stored their goods, or how many camels arrived at some particular time from some oasis or another and what they were laden with.

Using common sense, a healthy dose of twenty-first century skepticism, and modern historical techniques when necessary, it is usually not difficult to filter out blatant misinformation from the record. We must always keep in mind, however, that the narrative evidence we have access to, like that from archaeology and archival sources, is very selective, focusing most of all on what happened rather than on how it happened and least of all on why it happened. Even within these bounds our knowledge depends largely on what survived and what has been discovered – in other words, on luck. This changes as new information becomes available and, when it does, so will our interpretation of what really happened.

Chapter 2

In the beginning

If early hominids exchanged goods outside the immediate group to which they belonged, no archaeological evidence of it exists. Forager bands gathered materials in one location on their migratory rounds and transported them some distances – modern foraging groups normally do this up to a range of about 50 miles – but there is no indication they exchanged them with other groups. Archaeological evidence seems to indicate, for example, that Neanderthal groups, representing the closest relatives to anatomically modern humans, didn't trade with each other as the tools they made stayed with them. The same kind of evidence, however, seems to indicate that members of our own species may have engaged in such behavior very early on. Anatomically modern humans living in a cave in Tanzania between 100,000 and 130,000 years ago had tools made of obsidian, the closest deposit of which was 200 miles away, several times beyond the range of normal foraging. The most obvious conclusion is that this indicates the presence of an early exchange network.

Exchange between people living considerable distances from each other, beyond the range of normal movement, and perhaps other changes associated with the Late Paleolithic, may have been part of a strategy to deal with increased environmental stress, specifically the last glacial onslaught. One idea is that the earliest trade probably occurred when hunting bands accidentally bumped into each other and each discovered it had something the other wanted. This is certainly a reasonable, if unprovable, scenario, keeping in mind, however, that dealing with strangers in the Paleolithic world was unpredictable and may have been dangerous, so most exchange took place among groups who were connected to each other. Exchange was done through social networks determined by family and clan affiliations. Connected groups could stretch across vast areas although the exchanges that occurred were at best occasional and unsystematic. Social networks were held together by periodic meetings at special sites, during which a variety of activities was held to cement relationships. These included rituals and initiations, feasting, the selection of marriage partners, the exchange of information, and the exchange of goods particular to the area from which each group came. This was likely done in a group setting, not as an individual activity. The guiding principle was reciprocity, symbolizing the promise of mutual assistance, not profit.

Paleolithic exchange did not generally involve goods that were necessary for everyday living. Items could have some practical use as, for example, allies could exchange weapons made from local stone. Most likely, articles that traveled long distances had ritual or social value, such as carved figurines or ocher for skin application. The use of ornaments for personal decoration, including beads, necklaces, bracelets, and pendants made of bone, antler, animal teeth, shell, and stone, became popular. The distance an object traveled became a measure of its worth. Being exotic, that is, coming from outside one's immediate range, provided an appeal in itself and, because it was special, it made its owner special. By traveling far, even a mundane object could become valuable as in the case of certain kinds of flint and attractive seashells that were transported hundreds of miles.

Shell beads made from a certain snail species have turned up in Morocco dated to 82,000 years ago. The same style of beads from the same species made at roughly the same time has also been found in neighboring Algeria and distant Israel, prompting speculation on the existence of an exchange system or perhaps even an early form of currency, however improbable. Improbability turned into impossibility when in 2004 similar beads turned up in South Africa, sparking a media furor over the possibility of a prehistoric trans-African economy. But coincidence can play funny tricks; the skill is in determining where coincidence ends and serious consideration should begin. Most informed observers, trained to be skeptical of unfounded speculation and determined to use common sense in such cases, still consider the African snail enigma a curious bit of coincidence.

About 10,000 years ago, the world began a radical transformation as people settled down and started to domesticate plants and animals. According to one model, people tended to congregate in places that were crossroads for exchange and commercial activity. In the relatively small area of Southwest Asia where Asia, Europe, and Africa come together, the interaction of ideas and technologies and the exchange of goods were especially active. There, agriculture was first born, bringing a great increase in exchange. For a while, agriculturalists swapped products with the remaining hunter–gatherers such as, for example, wild animal meat and honey for grain, beer, and pottery, with neither of the participants dependent on the other for subsistence. The emergence of pastoralist societies offering dairy products, meat, and leather to agriculturalists provided an even greater stimulus for trade. Communities were still bound within ceremonial systems where valuables, as defined by their high symbolic content, were exchanged. Social alliances were the motivating consideration rather than cost–benefit analysis. Products could serve a range of purposes, and their significance could change as they circulated. Axes, for example, made from exotic stone and deposited as votive offerings, sometimes show considerable wear, indicating that at one time they were employed for practical use but later became ceremonial objects. Periodic meetings were no longer the principal venue for exchange; now groups were linked in chains, each link having access to some resource the others desired.

Commercial trade in a marketplace setting, where strangers were engaged in profit-driven entrepreneurial behavior, was as dangerous in the Neolithic as groups bumping into each other were in the Paleolithic. Dealing with people from different places with whom one did not have formal ties required assurances of security, which in the early Neolithic was usually not available. Goods generally moved in a linear fashion in what is referred to as a down-the-line system or percolated through one community to another in a trickle trade system so that, when traced, they decrease in proportion to the distance from their source. Items traveled farther than people so that no one had to move beyond his own territory.

In the later Neolithic, distribution patterns show signs of change. Most exchange was still between people who knew each other and was based on reciprocity although some transactions may have included elements of commercial trade such as bargaining. Likewise most goods continued to be sent down-the-line and often circulated over a period of generations but over increasingly larger areas. Some goods were also beginning to be sent directionally, that is, direct from their source to a specific location bypassing areas in between. Shells from the Indian Ocean have turned up in fifth-millennium BCE Syria, almost 1,000 miles away. As Neolithic economies allowed for steady population rise, more people fueled a demand for more goods. Larger, more stable communities attracted people with something to swap. Between 6250 and 5400 BCE, the largest of these communities was Catal Huyuk in south central Anatolia. At its height Catal Huyuk may have had a population of 4,000–6,000, making it the largest known settlement in the world at the time. Its inhabitants grew wheat and barley and traded cattle, which had the great advantage of transporting itself. They also traded obsidian from a nearby source, for which there was a great demand elsewhere. The ruins of Catal Huyuk contain an extraordinary quantity of imported material featuring shells from the Mediterranean and different kinds of exotic stones.

Around the Mediterranean long-distance trade did not wait for the rise of cities and states. People in boats were coast hugging from shore to island and island to island carrying and exchanging goods. This varied in scale from fishermen who did part-time trading to peddlers who stopped at villages along the coast to see what the locals had to offer. Many Neolithic sites were located near natural deposits of desirable stone. Cores and preforms, which had been roughed out or undergone some preliminary shaping and would be made into products elsewhere, as well as finished products such as blades, were sent out. Some settlements were composed of specialized craftsmen who manufactured products for export, such as ceramics or tanned hides. One rock that did not have to be crafted into a product was salt. The Paleolithic diet of wild animal meat had provided sufficient salt to satisfy human needs, but the Neolithic diet featuring principally cereals often did not, necessitating the development of the salt trade.

As agriculture spread into places such as central and northern Europe, vast forests had to be cleared, creating a demand for axes. The axe was a functional tool, but it also became an important prestige item, a symbol of maleness. Because it could be both utilitarian and ceremonial and was a high-demand product, the trade in axes may have had more of a commercial bent than either the giving of prestige gifts or the bartering of basic subsistence goods. Exactly when professional traders guided by an entrepreneurial ethos and operating on strictly market principles entered the scene, however, remains a matter of sometimes ferocious debate among archaeologists, anthropologists, and historians.

Some axe-producing operations were quite large. In the fifth and fourth millennia BCE, quarries in the Vosges Mountains of eastern France produced axe-heads of aphanite, a black rock with close texture. Partially finished objects were transported to nearby villages where they were made into polished axes, then exported over an east–west exchange network that extended as far as Switzerland. An even more widespread system involved jadeite, a fine-grained light green rock obtained from the western Alpine regions of France and Italy and sent over three different routes reaching from Scotland to southern Spain. The Irish made a large portion of their axes from porcellanite, a hard, dense, siliceous rock that looks like unglazed porcelain. Although only a few sources of it existed, all of which were located on the northeast corner of the island, porcellanite axes spread throughout Ireland and into Britain.

The most important stone used in Europe during the Neolithic Period was flint, considered especially desirable for making daggers, spears, and sickles as well as axes. Early exploitation of flint deposits was done seasonally by pastoralists or on an episodic basis by small groups rather than by permanently stationed workforces. Eventually some flint mines came to be quite large as at one site in Poland where the minefield covered an area 2.5 miles long and included 1,000 mineshafts, some reaching 36 feet deep. Archaeologists have located trader hoards of flint daggers in remote northern Sweden. Often in a given archaeological site both local and non-local flint implements can be found together, the non-local flint having come from different sources at varying distances away. Different varieties of flint were more highly prized than others, with chocolate-colored being the most favored even though from a purely functional standpoint it made no better implements. Indeed exotic axes in general were sometimes made from stones that were not as suitable as local varieties. Even more peculiar, people often chose to exploit rock sources that were difficult or even dangerous to access, working, for example, on narrow ledges in exposed highland areas, even when acceptable substitutes were available closer to home and under far more favorable conditions.

The increased prominence of prestige items in the archaeological record indicates an important socio-political change that appears in later Neolithic societies. Hunter–gatherers and early agriculturalists lived in basically egalitarian, acephalous societies. Different people enjoyed different status as, for example, elders and shamans, but there were no social hierarchies. Beginning in the fourth millennium BCE, the importance of social dominance and eventually the appearance of ranking and the assumption of power became more evident. In the struggle to determine who would emerge on top, the control over access to outside exchange networks became a key factor. Long-distance trade, social differentiation, and power concentration were all fueled by the development of metallurgy. During the Bronze Age, which began c. 3000 BCE, the trade in both raw metals and finished metal products grew enormously. Metals became associated with high prestige. Ornaments of gold replaced shell, and ceremonial axes came to be made of copper and bronze. Daggers and spears, drinking cups, lurs (large S-shaped bronze trumpets), equipment used for horseriding and charioteering, jewelry and other ornaments, and, above all, swords became the items of choice in exchange systems. Other products became available with the use of wool-producing sheep, which provided a basis for the textile industry, and the spread of horse domestication. Local communities became more interconnected, and regional exchange systems became interregional.

Trade helped to promote the rise of political power and the development of social inequality: where wealth accumulated, leaders emerged, and eventually states formed. If the key to power was control over wealth, those who controlled long-distance trade may have imposed themselves over the old kinship structure of society and emerged as a ruling class. Or perhaps the ruling class did not emerge from traders but came instead from the ranks of the tribal chiefs, that is, people who already had political power. Again, however, the procurement and distribution of wealth was the means to power. Wealth from trade provided a leader with the ability to pay for an army that could be used to get the rest of the community to obey him. And, by controlling trade, he had access to prestige goods from the outside, which he used to attract clients, creating a system of ranks in a structure that became the state.

In such a system, the ruler determined who would have access to what; in other words, he regulated demand as well as supply. The ruler and the elites who supported him would also have control over local specialists who made luxury items to be used as exports. Such a system was not based on commercialized market conditions in which luxury goods were sold to whoever was able to pay for them. Rather rulers defined the social and political status of others by controlling the system of wealth distribution. The flow of prestige goods as gifts determined the hierarchy, and wealth in the form of exotic valuables validated one's social status. Luxury goods were symbols of personal superiority, and the wearing, display, or consumption of them distinguished the elite from the common people. The larger a leader's capacity for dispensing gifts, the greater his hold over those to whom he gave them and thus the greater his power. Prestige markers distributed downward forged loyalty; it was on them that political power was based.

Utilitarian items continued to be exchanged, but the mass of common people reaped little immediate benefit from the metals revolution. A few copper sickles may have been made in copper-rich areas, but bronze plows don't usually appear next to bronze swords in hoards or among grave goods. As for the long-distance trade in luxury goods, its impact on the common people was hardly positive. Rather they ended up working harder in the fields, workshops, quarries, and mines to produce whatever was used for exchange by the elites to further their own status.

Long-distance trade in the Bronze Age impacted not only within societies but between them. Trade, gift exchange, and marriage links helped to lubricate relations between elites. Exchange systems were often designed so that elites could provide each other with the exotica needed to maintain power within their own spheres. Exchange did not have to take place directly between two parties. Participants were tied into a grid of exchange that allowed a giver to receive something in return from someone in the system that was not necessarily the direct recipient of his own gift. Rulers of equal stature were expected to exchange gifts equivalent in value, but if one could not match the other, he became obligated and thus inferior. A group that had better access to some prestige item through control over raw material could exert dominance over another group if its leaders needed the prestige material as a means for maintaining their superiority within their own group. But reciprocity was still the principle on which exchange was founded. The concept of making a profit in the sense of gaining a material surplus from an exchange was an idea whose time had not quite come.

The expansion of trade routes and the assertion of control over them by elites, the development of trade centers as places of wealth accumulation linking trade routes together, the formation of social hierarchies, the alignment of ranking among chiefs leading to paramount chiefs and ultimately chief-of-chiefs or king, and finally the emergence of state structures are best seen as interactive processes. By the close of the Bronze Age, long-distance exchange networks were in place from Italy to Sweden. Regions as peripheral as Hungary and Denmark were able to acquire large quantities of metal from considerable distances, transform it into finished products recognized for fine craftsmanship, and re-export them to other areas of considerable distance. Europe, however, was far from being the commercial center of Afro–Eurasia. Other, more central, places had earlier moved into more complex political and social forms, what is roughly referred to as "civilization." The earliest of these complex societies, Sumer and Egypt, arose in places that served as trade corridors. Sumer, in southern Mesopotamia, had the metal-rich Anatolian highlands to the north and the Persian Gulf, leading into the Indian Ocean, to the south. In Egypt, the Nile Valley provided the only direct access between the Mediterranean basin and the interior of Africa. It was here in hot lands with lots of river water and an abundance of grain that trade would begin to spread its tentacles from interregional to intercontinental systems.

A closer look: obsidian and amber

Two non-perishable commodities that serve as good examples of how long-distance trade worked in the Neolithic and Bronze Ages are obsidian and amber. Obsidian is volcanic glass formed by the cooling of viscid lava. It is black with a bright luster, spherulitic, hard but brittle, easily flaked, and almost indestructible. Amber is a yellow to brown translucent fossil resin that comes in different varieties depending on transparency and compactness. Compared to stone or metal, it is a soft, light material that is easily cut and takes a fine polish.

In the prehistoric world, nothing made a sharper edge for knives, daggers, scrapers, razors, sickles, and projectile points for spears, harpoons, and arrowheads than obsidian. It was utilitarian but not essential: other materials such as flint and chert were acceptable substitutes, and modern observers have sometimes referred to obsidian as "rich man's flint." It was the rock of choice for cutting as well as a status symbol. By Neolithic standards, it was a high-value item. Obsidian can be found only where there has been recent volcanic activity. Areas between deposits are completely devoid of it. Outcroppings are usually small and homogeneous in composition, and variations in trace elements make each source chemically distinct. As a result, testing can easily determine where a particular piece came from. This makes it a good indicator of trade routes, and indeed obsidian represents the earliest example of the widespread distribution of a non-perishable product. According to the Roman naturalist Pliny, obsidian was named for a fellow countryman, one Obsius, who discovered it in Ethiopia. Early man in Africa did use hand axes of obsidian although this was 100,000 years before Obsius lived. And Obsius did not have to go all the way to Ethiopia to find it since the Natufians, a proto-Neolithic culture of Southwest Asia, started trading for obsidian 10,000 years earlier. Obsidian may not have been the earliest commodity exchanged on a large scale across long distances, but it is the earliest for which substantial archaeological evidence remains.

Despite the advantage we enjoy in being able to determine the sources of obsidian, its trade was complex, and the various nuances involved are still not completely understood. We are not even sure whether it was ever traded on a for-profit basis by professional merchants. In certain instances, it was definitely not, but in others there is just enough circumstantial evidence to make us think, well, perhaps. And a good deal of flux is apparent in the obsidian trade. Over a period of time, a particular site can go from having 90 percent of its stone tools in obsidian to practically nothing and later back up to 90 percent. No doubt the trade was widespread, and today obsidian tools are found scattered across Southwest Asia and parts of Europe hundreds of miles from their source. Obsidian could travel in the form of raw nodules, preforms and cores, or finished blades. No wheeled vehicles or even pack animals were used; obsidian was carried by humans on foot or by boat. Initially this trade appears to have been down-the-line, but in some places, particularly where boat travel was involved, it became directional. Early Neolithic people inherited Paleolithic networks of contacts through which obsidian initially moved, and eventually the obsidian trade itself developed a whole new series of networks for subsequent generations of products to flow through.

Large-scale obsidian trade first appeared in Southwest Asia. The major sources were located at spots stretching from west to east across central Anatolia, ancient Armenia, and northern Iran. Most of the distribution shows a fall-off pattern with villages near a source using a very high percentage of obsidian tools and its presence declining with distance. Nevertheless, some Anatolian obsidian can be found up to 600 miles away, and Armenian obsidian reached as far as Bahrain in the Persian Gulf although nearby Qatar imported its obsidian from the opposite direction on the southwestern tip of the Arabian peninsula. Egypt also used the Arabian source and another in nearby Ethiopia, where a natural outcrop is reported to have been located near the mouth of a bay buried under a mountain of sand in the Red Sea. Obsidian from southeastern Slovakia and northeastern Hungary was traded to people living in southern Poland across a 5-day journey 120 miles over the Carpathian Mountains. In the meantime, the same people in southern Poland were exporting their flint to Silesia 120 miles to the west.

In Italy and the Aegean region, obsidian had to travel by sea. Italy was served by several islands, including Lipari off the north coast of Sicily, Palmorala between Rome and Naples, and southern Sardinia. In the early Neolithic one site in northern Italy began importing cores from Sardinia 270 miles away and Palmorala 300 miles away. In the middle Neolithic it added a small portion of imports from Lipari 500 miles away. By the late Neolithic, the Lipari product constituted almost 90 percent of this market, apparently because it was clearer and more glass-like. In this case, Lipari obsidian seems to have become a prestige item, and quality was considered more important than distance.

The Aegean Sea region had one major source, which was on the island of Melos directly north of Crete and east of the southern tip of Greece. Melian obsidian ultimately reached all around the area, including far inland. However, unlike Italy, there is no indication of directional trade, nor is there any question that the Melian trade was not profit-driven. Obsidian was being hauled off the island before anyone lived there and, after settlers did arrive, they did not live near the quarries and apparently made no attempt to establish a monopoly over them. Much obsidian was obtained by passersby – initially tuna fishermen and later merchant sailors transporting other goods such as metals and pottery, who stopped to collect it for ballast. When the transporters reached their ultimate destination, the obsidian was distributed down-the-line, accruing no real cost of transportation. Obsidian was also obtained from Melos by special-purpose trips made by knappers in the employ of the great Bronze Age palaces of Minoan Crete and Mycenaean Greece. In both instances, obtaining obsidian was a self-serve, cash-and-carry operation without the cash.

The Bronze Age did not bring an end to obsidian's popularity since few early tools were made of copper or bronze. The use of iron, however, spelled the decline of obsidian as a major item of trade although it continued to be used for ornamental objects such as statuettes and for decorative purposes in mosaics. The Egyptians made small elegant tables of it. The large-scale trade in amber came after that of obsidian and differed in significant ways. It was not used in bulk, was not utilitarian in function, and would oxidize and disintegrate under adverse conditions. Amber occurs naturally in various parts of the world and was often found in the soil, in beds of lignite, along sea and lake shores, and in coastal depressions. A few places around the Mediterranean, in particular Sicily, contained deposits, but the major source of European amber was around the Baltic Sea in a belt stretching from Britain to the Ukraine. The origin of this enormous deposit was a primeval forest that once existed in Finland but was eventually spread by glacial and water action to its present extent. All of the amber used in Neolithic and Bronze Age trade came from the Baltic amber belt.

During most of the Neolithic period, the use of amber was confined to its source area. It was gathered as nodules and taken to sites, a major one being in Latvia, where the raw material was worked into finished products such as beads and buttons. This began to change in the late Neolithic as amber spread in small quantities into Central Europe, but the trade came into its own in the Bronze Age, expanding south and west. The principal use was for ornaments, especially necklaces and pendants often deposited as grave goods, but amber workers also became more creative, turning out statuettes, reliefs, and incised plaques. While the possession of an obsidian knife may have brought status to an individual in an egalitarian society during the Neolithic, amber became part of the Bronze Age prestige exchange system that accompanied the development of hierarchies and the social stratification process. It was a product elites competed for; in one royal Mycenaean Greek shaft grave alone, 1,200 amber beads were found.

Amber became a major item of trade in the Bronze Age because places such as Denmark and other areas of northern Europe needed metals that were available in Central Europe. The north had to have something to exchange, which doubtless included perishables such as furs and perhaps fish and seal products, but all that remains in the archaeological record is amber. In Denmark amber was too common to be considered valuable and too widespread for its distribution to be monopolized by elites. The Roman historian Tacitus describes the far ends of Germania on the bounds of the sea "that girds the earth," where the Aestii, who collected amber, lived: "For a long time, indeed it lay unheeded like any other jetsam, until Roman luxury made its reputation. They [the Aestii] have no use for it themselves. They gather it crude, pass it on unworked, and are astounded at the price it fetches." So much amber was drained from Denmark its use there practically disappeared.

Ancient writers referred to an amber route running through Europe, but a series of trading networks would be more accurate. Indeed, Baltic amber reached many places that did not send bronze to Denmark because they lacked metal deposits themselves, indicating a complex and interrelated system. Raw amber was carried south to working centers where skilled craftsmen flaked it into finished products. One such center of production was in northern Italy, where craftsmen produced fibulae for re-export south and east. Other distribution systems were more circuitous as, for example, the one that brought amber first to the Wessex culture of south Britain, where it was fashioned into exquisite necklaces, then across Europe to Switzerland and south to the Adriatic Sea. Amber beads of Baltic origin were found on the Uluburun shipwreck off the southern coast of Turkey. At one point, rival amber networks, one running up the German river system and the other from the eastern Baltic through Poland, had to devise substantial detours to avoid each other's fortresses.

The Greek historian Herodotus tells an interesting story about an unnamed product that modern historians assume was amber. According to him, this product originated with a people called the Hyperboreans, whom he describes as living on the edge of the world. Periodically these Hyperboreans, in honor of a long-established tradition, would send "sacred objects tied up inside a bundle of wheat straw" to their neighbors with orders to pass them on from tribe to tribe until they reached the Adriatic Sea. From there they were conveyed to Greece and the Aegean Sea, where they ended up at the island sanctuary of Delos. These offerings were moved hundreds of miles through an unknown number of different peoples and places. Since nothing is reported to have been returned in exchange, for the Hyperboreans this cannot be considered as trade, but it does appear to refer to the route over which amber was carried southward for trade. Herodotus is detailing a classic down-the-line system in which items traveled long distances without the need for people to accompany them. However, directional trade was also used once the demand for amber was sufficient.

The popularity of amber fluctuated from time to time and place to place so that, for example, it was very much in evidence in southern Britain in the early Bronze Age but began to decline there just at the time it was becoming extremely popular in Mycenaean Greece. The Greeks of the classical period were not as impressed by it as their Mycenaean forebears, but their contemporaries, the Etruscans in northern Italy, apparently were and produced some fine products. The demand for amber remained long after the close of the Bronze Age although large-scale tribal migrations occasionally destroyed existing networks that had to be re-established once stability returned. In the first century CE Pliny felt it necessary to devote an extensive discussion to the various theories explaining what amber was, dismissing, for example, proposals that it was made from lynx urine, or from the tears of certain birds that lived beyond India, or from moisture formed from the sun's rays. Amber from Germany continued to flow into the Roman Empire even as the ancient era began drawing to a close.

Chapter 3

The first link

Once societies passed through the agricultural revolution, some began a process of transition toward social, political, and economic complexity that ultimately made them qualitatively and quantitatively different from earlier societies. Historians no longer draw a hard distinction between societies officially labeled as "civilizations" and others that do not quite meet the set of criteria that were once rigidly in place. But the word "civilization" is still convenient to apply to societies that went through this process, if we recognize that it represents a very ambiguous concept. With this in mind, the earliest civilization is considered to have emerged in Sumer, the southern part of Mesopotamia, a large plain lying between the Euphrates and Tigris rivers during the fourth millennium BCE.

The soil of Sumer was alluvial and very rich, allowing cultivators to produce a surplus of wheat and barley. Communities coalesced into city states such as Uruk, which undertook large construction projects that included temples and other forms of monumental architecture requiring vast amounts of building materials. Once built, these establishments needed to be furnished, indeed adorned. At the same time, the elite classes of priests and officials who directed and managed these societies did not hesitate to reward themselves with the luxury and prestige items they felt they so justly deserved. Armies needed to be equipped, ships built, infrastructure maintained, and other practical matters addressed. Once again trade increased enormously.

The trade of the early civilizations must be kept in perspective. Most people lived out their lives farming, herding, or fishing and consuming food, clothing, and other goods they produced themselves or obtained from their immediate locale. The Sumerian economy was never primarily directed toward export production, and the common people that comprised its base got no direct benefit from long-distance trade. Nevertheless, the importance of trade was disproportionate to its scale. Trade became an engine in driving socio-political complexity.

If the Sumerians wanted to build great cities and allow their elite classes to maintain a privileged lifestyle, they had to be great traders since Sumer was a resource-deficient area. Although it could produce a bounty of food once irrigation systems were in place, Sumer had no deposits of metals or useful stone, and its wood was unsuitable for heavy construction. Most of what Sumer lacked could be found in sufficient quantities in the areas that ringed Mesopotamia. Building an empire to incorporate these lands was not a viable option until the late third millennium: the Sumerian cities could not so much as unify themselves. The solution was long-distance trade. In the highlands to the east in modern Iran, copper had been worked as early as the fifth millennium BCE, and by the third millennium silver was coming from that direction as well. Beyond Iran was Afghanistan, from which tin and precious stones reached Mesopotamia, some probably through directional trade. The mountains to the north in Anatolia and the Caucasus were a storehouse of metals, and copper also came from the opposite direction on the eastern shores of the Persian Gulf. Syria and Lebanon to the west were a source of cedar and other hardwoods as well as wine and olive oil.

Imports have to be paid for by exports, and determining what the Sumerians used for this is somewhat tricky. They produced a surplus of grain and other foodstuffs, such as dates, dried fish, and lard. The problem was transportation, especially when goods had to be carried overland. Foodstuffs are a bulky commodity, and a lot of grain would have been required to pay for a rather small quantity of metal, not to mention precious stones. To make matters even less clear, food is among the most perishable of items and thus archaeologically invisible. Documentary evidence confirms that Mesopotamia exported textiles in the form of woolen cloth and clothing as well as leather products. Luxury goods flowed in both directions. The temples and palaces of Sumerian cities had great workshops that took in imported raw materials and turned out finely made jewelry, ceremonial and ritual items, weapons, and aromatic oils. Much of this was intended for the local elite, but at least some of it was exported with much value added. Over the years the Sumerians were able to create a market for their own surplus production. The consequence of this for the highland communities of Iran and other peripheries was to accelerate the process of social stratification as local leaders emerged to direct the production of Sumerian-bound exports and control the distribution of imports from Sumer.

As the cities of Mesopotamia became larger, richer, more centralized, and more complex, their needs expanded. Resources were sucked in from increasing distances as older networks of exchange broadened and new ones were created. Two systems evolved. In the first, trade expeditions, usually armed and under the banner of a king or temple, were sent out on a sporadic basis. The preferred way to trade was with partners with whom a relationship was already established rather than wandering around dealing with whomever one happened upon. In the second system, relay trade was used across a succession of middlemen. Rivers, especially the Euphrates, functioned as trunk lines for transporting goods with secondary linkages in the form of overland routes radiating outward in various directions. Trade routes and trading partners depended on changing circumstances, especially political factors such as the rise of new states or the collapse of old ones, creating new opportunities or ending old ties. But if the merchants of a particular city could exercise control over a trade route, they could ensure not only their own access to particular commodities but also assume some measure of control over other peoples' economies.

As early as the late fourth millennium BCE, the need for certain imports led to the creation of trading posts, enclaves, and colonies outside of Sumer. The best known of these was at Habuba Kabira on the upper Euphrates River in modern Syria, which was established under the auspices of the temple at Uruk. Habuba Kabira was located at a strategic position for controlling east to west trade running from Iran across northern Mesopotamia to the Mediterranean coast and could serve as a jumping off point to Anatolia as well. The inhabitants of Habuba Kabira, who may have numbered 6,000–8,000, did not produce their own food: the place was purely an entrepot. It lasted for about a century and a half, after which it disappeared.

The nature of early Sumerian trade is still a point of debate with two alternative models. One begins with the assumption that trade was initially conducted between societies, then institutions, and only later individuals. In a Sumerian city state, the government or temple engaged in gift exchange and held a monopoly over long-distance trade through its agents. Prices were set so that a guaranteed return could be expected on the safe delivery of a consignment. The other model has independent merchants, financed by their own or other private capital, calculating the difference in gains they would realize by bringing a particular commodity to a particular destination, reckoning risks, cost of transportation, and time spent. In other words, this model assumes the existence of a market economy. How far this went in becoming a truly self-regulating market based on supply and demand is questionable since in the ancient world the tie between production and price was a tenuous one. Over the long history of ancient Mesopotamia, both models are apparent, with the institutional agent prominent in the earlier period and the entrepreneur becoming more common later. Just how much later is the central point of the debate. When did the entrepreneur first appear and, more importantly, when was the change significant enough to matter? Although signs of entrepreneurial activity may be visible as early as the late fourth millennium BCE, the third and second millennia are seen as the crucial periods.

The earliest Sumerian traders did not constitute a middle class. In fact, they didn't constitute a separate class at all. The agents who represented kings and temples were part of the governing class, important men on a level with military commanders and high civil officials sometimes linked to the royal family by blood or marriage. Their livelihood was not dependent on market mechanisms but rather on their position at court. Their role was

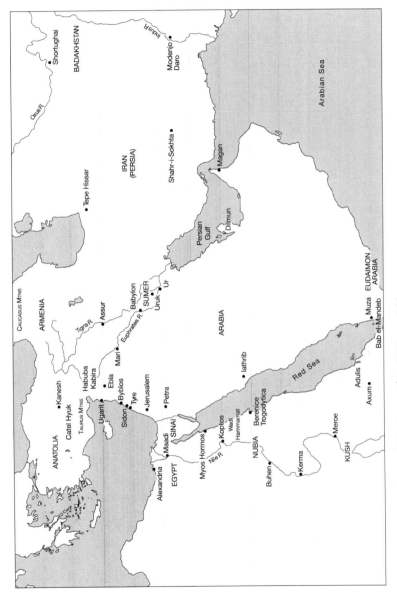

Map 3.1 Southwest Asia and Northeast Africa 5000 BCE–100 BCE

more akin to that of ambassador than peddler, and in the sources the words for "envoy" and "merchant' are often used interchangeably. In one Mesopotamian hymn, the high god Enlil is referred to as "merchant of the wide earth." At the other end of the scale, petty merchants involved in retail trade were not middle class either; they were solidly embedded in the lower ranks of society.

As duty-minded as the agent of a king or temple may have been, at some point agents also started trading privately, when the opportunity presented itself, for their own benefit. Merchants employed by the palace who accumulated capital on the side were in a position to survive the collapse of a dynasty or with some luck perhaps even a state. Others with capital, including members of ruling families, were not above joining in the pursuit of private gain through investment. Some merchants began operating independently of palace and temple, which the state does not seem to have opposed so long as it reserved the right to monopolize the trade in certain strategic commodities and the entrepreneurs paid their usually high tariffs. In fact, given the nature of the goods traded, the state and temples and the elites who controlled these institutions constituted the customer base for profit-driven trade. At times the palace and temple even encouraged private trade by lending money for a share of the profits or commissioning private traders to represent them in various commercial transactions. However, it should be noted that the development of early Sumerian cities was not uniform; different cities evolved in different ways, including how they carried on their long-distance trade, so merchants in various places at various times operated under different conditions. But during some times in some places, something like a true commodity market based on supply and demand, fueled by profit seeking, and made possible by capital accumulation and investment, did operate.

The Sumerian city states were finally unified by an outside force, their northern neighbors, the Akkadians, under Sargon. The creation of the first empire in history was due in part to Sargon's desire to control the trade in raw materials for the benefit of Akkad. Once the Sumerians were subdued, Sargon moved north into what is referred to in the texts as the "Silver Mountains" (Anatolia) and west to the "Cedar Forest" (Lebanon), assuming control over trade routes and commercial cities such as Elba and Mari. By his time, Mesopotamia was the hub of a system that stretched from India and Central Asia on one side to northeast Africa and the borderlands of Europe on the other, that is, far beyond Sargon's empire. Sargon's official policy was to support and encourage trade. When a colony of Akkadian merchants came under threat in the Anatolian city of Burushanda, he rescued it. But when the old city of Elba, a long-time axis for trade between Mesopotamia and Syria, appeared to be thwarting Akkadian interests, Sargon's grandson, Naran-Sin, destroyed it. During the Akkadian period (2350–2160 BCE), both state and private enterprise was evident with the state controlling certain commodities such as bulk metals and precious gems.

After a brief period of invasion and disorganization, the Akkadian Empire was replaced by a state centering on the Sumerian city of Ur that dominated Mesopotamia for about a century (2100–2000 BCE) and is referred to as Ur III (the Third Dynasty of Ur). It is a classic example of a state-administered economy, a highly centralized, bureaucratic structure in which external trade was the monopoly of the government, and merchants were government employees. The so-called "wool office" of Ur was a tightly controlled system of mass production that by one estimate employed 12,000 weavers and handled 6,400 tons of wool, producing a commodity directed mostly for foreign trade. Although by local standards they were considered to be of mediocre quality, these textiles were much in demand among highland peoples.

The collapse of Ur loosened the trading connections into and out of southern Mesopotamia, creating a vacuum private enterprise rushed to fill. Conveniently coming at the break between the third and second millennia BCE, it is sometimes used as an expedient cross-over point for the shift from a principally state–temple controlled system of external trade to a mainly profit-driven entrepreneurial system. This is a matter for debate, however, with the transition point sometimes seen to have occurred much earlier in the third millennium or much later at the end of the second.

The earliest and best example of second millennium private enterprise was the Old Assyrian–Cappadocian trading system. This operated in the first two centuries of the millennium, 1,000 years before the Assyrians conquered a great empire. These early Assyrians lived on the middle Tigris in the city state of Assur, which was strategically located along trade routes running north across the Taurus Mountains into the region of Cappadocia on the Anatolian plateau. Anatolia was divided at the time into small kingdoms; a reported 20 Assyrian trading colonies were located in proximity to the palaces of these kingdoms, the most important one being at Kanesh (Kultepe) about 700 miles from Assur. Modern historians would not have even guessed at the existence of the Old Assyrian–Cappadocian commercial system, one of the most important in the ancient world in helping to understand the mechanics of trade, except for the discovery of private archives at Kanesh, from which about 20,000 tablets have been unearthed. The trade, which was in metals and textiles, was probably initiated by Mesopotamian merchants seeking silver as Anatolia had the greatest supplies of silver-bearing ores in southwestern Asia. The Anatolians also had a plentiful supply of copper but needed tin for making bronze. This was provided by the Assyrian merchants. Initially this trade probably required the strong centralized authority of a state, but as bronze became increasingly used for practical purposes and not just for status or ritual products, its demand became more widespread, and control slipped into the hands of private traders.

The origin of the tin, which was so central to this trade, has not been pinpointed since no local deposits of this metal were available in

Mesopotamia. The best guess is that it came from sites in Afghanistan and possibly Iran. Mesopotamia did produce the other Assyrian export, woolen textiles, in the form of cloth and clothing. Much of this came from Babylonia in southern Mesopotamia, which was renowned for its high-quality products, but Assur also made and exported its own cheaper version. The matter of quality is interesting since the people of Anatolia themselves also produced textiles using essentially the same technology as the Mesopotamians. However, Mesopotamian textiles were perceived as finer and had much higher prestige value. Since no examples of the cloth are available for comparison, this has raised the question of whether the imported product had an inflated value largely because of its exotic appeal. In any case, for the Assyrian merchant, the net profit for textiles was higher than for tin.

The tin was packaged and placed on the sides of donkeys, over which the textiles were piled. A donkey load constituted about 200 pounds; its composition depended on current market conditions, that is, on the cost of tin and textiles in Assur and the prices paid for them in Anatolia. Goods were sealed and accompanied by a manifest that was checked on arrival to prevent pilferage. Usually the goods of several merchants, each with up to 20 donkeys, were represented in a caravan. Caravans moved an estimated 12–15 miles per day, and there were staging posts along the way where fresh donkeys could be obtained. Merchants could accompany their goods, but in general the caravans were in the hands of professional transporters who were paid a flat rate and were entitled to interest-free loans, which they used to engage in their own trading on the side.

On arrival at its destination in Anatolia, a caravan first headed for the palace of the local ruler. The palace provided some protection on the roads, helped to collect debts owed to the merchants, and could also store goods and lend or borrow on credit from the merchants. In return it was owed taxes and the right of first refusal. Palace officials bargained for a special price on a portion of the arriving cargo, after which the merchants were free to sell the rest on the open market. Tin and textiles were exchanged directly for silver or for copper, which was then re-traded for silver. If silver was unavailable or too costly, gold could be substituted. The silver or gold was then sent back to Assur, where it was used to buy more tin and textiles. The trade was in the hands of certain families who constituted merchant houses headquartered in Assur. Wives of merchants commonly supervised the textile production back home. Moneylenders, including temples, extended credit, and individual houses sometimes pooled their capital to spread the risk in particular ventures. Agents representing the Assyrian commercial houses were permanently stationed in the trading enclaves located in close proximity to the Anatolian palaces. Their relations with local merchants and their participation in local trade were closely regulated by their hosts. They remained to some extent insulated from the local population, using their own system of weights and measures, calendar, and language, but they lived in Anatolian-style houses, used Anatolian utensils and pottery, and could take local wives.

Central to the Old Assyrian–Cappadocian trading system was the karum, a merchants' association charged with representing the collective interests of the Assyrians in dealing with local authorities. The origin of this institution was in southern Mesopotamia: karum is Akkadian for "quay" or "wharf," referring to places along the rivers where goods were unloaded and business transacted. Eventually the term was applied to the community of merchants in a town. Rulers found it convenient to deal with private merchants as a group, especially if they were resident foreigners, and in some places the karum assumed such functions as lending money and operating warehouses. In the Anatolian trade, karums were connected together in a network with the chief branch in Assur and the next most important in Kanesh. Included in its duties was the enforcement of proper ethical standards among its members to ensure the overall integrity of the group. To maintain its officials and carry out its functions, the karum extracted its own tax from the traders.

The karum in the Anatolian trade never evolved into a loosely organized company. Political authorities on both ends regulated and taxed but never controlled or administered the trade. This was private enterprise, early second millennium BCE style, using private capital with the goal of accumulating wealth by professional merchants taking advantage of market conditions based on supply and demand. Trade was structured and scheduled within a large-scale wholesale system: this was not peddling. Silver and gold were units of exchange; in other words, they served a money function. Most of the time prices were relatively stable. Normally in Assur 1 unit of silver was valued at 15 units of tin whereas in Anatolia the ratio was 1 to 7. This would make the gross profit on tin about 100 percent where the gross profit in textiles appears to have been closer to 200 percent. However, the price of tin is known to have fluctuated as much as 20 percent over short periods. Taxes amounted to 10 percent paid to the palace in addition to other payments on departure from Assur, en route, and to the karum.

For Anatolia, the Old Assyrian–Cappadocian trade system helped to stimulate the process of state building by providing a steady source of government income, and it was in this region that the Hittite Empire would soon arise. As for the Assyrians, their system enriched several generations of merchant families, then disappeared around 1750 BCE probably due to unsettled conditions back in Assur. Under the next great empire to arise in Mesopotamia, the Babylonian, the role of the state and the temples in trade was greatly reduced when compared with that of Ur III. The government still had a hand in some commodities, including food, but used private operators as its agents. Through the second millennium BCE, the trend toward privatization was unmistakable. By the first millennium BCE, entrepreneurs could operate independently, buying and selling whatever commodities would make them the largest profit rather than being directed by the specific demands of the elites. The impact of trade began to reach farther down the social ladder.

Mesopotamian trade was also spreading out geographically. From the time they began exchanging products with each other and with their neighbors to the north and west, the Mesopotamians used their rivers to transport goods, especially when heavy loads such as grain and timber were involved. Long stretches of both the Euphrates and Tigris were navigable, and in the southern regions many canals were also used. The main problem limiting riverain traffic was that the prevailing wind blew from the north and the river current also flowed from that direction, making it difficult to go upstream. The scarcity of suitable trees for boat construction was addressed in the early period by using bundled reeds or hides stretched over a wooden frame to form a hull. These skin boats were strong enough to carry heavy loads of stone and at the conclusion of the trip could be disassembled and packed up for the overland trip back home. On the upper reaches of the rivers where rapids often tore up conventional boats, the hides were inflated to serve as cushions, giving the boats a rounded appearance. Herodotus reports that they were still in use in the fifth century, calling them "the most amazing thing in Assyria [Mesopotamia] after Babylon itself."

If the Sumerians learned their water skills on the rivers, by the third millennium BCE they were applying them to a much larger and more challenging body, the Persian Gulf. The Gulf connected the Indian Ocean with the Mediterranean in one direction and Central Asia in another, both via Mesopotamia. While at times it could suffer devastating storms, the Gulf is relatively shallow and under normal conditions not considered to be among the more turbulent of seas. And it had numerous islands and promontories inviting point-to-point sailing although its coasts were not equally attractive. Pliny proclaimed that the area off Bahrain was impossible to navigate, and although this is characteristically overstated, it does signal a significant difference. Long stretches on the Arabian side have dangerous reefs and shoals, and the coasts are barren whereas the Iranian side is deeper and less plagued by problems. Most ships traveling between the top and bottom of the Gulf stuck to the Iranian side, crossing at certain points if they were stopping at places like Bahrain.

Sumerian interest in the Gulf dates from the beginning of the third millennium BCE as part of a general reorientation of Mesopotamian trade from north and west to south and east. Over the next few centuries, the land of Dilmun – as a specific place, the island of Bahrain; as a region, the coastal area and oases from Kuwait to Bahrain – became a major trading partner. From Dilmun came copper, gold, ivory, gems, special types of wood, pearls, and mother-of-pearl in such quantities the Sumerians assumed that these products originated there. Actually only the pearls, which the Sumerians referred to as "fish eyes," and the mother-of-pearl, the iridescent interior layer of mollusk shells used for inlays, were products of Dilmun. The Dilmunites were middlemen although it is uncertain how proactive they were. In one scenario Dilmun was a neutral meeting ground where foreign merchants connected with each other to trade unmolested. In another the Dilmunites made the connections themselves and did the carrying. Sumerian sources make frequent reference to the Dilmunites as "great seafarers," which would tend to favor the more proactive model.

In the third and second millennia, Mesopotamia appears to have been an inexhaustible market for copper. At the same time that donkey caravans were bringing it down from Anatolia and Iran, ships from the Gulf were arriving with consignments, according to temple records, of up to 18 tons in the form of ingots, oblong pieces, and occasionally finished objects such as kettles. The source of this copper was actually Magan (Oman with portions of Iran on the opposite shore) at the mouth of the Persian Gulf. The mining was done in the mineral-rich mountains at numerous small-scale sites by people practicing subsistence activities such as agriculture and herding who engaged in mining as a supplementary activity. Other Magan-made products that arrived on the docks of Sumerian cities included diorite, a hard, black, igneous stone favored in making sculpture, and red ocher used as a pigment. The Sumerians also acquired a taste for high-quality dates and for a peculiar type of local onion (perhaps garlic or asafetida), which was imported in large quantities. Magan was also known for its special breeds of donkeys and goats but no gold, ivory, gems, or special wood products – these had to come from still farther afield.

An Akkadian tablet boasting of Sargon's achievements mentions in passing that "ships of Melukha, Magan, and Dilmun moored at the quay of Agade," the Akkadian capital. A poem from the time of Naram-Sin speaks of elephants and apes, "beasts from distant lands jostling in the great square." Elephants and apes could not have originated in Dilmun or Magan, but reference to this third place, Melukha, provides the key for understanding the full extent of this early trade system. Melukha was India, or more specifically the Indus River Valley culture known as Harappan civilization. Among the early alluvial riverain civilizations, the Harappan was the most extensive, covering much of modern Pakistan and parts of northwestern India with sites along the coast from just north of modern Mumbai to the Iranian border. By the time it reached its mature state of development in *c.* 2600 BCE, Harappan civilization contained a multitude of centers including five major cities, the largest of which was Mohenjo-Daro with a population estimated at between 30,000 and 50,000. Urban concentrations appear to have been located to take advantage of specific resources or to occupy strategic nodes in the transportation system. Urban planning is evident in the layout of cities that included neighborhoods of artisans and craftsmen with small shops lining the streets. The system of government, the nature of society, and the mechanisms driving the economy are all matters of endless debate since Harappan writing remains undeciphered.

The Harappans traded with each other locally and regionally on an extensive basis through an elaborate internal network. The importance of foreign trade for the Harappans, however, is not quite so clear. One interpretation is that external trade was just as important as internal trade. It played a crucial role in the founding of this civilization, and it continued to keep the urban centers economically viable. A contrary view is that trade outside the Harappan zone was mostly in luxury items through middlemen such as the Dilmunites and was essentially irrelevant to the economy as a whole. Early contact was made to the north in Afghanistan and Turkmenistan with sites established on the Oxus River and in the Pamir Mountains. The Harappans knew how to make bronze although in metallurgy their technology was not on a par with Mesopotamia. And although copper and some tin were available in the Indus region, the Harappans appear to have brought their tin from Afghanistan and perhaps Uzbekistan and imported some bronze from Iran rather than bothering to make it themselves.

From their northern contacts the Harappans obtained significant quantities of lapis lazuli, which they did not use much of themselves but re-exported to the Sumerians. Jade was carried from Tibet and amazonite from southern India. Other semi-precious stones were available within the Harappan area itself, particularly carnelian, a hard, translucent, flesh-colored, red chalcedony from the Narmada Valley and Vindaya Mountains of western India and the Hindu Kush to the north. Carnelian was made into etched, drilled beads, a signature product of the Harappans considered to be so valuable by the Sumerians that they buried it with their kings. Bead-making using stones, gems, gold, copper, shells, and ivory was an extensive industry for the Harappans as was the manufacture of other ivory products including inlaid furniture, figurines, breast plates, boxes, spoons, and particularly combs, another signature product.

The special types of wood that came into Sumer doubtless included teak and probably deodar and sissoo. In later centuries India's greatest export would be cotton textiles, and the Harappans spun and wove cotton. However, there is no textual or archaeological evidence to show that they exported it to Sumer or the Persian Gulf; indeed textiles in the form of woolen products continued to be a major Mesopotamian export. The most commonly recognized Harappan remains recovered in Sumerian sites are small, square or rectangular carved seals usually made of soapstone or steatite. Although some of these are quite exquisite, virtually miniature works of art, they served a practical purpose. Seals were used for stamping an impression on clay, usually an inscription in the Harappan script (60 percent of all Harappan writing comes from seals) along with the image of an animal, the most common being the unicorn but including bulls, elephants, tigers, and composite human figures. This served as a means of identifying ownership and perhaps contents, destination, and other necessary information on packaged goods.

The great enigma of Harappan foreign trade is not exports but imports. In some way the Mesopotamians had to pay for those carnelian beads and ivory combs, but no clearly identifiable remains of Mesopotamian goods have been recovered at Harappan sites. This suggests invisible exports, and the Sumerians are known to have traded grain and textiles to other people. Unfortunately, this does not fit well since the Harappans also produced a grain surplus and had their own fine textiles. A more likely import would be copper from Magan, indicating a more complex system in which Harappan products could end up in Ur, but Sumerian products did not necessarily have to end up in Mohenjo-Daro. Nevertheless, the Sumerians had to be more than consumers.

The island of Bahrain had springs that allowed for the cultivation of some grain and dates, but overall both Dilmun and Magan had very limited agricultural potential. Sumerian documents always mention cereals, especially barley, as one of two major exports to the Gulf, and Sumerian food allowed for the development of a considerable urban population in Dilmun. The other major Mesopotamian export was wool and woolen textiles, especially garments, huge quantities of which could be turned out in royal workshops. Other products included sesame and linseed oils and leather goods. From beyond Mesopotamia came silver and possibly cedar wood. One temple document specifies that the following consignment of goods be traded for copper: 3,600 pounds of wool, 70 garments, 330 gallons of linseed oil, and 180 leather products.

All of the Mesopotamian exports were perishable except for silver, which was recyclable: in other words, they are all archaeologically invisible. Fortunately, there are textual sources; unfortunately they often designate Dilmun as their destination regardless of where the product ultimately ended up. Thus, there is no indication of what, if anything, went all the way to India. Probably the safest guess is that the Harappans imported metals, copper from Magan and silver from Mesopotamia, which the Sumerians got from Anatolia. With the Sumerians supporting the Dilmunites and Maganites with food, and the Dilmunites handling and finessing the overall exchange, the Sumerians did not have to give the Harappans the exact value of goods they received from them.

The organization of Persian Gulf trade from the Mesopotamian side was similar to land-based trade in that government and temple control were prominent in the earlier period, reaching a peak under Ur III. This changed in the early second millennium BCE when commerce shifted into private hands directed by Sumerian families referred to in the texts as the "Dilmun traders." Under Sargon's empire, Dilmun, Magan, and Melukha were all considered to be trading partners. Mention of Melukha fades under Ur III, but Magan is still prominent; later only Dilmun is mentioned. This may be connected with the shift to private enterprise. Merchant families, however wealthy, could not provide the capital put up by the state and temples, and whereas donkey caravans carried less than ships, they also represented less capital investment. Private ventures would tend to be less risky, which may have confined them to nearby Dilmun, thus consolidating the middleman monopoly of the Dilmunites.

Traffic, however, did not fall off in this period but rather increased. Partnerships were common between investors and the traveling Dilmun traders but only on a transaction-to-transaction basis. Terms varied according to whether the investor shared in the risk and thus in the profit or received a fixed return regardless of outcome. On the positive side, the necessity of having the capital, ships, navigational and commercial knowledge, and contacts with counterparts in Dilmun all meant that the class of Dilmunite traders must have been very small, limiting competition. On the negative side, even private enterprise was subject to royal supervision and was heavily taxed – ships carrying 10 tons of copper, for example, could expect to pay up to a ton in duties – despite the merchants receiving little in protection or other services from the state.

Mesopotamian sources indicate that the Persian Gulf–Indian Ocean trade system peaked in *c.* 1800 BCE. If so, at least one of the partners was already in full decline and would soon disappear. Harappan civilization began with a massive population shift to urban areas and ended with a reverse shift that may have started in *c.* 2100 BCE and appears to have run its course by 1750 BCE. This total urban collapse may be at the top of the list of ancient India's many mysteries. Natural disaster in the form of severe flooding caused by a shift in the course of the river or environmental degradation and climate change leading to ecological collapse are the most likely culprits. It is unlikely that a problem with trade provided the triggering mechanism, but once trade was disrupted, it could have quickly led to deurbanization given how dependent this society appears to have been on internal trade.

Viewing the trade from the Mesopotamian perspective, indirect contact with the Harappans seems to have continued up to the end of their civilization. Once it was gone, the Mesopotamians compensated by reinforcing their contacts with old trade partners to the north and west. Even the tie with Dilmun slipped. It was reconnected a millennium later under the Assyrian Empire, which needed all the copper it could get for its war machine. Other commodities the Dilmunites later sent to Mesopotamia included spices, perfumes, and exotic woods, indicating that once again Dilmun was playing a middleman role. As for Magan and Melukha, these names became assigned to other places including East Africa probably because it supplied some of the same products as the Harappans once did.

A closer look: lapis lazuli

To the Mesopotamians gold was the most valuable commodity whereas in Egypt, considered to be the land of gold, silver was in greater demand. But for both the most sought after among precious stones was not diamonds, rubies, sapphires, or emeralds; it was lapis lazuli. Today lapis lazuli is considered a semi-precious stone, but among the ancients, there was nothing "semi" about it. Lapis ranged in color from violet to green, with the finest quality being a rich azure blue. It had no real utilitarian value but was thought to represent the powers of both divinity and royalty and was used for ritual and ceremonial purposes. It has been recovered in the remains of temples and palaces as well as from hoards and elite graves with one shaft burial containing 500 beads. Lapis was prized for prestige reasons, and for personal adornment it was cut in numerous ways and often set in gold. Jewelry included necklaces, pendants, beads, discs, and amulets representing various animals ranging from bulls to frogs. It was also made into hair combs, dagger handles, and seals, depicting scenes from mythology or containing cuneiform writing, and used as veneer for boxes, boards, and bowls as well as inlay for eyes, eyebrows, and beards in anthropomorphic sculpture. It was the stuff of gods.

Lapis lazuli is a mineral composed of sodium silicate containing sulfur. A product of metamorphism, it is formed in crystalline limestone. When classical authors referred to sapphires, they meant lapis. If obsidian and flint represented an older trade, lapis and other semi-precious stones such as carnelian, turquoise, and agate were the first luxury trade. Archaeologists use lapis as an important marker for determining trade routes. Metals were melted down or could corrode, but lapis had a high survival rate because beads were usually too small to be reworked. And unlike other valuable stones, lapis had a unique source.

Lapis lazuli occurs naturally in very few places worldwide. The closest to the ancient centers of civilization was in Badakhstan in the snowy mountains of northeastern Afghanistan 1,500 miles as the crow flies from Mesopotamia and twice that far over the circuitous routes traders actually traveled. From the beginning of the trade, four small mines in Badakhstan have been the only source for lapis from India to Greece. The mines, which ranged in elevation from 6,000 to 17,000 feet, were connected to the outside world by little trails that were snowbound much of the year. The stone was quarried in the most primitive of ways. Wood was carried in on the backs of donkeys and a fire built at the rock face. Once it was sufficiently heated, cold water was splashed on the rock to crack it. The lapis was then chipped out by pick, hammer, and chisel.

Lapis first appeared in northern Mesopotamia in the form of beads at the end of the fifth millennium BCE although it did not become abundant until the middle of the fourth. From northern Mesopotamia lapis was passed on to Syria and Egypt and by the end of the millennium was being deposited as grave goods as far away as Nubia. Lapis did not become evident in Sumer until about 3100 BCE, reflecting the dominance of northern Mesopotamia as the hub of international trade routes during much of the fourth millennium. In the late fourth this dominance began to shift to southern Mesopotamia, signaling the economic and political rise of Sumer. Events in Iran were responsible in the early third millennium for a sudden collapse of the trade, during which no lapis reached Mesopotamia, Syria, or Egypt for two centuries. This so-called "lapis crisis" left such an impression on the Sumerians they immortalized it in an epic known as *Enmerkar and the Lord of Aratta*.

Enmerkar was the King of Uruk. He wanted to adorn a temple for the goddess Inanna, but there was no lapis because the King of Aratta, said to be located beyond seven mountain ranges to the east in Iran, was trying to monopolize all the prestige goods he could get his hands on to embellish his own temples. Enmerkar sent an ambassador to Aratta, who attempted to negotiate but was rejected as apparently Aratta had no need of any product from Sumer. This was followed by a series of threats, challenges, and the solving of riddles until finally negotiations brought about an equitable exchange after Aratta was stricken with famine sent by Inanna. A donkey caravan loaded with grain was dispatched for Aratta, and in return Enmerkar received his lapis. This story may represent an actual instance when prestige goods were received in exchange for food during a famine and evolved into ongoing trade since by the mid-third millennium vast quantities of lapis were being imported into Sumer.

The story of Enmerkar seems to imply that either Aratta was very close to the mines and had a monopoly over production, or that there was only one principal route the lapis was sent across, or that Aratta was large enough to control all the routes. In fact, over the centuries the precious blue stone reached Mesopotamia from three major directions, one that ran north and another that ran south of the mines, both connecting to east–west trunk roads, and one that ran to ports on the Indian Ocean. It is not likely that this was down-the-line or trickle trade. It could have been directional trade: in the fourth millennium lapis was available in Mesopotamia but does not appear to have been used near its source nor along the way. Or this could have been what is called central place trade, in which producers sent their product to a nodal point where traders from consuming lands went to buy it. In the lapis trade there are two likely candidates to have served as central places, Shahr-i-Sokhta in the south and Tepe Hissar in the north.

Shahr-i-Sokhta, now located in a desert in southeastern Iran, was once a prosperous urban center where lapis as well as carnelian from the Hindu Kush Mountains was brought in raw blocks. There, stoneworkers shaped and trimmed the material, removing a large amount of impurities to reduce the cost of further transport. Some beads and other items were also produced there, but for the most part the Sumerians wanted to finish their own products. The archaeological record provides no evidence as to what was imported from Mesopotamia in return, and lapis was not traded within the local economy. Shahr-i-Sokhta may have been the mysterious Aratta although its location does not match the description in the epics. For lapis carried across the northern route, a similar center existed at Tepe Hissar.

Some lapis also reached the Harappans, who had links with trading stations at Shortughai in the Oxus River valley west of the lapis mines. It has been suggested that these stations may have directed the mining process. Lapis was carried from Badakhstan to Kabul to Peshawar and down the Indus River to ports on the Indian Ocean. The transporters in the early part of the trip may have been nomadic tribesmen making their yearly rounds seeking pasture. Curiously, the blue stone was never valued among the Harappans as it was in Mesopotamia and Egypt. Once trading contact with Sumer was established, the Harappans transshipped all but a small quantity of their lapis westward.

The great lapis crisis may have been the first good opportunity for lapis from the Indian Ocean to enter the Sumerian market along with other products such as carnelian and ivory. Sumerian records designate Dilmun as a major source of lapis, and indeed Dilmunite ships probably carried it from India to Sumer via Dilmun. A later opportunity for the Dilmunite–Harappan connection came during the Akkadian Empire when the Akkadians were seeking to establish a monopoly over trade in the lands they conquered. Their aggressive policies caused some trading partners outside their orbit to shy away, including the Iranians who were responsible for the Shahr-i-Sokhta trade. The loss of the overland Iranian trade proved to be a gain for the Indus-to-Persian Gulf connection.

As civilization spread westward over the following millennia, lapis lazuli continued to be a popular trade item. But even Pliny, who wrote 4,000 years after lapis first appeared in Mesopotamia, didn't get his lapis facts right: "The best," he tells us, "is found in Persia." Moreover, lapis stones "are useless for engraving because cores like rock-crystal interfere with this." The long-gone Sumerians would have been surprised to read this.

Chapter 4

Land of gold

If Mesopotamia boasts the earliest civilization, the lower Nile River valley is credited with being second by only a few centuries. Egypt and Mesopotamia shared many similarities, but in long-distance trade, they also show many differences. Mesopotamia was bordered by diverse environments containing a variety of raw materials and peoples. Egypt was surrounded by desert, a comparatively sterile environment supporting few potential trading partners. Egypt opened to the outside world only at two main points. Control over the Nile delta meant a monopoly over trade north into the Mediterranean and eastward to Asia. On the other side, control over the entry to the cataract region in the south meant a monopoly over trade with Nubia and the interior of Africa. This was a very different situation from Mesopotamia, where numerous routes criss-crossed, and it was impossible to monopolize the multitude of entry points except under a powerful empire like the Akkadian.

Geography determined that the Egyptian economy would be far less impacted by foreign trade than the economy of Mesopotamia, but Egypt was never completely isolated even in the period before the rise of the pharaohs. In the fifth millennium BCE, Upper (southern) Egypt traded with nearby desert regions importing metals, pigments, and beads of jasper and carnelian, as well as shells from the Red Sea and ivory from Nubia in exchange for finely made eggshell-thin pottery. In the fourth millennium, the city of Maadi at the base of the Nile delta in Lower (northern) Egypt served as the nodal point for trade with Sinai and Palestine. Copper and turquoise arrived from Sinai carried on donkey caravans by local tribesmen, and there was a steady trickle trade with Palestine for products such as wood, wine, and olive oil. At the time, Palestine enjoyed overland contacts stretching north to Syria and beyond to Anatolia, Mesopotamia, and Iran. Maadi seems to have traded more with Palestine than with Upper Egypt as witnessed by the obsidian trade: obsidian coming into Lower Egypt originated in Anatolia, but obsidian used in Upper Egypt came from the areas of modern Yemen and Eritrea.

In the late fourth millennium BCE, the struggles between warrior groups up and down the Nile Valley for control over internal trade and access to external routes were a major factor leading to the unification of Egypt. From the beginning of the pharaonic period, long-distance trade, like the rest of the Egyptian economy, was under strict state management and remained so for the next several thousand years. During this time foreign trade always existed but had less impact on the overall economy than in most other complex societies. Foreign goods entered Egypt through large-scale expeditions organized and directed by royal officials to obtain specific items. Some observers have concluded that expeditions could not have satisfied all the country's needs; therefore, something like ongoing trade, entrepreneurial or not, must have existed. If so, this remains a well-kept secret. In all the official documentation left by the Egyptians, virtually nothing refers to trading practices outside of expeditions. Imports were consumed directly by the court in its enormous building projects or redistributed to the country's elite in the form of luxury goods. Egypt provides a classic example of a general rule among powerful states in the ancient world: trade with the outside was designed to secure desirable imports, not to create export markets.

Sometime in the late fourth to the early third millennium BCE, overland trade with Palestine began to taper off in favor of sea contact between Egypt and the Levantine littoral, the eastern shore of the Mediterranean extending north of Palestine to the border of Anatolia (today comprising Lebanon and northwestern Syria). This shift may have been due in part to the construction of larger, faster, more seaworthy ships; which side, the Egyptian or the Levantine, initiated the contact is not certain. Lebanon–Syria offered a much wider range of products than Palestine, foremost of which was high-quality timber strong enough for heavy construction. Timber in large quantities was a difficult product to pass along through trickle trade; fetching wood meant sending out expeditions.

The new tie with Lebanon and Syria plugged Egypt more directly into the main trunk line of the long-distance commercial network that ran from Anatolia to Afghanistan. The cities of the Levantine coast became emporia for products bound for Egypt, ranging from silver and precious stones to perfumes and oils. Egypt, in return, had a product the rest of the word was eager to get: gold. And Syria was directly connected to Sumer, a relationship facilitated by inland cities such as Elba, Mari, and the Sumerian colonies on the upper Euphrates. A direct route from Sumer to Palestine, although shorter than from Sumer to Syria, was not operational due to desert in between since camels were not yet used as pack animals. Palestine became a commercial cul-de-sac. The earliest Sumerian objects recovered in Egypt are from the late fourth to the early third millennium BCE and consist of stone cylinder seals. Some Mesopotamian ceramics in the form of small liquid containers also reached Egypt, but no object of Egyptian manufacture has been found in Mesopotamia from this period. Considerable speculation has been made about a Persian Gulf to Red Sea maritime connection tying Sumer and Upper Egypt. Curiously, for a brief period, some indications of

Mesopotamian and even Iranian cultural influences appear in Upper Egypt that are not found in Lower Egypt. However, there is no conclusive evidence for an early sea-route trading relationship, and whatever contacts were made were not sustained into the pharaonic period. Egypt and Sumer did not become direct trading partners.

Egypt's integration into the long-distance trade network that spanned southwestern Asia must have been heartily welcomed even if it often led to war with Mesopotamian and Anatolian states over control of the lands bordering the eastern Mediterranean shore. As a trading partner, Egypt had much to offer. From the pharaoh's workshops came exquisite craft goods ranging from ivory-inlaid furniture to amulets in the form of scarabs (dung beetles, which became a widely used motif symbolizing resurrection) cut from semi-precious stones or products in faience, a ceramic made from powdered quartz. These were mostly luxury items designed to reinforce the status of elites. Like Sumer, Egypt also produced a huge grain surplus, an archaeologically invisible product that is assumed to have been traded to people who lived in less bountiful environments like the desert or mountains. Nevertheless, what the outside world wanted most from Egypt was gold.

Gold deposits were located in Upper Egypt, the most productive being in the wadis (dry river beds) of the eastern desert between the Nile Valley and the Red Sea. It was this gold that first attracted outside traders, including, perhaps, Sumerians, to Upper Egypt. The need to organize the mining and control the trade prompted the early states of Upper Egypt to become more centralized and militarized: it was no accident that Egyptian unification was achieved by the rulers of Upper Egypt who conquered Lower Egypt. Early in Egyptian history royal expeditions were dispatched to the most productive of the wadis, the Wadi Hammamat, but in later periods permanent camps were established in some wadis and the mines worked by gangs of criminals, political prisoners, and slaves under the most horrid of conditions.

In addition to exploiting their own deposits, the Egyptians got much gold from Nubia, the land immediately south of Upper Egypt. The Nile below Egypt has a deep channel that in places provided a good transportation corridor but is broken over the length of 1,000 miles by a series of six cataracts, each a lengthy sequence of impassable rapids. Land caravans had to move traffic around the cataracts, or there was an alternative route that took travelers west of the Nile Valley across the desert through a series of oases that exited in Upper Nubia. This was the quickest, if not the most comfortable or sometimes most secure, road for tapping into the products of Africa's interior.

In Nubia gold could be found in shallow surface workings as well as in riverside deposits. Amethyst, carnelian, and diorite were also available; one quarrying operation is reported to have involved 1,000 men and an equal number of donkeys. The Nubians and the Kushites further up the Nile were famous for their herds of cattle, which brought high prices in Egypt. An interesting piece of Nubian ware from the late fourth millennium BCE has turned up in the Sumerian colony of Habula Kabira in Syria, which doubtless came via Egypt. Other products from farther south included ivory, animal skins (particularly leopard), ebony, and incense, for which there was a tremendous demand in Egypt. What the Egyptians used in payment is less clear but is believed to have included copper, gems, textiles, clothing, wine, beer, oil, honey, faience, and stone products. The Egyptians established a trading post at Buhen near the second cataract early in the third millennium, from which expeditions set out southward to the Dongola Reach area of Kush between the third and fourth cataracts. In $c.$ 2300 BCE they dug five channels to overcome obstacles in the first cataract that allowed ships to penetrate by river. Four centuries later these passages were cleared so that much larger vessels could be accommodated. Work was also done on the second cataract to allow ships to be dragged across it.

The best documented Egyptian expeditions southward were led by Harkhuf, who lived in the late twenty-fourth to the early twenty-third centuries BCE and left an account of his adventures on the walls of his tomb. Harkhuf was no petty trader but a high court official with a list of impressive titles, including "Adviser to the Pharaoh for All Affairs South of Upper Egypt." He made four trips to the land of Yam, which is difficult to pinpoint except that it was somewhere south of Lower Nubia. His father accompanied him on the first of these, which was intended mainly to find the best way to get to Yam although it is clear that they were not the first Egyptians to go to this country. They accomplished their mission in seven months and returned with an unspecified load of goods identified as "gifts" or "tribute" (depending on translation).

Harkhuf went on the second expedition alone, which took eight months, and again he returned with large quantities of goods "of a kind which nobody had ever brought to Egypt before." On the third trip he took the oasis road. He found the King of Yam busy fighting the Tjemehu (Libyan desert nomads), who were also enemies of the Egyptians, so Harkhuf joined him. After what was apparently a successful campaign, Harkhuf returned home via the river road with 300 donkeys "laden with incense, ebony, hekenu oil [for perfume], grain, panther skins, ivory, boomerangs, [and] all kinds of beautiful and good products." The King of Yam provided him with a substantial military escort lest the King of Irtjet, who controlled Lower Nubia, attempted to plunder the caravan. The King of Irtjet was so intimidated he sent bulls and other livestock to Harkhuf as his own gifts and personally guided him through some tricky hill passages. As for the fourth expedition, it is not mentioned in the account detailing the other three but is referred to in a letter the pharaoh sent to Harkhuf that was copied verbatim on another part of the tomb. Gifts are mentioned, but, as in expeditions one and two, they are unspecified except for a dancing dwarf (sometimes translated as pygmy), which especially pleased the pharaoh.

Harkhuf's trips are usually seen as trading ventures even if he claimed to be returning with gifts or tribute and never mentions any reciprocal gifts. Egyptian pharaohs preferred to interpret their exchanges with other states in this light rather than as straight commercially based trade. Yam was obviously beyond the reach of Old Kingdom Egypt's limited striking force, and if Harkhuf's expeditions were designed for nothing more than extorting gifts or tribute, the King of Yam probably would have become pretty tired of it. Instead Harkhuf seems to have received more and better gifts on each successive trip doubtless because he was bringing his own gifts. This little detail just did not make it on to an already crowded tomb wall.

The most commonly proposed site for ancient Yam is the area around Kerma above the third cataract. A great brick structure was built there, although dating from the second millennium BCE several centuries after Harkhuf's visit. This was once believed to have been the site of a Middle Kingdom Egyptian trading colony but is now recognized as the center of an independent state that reached its peak during Egypt's Second Intermediate Period (1783–1540 BCE) and was bound to Egypt by strong commercial ties. The role of Nubian states in Egypt's trade with the interior of Africa is still not completely clear; scholars are uncertain whether they were actively involved as middlemen or were content merely to extract tariffs and duties from caravans passing through.

Egypt's interest in the south was not confined to overland and riverain traffic. To the immediate east of Egypt lies the great ditch that separates Africa from Arabia, the Red Sea. Like the Persian Gulf, the Red Sea was a corridor into and out of the Indian Ocean. However, it was larger and less inviting than the Gulf owing to its dangerous shoals and wind pattern that brought rough weather from June to December. Its main advantage was that it was closer to the Mediterranean Sea than the Persian Gulf, an important consideration since the Gulf and the Red Sea often competed for commercial preeminence. Occasionally a powerful empire would control both waterways, giving it a monopoly of trade between the Mediterranean and Indian Ocean, but this was unusual.

During the Old, Middle, and New Kingdoms, ships sailed down the Red Sea to a land the Egyptians called Punt, determining the location of which has been a favorite pastime of ancient armchair geographers. From its flora and fauna as described by the Egyptians, it was clearly in Africa not Arabia, but the Egyptians always went to Punt by the Red Sea, never overland even though under the New Kingdom Egyptian control penetrated far up the Nile Valley. Recent studies appear to show Punt as being located in modern Eritrea or on the coast of southeastern Sudan although proposals putting it even farther northward, closer to the Egyptian border, or much farther southward, in Somalia, have their advocates. Punt may have been a crossroads for trade coming from the interior of Africa, the western and southern coasts of Arabia, and points in the Indian Ocean as many of the products Egyptians brought back could not have originated there. The Egyptians sometimes referred to Punt as "God's Land" because it was blessed with products often used for religious purposes. Foremost of these were the gum resins frankincense and myrrh, burned as incense in temples and used in embalming and perfume. The trees that produced these grew only in Somalia and on the southern reaches of the Arabian peninsula. Ivory and the skins of giraffes, leopards, and cheetahs, all of which were worn by temple priests, probably did not originate in Punt but from farther into the interior as did live animals such as a particular type of baboon the Egyptians considered to be sacred. The Egyptians could also obtain gold and cinnamon in Punt, both of which came from elsewhere.

The earliest known expedition to Punt was sent out by Sahura (2458–2446 BCE), a pharaoh of the V Dynasty. It returned with 80,000 units of myrrh plus some electrum (a mixture of gold and silver) and two commodities that cannot be identified. Other expeditions followed, the normal procedure being to march from the Lower Nile across the desert to the Gulf of Suez, where boats would be constructed on the beach. Under the VI Dynasty (2345–2184 BCE), the members of one such expedition were attacked by desert raiders while in the process of building their boats and massacred. Such expeditions could bring back very large quantities of goods, but they did not represent a regular or continuous trade, and long periods often intervened as, for example, between the VI and XI dynasties. One expedition sent out by Pharaoh Mentuhotep III (2004–1992 BCE), consisting of 3,000 men, marched from the Upper Nile down the Wadi Hammamat to the sea with a caravan of donkeys carrying materials to build the ships. Wells had been dug by an advance party and soldiers sent ahead to secure the road.

The most celebrated of Egyptian expeditions to Punt was that of Queen Hatshepsut (1473–1458 BCE), who ruled as pharaoh in the XVIII Dynasty. She was reportedly told by an oracle to send an expedition to Punt and in compliance dispatched five ships, galleys that may have been up to 90 feet in length. Hatshepsut commemorated the event in a series of reliefs depicted on the walls of her mortuary temple, which include lengthy inscriptions. The ships are shown arriving in Punt, where they are being greeted by a bearded chief and his deformed wife, who seems to have been suffering from some disease like lipodystrophy. The local people lived in beehive-shaped reed houses raised on stilts above the water. They did, however, have many riches, "marvels of the land of Punt" as the inscription reads, including bags of myrrh and frankincense, ebony, ivory, gold, fragrant woods like cinnamon and khesyt, eye cosmetics, panther skins, and live animals, including monkeys and dogs. In return, the Egyptians are shown trading beads, bracelets, weapons, and tools.

Hatshepsut's expedition reestablished contact with Punt that lasted several centuries to the reign of Ramses III. Trade remained a royal monopoly managed through organized expeditions using a port on the Red Sea, but no permanent Egyptian post was established at Punt. Visiting Egyptians would stay there for several months, occasionally penetrating into the interior to seek goods. In return, Puntite boats, looking more like rafts, sometimes reached the coast of Egypt to trade or bring royal visitors. With all of this activity over such a long period on a fairly continuous basis, it may be reasonable to assume that at one time or another the Egyptians ventured farther on through the Bab el-Mandeb, the straits separating the tip of Arabia from Africa, and out into the Gulf of Aden to Cape Guardafui at the tip of the East African Horn. Beyond lay India and Southeast Asia in one direction and the coast of East Africa in another. But the Egyptians were not the most adventurous of ancient peoples, and no evidence of this exists.

Although trade to the south with the lands of Yam and Punt brought exotic materials to Egypt, in terms of quantity and overall value this never matched Egypt's trade to the north with the cities of the Levant. The coastal rim of what is today Lebanon was marked by little bays, inlets, headlands, and islets. Shipping lanes led south to Egypt and northwest to Cypress and the Aegean Sea. Inland, running parallel to the coast, stood a range of mountains once covered with forests of cedar, cypress, pine, and juniper. Passages ran through these mountains linking the coast to a caravan thoroughfare connecting to the Euphrates Valley. Beyond lay Mesopotamia to the south, Anatolia and Armenia to the north, and Iran and Afghanistan to the east. The little strip of coastal plain was well positioned to become the hub of intermeshing trade networks.

Historians refer to the people who lived along the Levantine coast and in much of its interior down to the second millennium BCE as "Canaanites," which appears to be what they called themselves. In the first millennium the Greeks designated those Canaanites who lived in the coastal cities of Lebanon by the term "Phoenicians," and historians have dutifully followed suit. The Canaanite–Phoenicians did not form a unified nation, preferring to live in small commercialized states that competed fiercely with each other in trade but, unlike the Sumerians and Greeks, generally not in war. Beginning in the fourth millennium BCE, the greatest of these cities was Byblos (Jubayl), which originally was the center of a silver trade between Egypt and Anatolia. This withered in the third millennium (at about the same time the lapis trade was interrupted), but Byblos continued to enjoy a special relationship with Egypt through the second millennium.

Other cities of note that would eventually surpass Byblos in the first millennium included Sidon ("the Fishery"; modern Sayda) and Tyre ("the Rock"; modern Sur) to the south. Ninety miles to the north lay Ugarit (Ras Shamra) with a cosmopolitan population that blended Canaanites with other trading peoples. Ugarit had the advantage of being closer to Anatolia and

Cyprus, which became the great suppliers of copper in this part of the world in the mid- to late second millennium. Ugarit could also tap into nearby Syrian products such as ivory (elephant herds still roamed the area) and fine wines. Between 1400 and 1200 BCE it was perhaps the greatest port in the world of its time.

Goods from many places passed through the Canaanite ports, but the most important were homegrown, beginning with timber from nearby mountains. The Egyptians used this to build ships, furniture, and other wood products and for resin in mummification. To much of the outside world the most sought after commodities were woolen textiles, particularly high-end garments such as robes dyed reddish purple. The color came from the murex, a marine gastropod that was collected along the shoreline. These little creatures were crushed, then dumped into boiling vats from which a minute amount of precious secretion was extracted. The Greeks called the people who traded in this cloth the "phoinikes" (purple men), hence the name Phoenician. Other commodities included olive oil, wine, foodstuffs ranging from dates and figs to honey and cheese, aromatic oils from cedar and other woods, carpets, sandals, baskets, hardware, precious stones, glass beads, and slaves. A thriving metallurgy industry made possible by the abundant fuel source in nearby forests turned out finished metal goods including bronze swords.

Byblos and its neighboring cities became Egypt's main commercial outlet to the rest of the world. The Egyptians first ventured into the Mediterranean in the fourth millennium BCE using river boats without keels but having sails. Six days of coastal hugging from the Nile delta would bring a ship to Byblos and 12 days to Ugarit under good conditions, but the return trip would take twice as long fighting countervailing winds and unfavorable currents. Nevertheless, a few ships could carry the equivalent of many donkey caravans, and soon ships from both sides were scurrying back and forth. Commercial contact escalated during the period of the Old Kingdom in the third millennium as ships improved and sailors discovered new tricks such as sailing due west on the return voyage to pick up southbound currents and winds. By 2300 BCE large cargo vessels exceeding 100 feet in length, known as Byblos ships, were sent out in fleets of 40 to pick up loads of cedar. Egyptian exports included glass, jewelry, perfumes, and papyrus, Egypt's most important trade commodity after gold. Papyrus, which grew as a weed along the Nile, could be used for making boats, cloth, sandals, and cord and even eaten if properly prepared, but its most important use was as a material to write on (from which our word "paper" comes). The pith of the papyrus was cut into strips, arranged crosswise in layers, soaked in water, dried in the sun, and pressed into rolls. As the main supplier of Egyptian papyrus to places outside of Egypt, Byblos became associated with the writing of books (ultimately providing the word for "Bible").

By the period of the New Kingdom (1539–1069 BCE) in the second millennium BCE shipwrights were using bronze tools to build much stronger hulls capable of making long voyages across open seas. Large, slow freighters with square sails, high sides, decks, and deep-bellied cargo holds were now capable of carrying vast amounts of merchandise. Canaanite ships were sturdier and stubbier than Egyptian ships with heavy hulls rounded at both ends; the Greeks later dubbed them "gauloi" (tubs). One estimate is that by 1200 BCE the largest of these ships could hold up to 450 tons. Some idea of the number of ships involved in this trade can be seen from the account of Wen-Amun, an Egyptian envoy to King Zakarbaal of Byblos in the early eleventh century, in which Zakarbaal told Wen-Amun he had a fleet of 70 ships, 20 of which traded in partnership with the Egyptian pharaoh and 50 in partnership with a private merchant from his own country who resided in Egypt.

Although the Egyptians and the Canaanites were close trading partners for many centuries, their systems could not have been more different. Among the merchants of the Levantine coast, the basic commercial unit was the private family business, which sometimes formed partnerships to provide sufficient capital and spread risk in large-scale enterprises. At times merchants competed directly with the palaces; at other times kings joined private concerns in partnerships with profit-making as their primary motive. Egyptian trade, on the contrary, was highly centralized under the direction of the Pharaoh with market forces and profit-making playing negligible roles. This remained the case even during Egypt's most dynamic period under the New Kingdom, a time of many cultural, technological, and political changes. Although foreign trade became a more complex business, the main mechanism was still direct royal gift exchange. In one of these a pharaoh sent to the King of Babylon gifts amounting to 26 pounds of gold, 6.5 pounds of silver, 18.5 pounds of bronze, more than 1,000 textiles (probably linen), more than 1,000 stone vases filled with aromatic oils, 163 empty stone vases, finger rings, necklaces, mirrors, ivory boxes, and other items. From the King of Babylon, the Egyptians received such goods as horses and chariots, silver, bronze, lapis lazuli, and oil. Regifting was considered an honorable practice. A Hittite king in a letter to a fellow ruler notes that he was sending a gift consisting of a rhyton of gold and a rhyton of silver (a standard gift item, a rhyton was a drinking horn with a base representing the head of a woman, animal, or mythological creature) that had previously been sent to him as a gift by the pharaoh.

By this time, gift exchange between courts was no longer based on the old concept of better-to-give-than-receive. Wen-Amun's expedition to Zakarbaal sought timber initially as tribute. Zakarbaal reminded Wen-Amun that he no longer paid tribute to Egypt but would provide what Wen-Amun wanted for a suitable quid pro quo. Wen-Amun got his timber only after new ships arrived from Egypt bringing gold, linen, cowhides, ropes, bags of lentils, baskets of fish, and 500 rolls of papyrus. In some places, like Mycenaean Greece, the inferior party was now expected to outgive his superior as a mark of subordination. Rulers kept careful inventories of gifts sent and accepted and frequently noted in their records the exchange value of a gift in relation to other commodities, particularly silver. Occasionally the king on the receiving end openly complained that the exchange value of a gift was less than what was expected. In one letter, a Hittite king complained to the King of Babylon: "Why did you send me lapis lazuli of poor quality?" The Biblical King Solomon enjoyed a reciprocal relationship with Hiram, King of Tyre, who provided timber and gold to help Solomon build his temple. In return, Solomon sent grain and other foodstuffs, but at one point the ledger swung too far, so to compensate, Solomon offered Hiram a one-time gift of 20 cities. On inspection, however, Hiram sent a message saying, "What kind of cities are these which you have given me, my brother?" And he called them the "land of Cabul [garbage]."

Rulers do not appear to have taken such rebuffs personally. In the incident involving the "garbage cities," for example, Hiram and Solomon continued as allies and business partners who combined to develop the only substantial commercial enterprise in the Red Sea since the end of the Egyptian expeditions to Punt. Together they built a merchant fleet at Ezion-geber on the shore of the Gulf of Aqaba. Their intention was to open a new market with the inhabitants of Ophir, a place whose identity remains more mysterious than that of Punt. Ophir may have been Punt or any other place on the East African or Arabian coast, or, since ships were said to return every 3 years, Ophir could have been much farther away, almost anywhere in the Indian Ocean.

The Ophir trade is described in the Bible (1 Kings and 2 Chronicles) as bringing back "gold and a very great amount of almug wood and precious stones." Almug wood was used in the construction of Solomon's temple and palace, and what was left was made into lyres and harps for his singers. But the primary objective was gold. Prior to this time the Egyptians not only controlled their own production and that of Nubia but also gold coming from Punt, which may have originated in the African interior or somewhere in Asia. Hiram and Solomon intended to break the Egyptian monopoly, and initially they enjoyed great success: "They went to Ophir and brought from there gold to the amount of 420 talents; and they brought it to King Solomon" (a talent was the equivalent of 60 pounds).

Both monarchs used their gain for building projects. Hiram initiated a massive program to expand his city, including the harbor in preparation for the great age of Phoenician expansion that would soon follow. Solomon spent much of his profit on his temple: "Thus King Solomon excelled all the kings of the earth in riches and in wisdom." Solomon's reputation eventually reached the Queen of Sheba (Saba in modern Yemen), who came to Jerusalem with a caravan of camels bearing spices, precious stones, and "very much gold." She was so impressed with his wisdom she gave him an additional 120 talents of gold plus more precious stones and spices. This was intended as an act of competitive gift exchange, and when the queen departed, Solomon gave her "all that she desired, whatever she asked besides what was given her by the bounty of King Solomon."

The new commercial and geopolitical configuration in the Red Sea did not last long. When Solomon died, Israel split into two states. In Egypt a new and more vigorous pharaoh, Sheshonq (945–924 BCE), conquered Jerusalem in 930 BCE, reestablishing Egyptian influence in the region. The connection with Ophir was broken. In the mid-ninth century a later king, Jehosaphat, attempted to reestablish it, going so far as to build a new fleet at Ezion-geber, but the ships were wrecked (no details are given), and Jehosaphat died shortly thereafter. As for Tyre, by this time its interests had turned elsewhere, and the old commercial tie between the two peoples faded.

Despite Sheshonq's muscle flexing, for Egypt the golden age had passed. With the exception of the energetic XXVI Dynasty (664–525 BCE), the great expeditions were over, and Egypt slipped into a mode of passive trade in which others, particularly Phoenicians and Greeks, came to Egypt. The kings of the XXVI Dynasty were more interested in business than was usual, and one in particular, Necho II (610–595 BCE), was responsible for one of the most audacious adventures of the ancient world. In $c.$ 600 BCE, according to Herodotus, Necho sent out ships manned by Phoenicians to circumnavigate Africa by sailing south from Egypt through the Red Sea. To keep from starving, they landed periodically and planted crops. After more than 2 years they returned to Egypt via the Straits of Gibraltar although how they conquered the African winds and similar problems have given skeptics a field day. Assuming this trip was actually made, the Phoenicians found no new sources of wealth nor opened any new trade routes. At the time the kings of the XXVI Dynasty were making plenty of money closer at hand, so from a commercial perspective the great voyage was a bust.

Necho's schemes were not all wild-eyed and pie-in-the-sky. Closer to home he was particularly interested in the Red Sea and in reopening the Punt connection. According to Herodotus, Necho attempted to dig a canal from a branch of the Nile to the Gulf of Suez during which 120,000 Egyptians died. The work was stopped before completion because an oracle warned Necho that he was making it easier for an invader to penetrate into the delta. Necho's canal was eventually completed in 497 BCE by King Darius after Egypt was invaded and conquered by the Persians. Sailing through the canal took four days as it was quite crooked, but it was wide enough for two triremes to be rowed abreast. Herodotus provides no information on its commercial impact. Both Strabo and Pliny tell other stories about this canal. According to both, Ramses II (1279–1213 BCE) had the original idea, and Strabo claims that under him "the canal was first cut."

Both agree that Darius also played a role, but in Pliny, Darius just thought about it whereas in Strabo he had it near completion when he was "persuaded by a false notion" to abandon the project. For Pliny the first ruler to do any digging was Ptolemy II (282–246 BCE), who had a trench 100 feet across and 30 feet deep dug for 34 miles, a little over half the distance between the Nile and the Red Sea. He called a halt after being warned that the level of the Red Sea was higher than that of the Nile Valley so that if connected the sea would pour into Egypt and flood it. So, according to Pliny, the canal was never completed. In Strabo, Ptolemy II cut all the way through "so that when they wished they could sail out without hindrance into the outer sea and sail in again." Unfortunately archaeological evidence has not clarified the issue.

By the time the Romans invaded in 30 BCE, Egypt had undergone 1,000 years, more or less, of slow decline. Yet the Romans still considered it to be the richest country in the world.

A closer look: trade and the authorities

The relationship between long-distance traders and the political authorities who ruled in the places where they did business varied greatly across time and space, ranging from the Egyptian example, in which trade was a royal monopoly, to situations in which rulers partnered with private traders, to conditions under which the authorities were less than supportive or on occasion even hostile. By their nature the roles of ruler and trader operated at cross-purposes: traders were capital accumulators; rulers were capital consumers. But rulers who mistreated traders discovered to their detriment that this did not benefit their own long-term interests. Expropriating the goods of visiting merchants, cheating them, taxing them excessively, or abusing them in some other way would likely rechannel the flow of traders, their products, and their taxes in the direction of rival states.

Ideally the interests of rulers and traders were complementary. Merchants needed the stability and protection a political authority could provide, and governments saw merchants as a source of revenue that was usually more willing to be taxed than other groups with surplus income such as warrior or religious elites. The state usually acted in the interests of special groups it favored, including the ruler and his family, which determined the parameters under which trade was allowed to operate. Government interference could come in the form of import or export restrictions, price controls, or other hindrances intended to benefit someone in some way at the cost of undermining strict economic efficiency. In the main, governments did not bother to become involved as a matter of public policy intended to benefit society at large.

Relations between traders and host societies were not always symbiotic. In China, merchants were considered to be parasitic as, unlike farmers or craftsmen, they produced nothing but were thought to live off the labor of others. Where commerce was viewed as an unpleasant or degrading occupation, as in Homeric Greece, foreigners were allowed or even encouraged to engage in it. The merchant foreigner represented the unknown outside world and as such was usually suspected of being in some way potentially dangerous. A curious insight into the contradictory image of the long-distance trader is provided in the *Arthashastra*, a handbook written for rulers in India between the fourth century BCE and the second century CE. In it trade is recognized as one of three economic activities constituting the main sources of wealth for a country (agriculture and cattle husbandry being the other two). Rulers are advised to promote trade to fill their treasuries with taxes and obtain war material. Nevertheless, the *Arthashastra* specifically warns: "Merchants ... are all thieves, in effect, if not in name; they should be prevented from oppressing the people."

Commercial boundaries and political boundaries did not as a rule coincide. If rulers and elite classes wanted access to particular products beyond their borders, they could raid or invade the territory where these goods originated, or they could participate in consensual trade. Long-distance trade operated through commercial networks, and political power could impact on segments of a network. In the worst case scenario of a state inflicting enough damage on a network to mortally wound it, new networks would likely arise or existing networks adjust, provided market forces remained constant. In many instances, there was a direct correlation between strong government and commercial prosperity, especially if a strong government attempted to support trade even in some minimal way. On the other hand, political disunity did not necessarily mandate commercial decline. In some places, prosperity could result from not having to suffer interference by strong political authority. India enjoyed one of its greatest periods of commercial growth between the collapse of the Mauryan Empire in 184 BCE and the reestablishment of centralized control under the Gupta dynasty in 320 CE. A similar situation occurred during the Late (Eastern) Zhou period when the Chinese state fragmented.

Throughout history war has had one of the most profound impacts on long-distance trade. War can open new routes, create new demands, and introduce new commodities. Generally, however, war has been a disruptive factor. Unlike raiding parties or pillaging hordes, organized armies on the march usually left merchants alone, but the same cannot be said for cities. Plundering a prosperous trade center was one of the great rewards of fighting a successful campaign even if in a war of conquest the conqueror was, in effect, despoiling himself. If a commonsensical formula exists in which peace equals increased trade equals increased prosperity, those who had the authority to make war often did not think this out from a commonsensical perspective. The opportunity for immediate gain without remuneration had too strong an appeal.

Most economically motivated wars resulted from the desire to take control over the means of production – land and people – or the means of exchange – markets, ports, and trade routes – or simply to appropriate accumulated wealth. The imposing of favorable trade terms on a defeated neighbor or the seizing of some valuable asset such as a metal deposit was often the outcome of a successful war. But states rarely admitted that trade or some other economic issue was their principal motive for engaging in hostilities, preferring to use political or ideological arguments. Historians, on the other hand, may too often be inclined to impose economic motivations on the many conflicts of the past for which we don't have adequate documentation to determine cause since from the outside this appears to be the most obvious and rational explanation.

In examining the various ways in which rulers, governments, and states related to long-distance trade and traders, the most important consideration was the type of economy a state had. In this, states could be divided into two ideal categories, each with an infinite range of varieties. The first and more common type had an essentially agricultural economy ruled by a bureaucratic monarchy based on taxing peasant surpluses. Most cities were primarily political, administrative, or religious in nature, with trade playing a secondary role.

The second type was generally smaller, often a city state ruled by a commercial oligarchy. These "trade states" existed only under special conditions in which they served as hubs or nodes for long-distance trade. They were more interested in controlling routes and strategic points than large chunks of land and masses of people. In outward expansion their main interest was in establishing stations or at most colonies, which in due time usually became independent. Sometimes trade states created their own empires, as in the cases of Carthage, Athens, and Srivijaya, in the hope of taking over whole networks or commercially valuable regions. Trade in such states was much less government directed and dependent on the needs of military or religious elites and more responsive to market pressures. The manufacturing sector tended to be highly specialized, and often the people depended on the import of food and raw materials for their very existence.

Chapter 5

Into the Aegean and out of the Bronze Age

During the second millennium BCE the maritime trading system of the eastern Mediterranean spread westward into the Aegean Sea. Our knowledge of this expanded network has been greatly enhanced since the discovery in 1982 of a wreck off the rocky promontory known as Uluburun near the modern Turkish town of Kas. Sometime *c.* 1300 BCE a merchant vessel 50 feet in length sank here in waters about 150 feet deep. Its origin and crew are uncertain but were probably Canaanite. The principal cargo was copper in the form of 400 ingots totaling 10 tons in addition to a ton of tin ingots, enough to equip a good size army. Bronze weapons and tools were also found. Next to copper, the most abundant cargo was a resin made from the terebinth tree used by Egyptians in burial rites. It was carried in 150 terracotta amphorae carefully cushioned by dunnage made from shrubs. Other amphorae contained glass beads and orpiment, a yellow arsenic that could be used as a pigment or mixed with beeswax to make writing material. Also there was a number of pithos, large open-mouth storage jars used as barrels. One of these was filled with whole pomegranates; another was used to store smaller pieces of pottery, including juglets, oil lamps, and bowls. Among personal effects were drinking flasks, musical instruments, and a diptych (writing board).

The ship also carried exotic goods, including a piece of unworked ivory, four hippopotamus teeth, tortoise shell, and logs of African blackwood. From the north came Baltic amber beads and a ceremonial axe likely originating in the lower Danube River region of Romania. From the south were faience beads and a faience rhyton in the shape of a ram's head, pieces of ostrich eggshell, a rectangular plaque made of green stone with hieroglyphs praising the Egyptian god Ptah, and two cylinder seals, one of quartz with gold caps and the other of hematite, a blood-red crystal. Old cylinder seals were a common gift item in this period. The hematite seal is especially interesting because it had been partially recycled depicting one scene of a king and a goddess with a horned headdress from eighteenth-century BCE southern Mesopotamia (Old Babylonian) and a later design from fourteenth-century BCE northern Mesopotamia (Assyrian) depicting a warrior facing a winged griffin engraved over a portion of the earlier design.

Exotic bric-a-brac is important in providing historians with an idea as to how far connections extended, but they do not represent the ship's basic cargo, which consisted of raw materials. Next in importance to the copper, tin, and terebinth resin were almost 200 "inekku stones," cobalt blue glass ingots in the shape of discs 6 inches in diameter and 2.5 inches thick. The ship also carried opercula, shelly plates attached to murex that were used in making incense. Miscellaneous pieces of gold and silver were found, including rings and bracelets; four gold pendants bearing Canaanite motifs, one showing the figure of a nude woman, probably a goddess, holding a gazelle in each hand; a gold chalice; and a small gold scarab with the inscription "Nefertiti," wife of the heretic pharaoh Akhenaton. The gold and silver were apparently carried as scrap to be melted down and reused.

The ship appears to have been traveling westward when it met its doom. This suggests a counterclockwise maritime system that brought goods from Egypt to Levantine cities such as Byblos and Ugarit, then across to Cyprus and westward along the coast of Anatolia to Crete, the Aegean islands, and the Greek mainland before turning southward to cross the open sea – not an especially difficult leg of the voyage owing to favorable currents and winds – to the African coast and back to Egypt. Some more adventurous ships may have occasionally wandered west to Sardinia for metals and perhaps as far as Spain. The huge variety of products on the Uluburun shipwreck seems to indicate it had been tramping, that is, sailing from port to port taking on whatever was available and selling whatever would turn a profit. Tramping could be combined with directional trade; a ship could be traveling under the aegis of a king, perhaps sending gifts to another king, and engage in buying and selling on the side. Or the ship could have been in a long-distance haul headed for a single destination that served as the distribution point for a whole region. This would have required a very complex system of local distribution since the large quantity of metals, resin, and inekku stones would have been quite beyond the needs of any single city or even all but the largest of states.

Some of this cargo is likely to have been on official consignment, in particular the copper, which may have been sent by the King of Alashiya (Cyprus) to the Egyptian pharaoh. However, much of it, including the valuable scrap, appears to represent private enterprise. The capital investment for such a load must have been huge for its day, making the loss catastrophic. Over 1,000 items were recovered at Uluburun, an enormous quantity compared to what is normally found in land sites. If this ship had not sunk, most of the articles on board, particularly the perishables and raw metals, would never have made it into the archaeological record.

How and when the peoples of the Aegean began to trade directly with the Levant and Egypt remains unrecorded. They had been exchanging obsidian and many undetectable goods among themselves for thousands of years. The introduction of metals energized this trade, which in turn stimulated the development of more complex social structures and ultimately the rise of states. The island of Crete, lying at the entrance to the Aegean Sea 60 miles from Greece, 120 from Anatolia, and 200 from the coast of Africa, was home to the first advanced European civilization known today as the Minoan. In the early to mid-second millennium BCE Minoan political, religious, and economic life centered on great palaces from which bureaucracies directed an ordered society. Palace workshops were production centers for pottery, metalwork, and textiles, and the state controlled long-distance trade. Crete was a relatively small place with a growing population and a heated economy. The result was a hybrid system, at the same time a trade state and a bureaucratic monarchy, but 100 percent maritime in orientation. No remains of Minoan ships have been found, but they were not the large bulky vessels that characterized the Egypt to Levant trade. Aegean ships were probably about 30–50 feet in length, small enough to drag onto a beach. They used sails but were mainly oar-driven. A signet ring depicts one vessel with 15 oars on each side and a high stern, although high prows and low sterns are believed to have been more common. A Minoan naval procession depicted on a frieze from c. 1600 BCE shows galley-type ships being paddled (actually oars had long before replaced paddles) with a single mast and an Egyptian style square sail with a boom.

The first product the Minoans had to trade was probably high-quality timber suitable for shipbuilding since great forests originally covered the island. Once cleared, much of the land was replanted in olive trees and grape vines. In the Mediterranean world, the importance of the olive can scarcely be overstated. First cultivated perhaps in Syria, it spread to Crete by the third millennium BCE. In places where the climate was suitable, the olive combined remarkable endurance with copious amounts of fruit. Olive trees thrived on rocky and barren landscapes, and their deep root systems had no problem surviving summer droughts; they didn't require much attention and could remain productive for the better part of a century. The olive proved to be a nourishing food, and its oil remained the principal edible fat in the Mediterranean basin for thousands of years. Olive oil lamps lit the interiors of buildings, and oil soaked in aromatic herbs was used as perfumed unguents, medicine, and body cleansers in the age before soap. Hundreds of massive jars holding thousands of gallons of olive oil were stored in Minoan palace warehouses awaiting export. The grape vine, which required much the same growing conditions, provided thousands more gallons of exportable liquids. On land where olive trees and grape vines were not grown, the Minoans raised flocks of sheep, allowing for a considerable export of woolen textiles.

Olive oil and wine needed to be stored and shipped in containers as did other commodities, including perfumes, resins, spices, and even opium, hence the need for a large pottery industry. Some pottery was decorated, painted, and shaped so finely it became valuable in its own right. The craft industries of the palace workshops turned out other high-quality goods in gold, silver, bronze, ivory, and precious stones from figurines to cups and swords and even ostrich eggs decorated in faience. Among the most exquisite products of Minoan manufacture were vases, bowls, jars, and lamps cut from solid stone, initially soft stone such as chlorite and serpentine but, as techniques evolved, craftsmen moved to alabaster, breccias, marble, and finally obsidian and rock crystal.

The island of Crete could not supply itself with the gold, silver, and copper it used, leave aside the ivory, tin, and ostrich eggs. Clearly the Minoans were a people who imported raw materials and exported manufactured goods. The Uluburun shipwreck accents the importance of trade in bulk metals, which was the most important trade commodity in the Bronze Age. As for finished products, Babylonian seals have been found on Crete along with the remains of Canaanite and Cypriot pottery although what was contained therein remains a mystery. Egyptian stone vessels from the third millennium BCE reached Crete, where they remained in circulation for a long time providing models for the Minoans' own stone industry. Other imports from Egypt included linen, papyrus, alabaster, amethyst, carnelian, ostrich eggs, and finished goods such as scarabs, beads, jewelry, and even a Middle Kingdom statuette. Crete also enjoyed an active trade with Ugarit, exporting finished goods such as weapons, textiles, pottery, and sandals in exchange for raw materials such as tin, gold, ivory, and precious stones. The Minoans may have had a small colony in Ugarit.

In the fifteenth century BCE Minoan power began to wane in favor of a people from the Greek mainland, the Mycenaeans. How this happened remains uncertain although speculation sees trade as playing a central role. One suggestion is that the Mycenaeans were essentially pirates who over a long period bled the Minoan commercial system dry; however another proposes that Minoan society self-destructed as a result of deterioration in the relationship between the Minoans and their commercial partners.

The Mycenaeans lived in separate but powerful city states. Like the Minoans, these were palace-centered with state bureaucracies controlling all large-scale economic activities. Much of the foreign trade was probably carried out in the form of gift exchange although private traders, particularly those coming from the Levant and Cyprus, may have operated in some capacity. This trend became more evident in the thirteenth century BCE when government control over trade appears to have slipped. Nevertheless, it is instructive that linguists have not been able to identify words for "buy," "sell," "merchant," or "money" (referring to a medium of exchange) in the Greek Mycenaean vocabulary. The Mycenaeans imported and exported the same products as their predecessors although on a larger scale, over a wider geographical range, and for a shorter time, reflecting a general trend in the increased growth of sea trade during the last centuries of the Bronze Age. Mycenaean pottery, which is characterized by graceful, flowing, decorative motifs that included birds, octopi, and papyrus, became so popular as an item of exchange it is found today in places the Mycenaeans never went themselves and probably never heard of. Olive oil remained at the center of Mycenaean trade along with wine: almost 3,000 stemmed drinking cups were found in one room in the Mycenaean palace at Pylos, an indication of the enormous quantity of wine produced.

In the east, the Mycenaeans were aggressive traders who operated from commercial outposts at Ugarit and other Levantine cities. To the south, shards from Mycenaean stirrup jars used for shipping oil have been found as far as Nubia. To the west, Mycenaean activity extended to Sicily, southern Italy, and Sardinia. This is most evident in the thirteenth century when the Mycenaeans appear to have shifted their trade westward to compensate for deteriorating conditions in the east. To the north, there is little in the way of pottery or other indicators of Mycenaean trade except for weaponry, such as bronze swords, double axes, spear heads, and even war chariots that turn up as grave goods, and items that are believed to have been symbols of high rank such as razors, tweezers, and folding stools. Along with the actual imports are many local imitations. Curiously, Mycenaean contact is more evident in the Nordic–Baltic region than in Central Europe. The explanation may be amber, the one detectable item from the far north for which the Mycenaean elite appears to have had an inexhaustible appetite. Assuming a Baltic-to-Aegean commercial link based on an exchange in prestige goods – amber for heroic weaponry – several mechanisms could have been used: directional trade involving long-distance professional traders, large-scale expeditions up the river systems, or inter-elite prestige chain gift exchange. Another possibility is that the Mycenaeans simply plugged into preexisting trunk routes running across central and northern Europe and did receive goods from central Europe, such as horses and slaves, which are archaeologically invisible.

By the late Bronze Age a series of overlapping commercial exchange systems extended from the western Mediterranean to Afghanistan and India. This structure would not make an orderly transition into the next period, the Iron Age. In the last centuries of the second millennium BCE, the Bronze Age cities and states came crashing down, destroyed by fire and sword. Cities like Ugarit were destroyed, states as powerful as the Hittite Empire were crushed, and whole civilizations including that of the Mycenaeans faded into oblivion. Egypt might have been overrun by the enigmatic Sea Peoples except that, by luck, it was under the rule of one of its greatest warrior pharaohs, Ramses III. New peoples such as the Philistines and Dorians seem to appear ex nihilo. Farmers, craftsmen, and miners stopped producing for a market economy, sea lanes swarmed with pirates, roads fell into disuse, trading centers were abandoned, and whole trade systems became dislocated. The remaining traffic dwindled to a trickle.

The cause of this cataclysm has not been completely sorted out, but the usual suspects – warfare, demographic shifts, large-scale migrations, social upheaval, famine from poor harvests, epidemics, and natural catastrophes – have all come in for a share of the blame. One factor is certain: the magnitude of this phenomenon can be explained only by the interconnectedness of the Bronze Age world. In the late second millennium BCE, the domino theory was played out with a vengeance. The result was a near total systems collapse. The world as the peoples of the eastern Mediterranean and Southwest Asia had known it simply disintegrated.

A closer look: trade and the Trojan War

The most celebrated adventure of the Mycenaean Greeks, referred to in this context as the "Achaeans," was the Trojan War, doubtless the most famous war in ancient history. With over 130 years of on-and-off fieldwork on what may be the most exhaustively worked archaeological site in the world and detailed descriptions from the most celebrated literary work to survive the ancient Mediterranean world, the *Iliad*, we should know everything that was important about Troy and the Trojan War, including the role trade may have played. That we do not provides a cautionary lesson as to what we can and cannot learn about the past.

The Classical Greeks knew the lands that ringed the Black Sea as a rich region, and they sailed there to obtain grain, gold, and slaves, but the earliest archaeological evidence for such trade comes only from the seventh or possibly the eighth century BCE. Their predecessors, the restless Mycenaeans, went east, west, and south, but did they also go north? The city of Troy was located on the northwestern corner of Anatolia on the eastern side of the Hellespont (Dardanelles), a channel 40 miles long and 1 mile wide, one of two water passages separating the Aegean, and thus the Mediterranean, from the Black Sea. For ships sailing northward from Troy, the current is unfavorable since it flows down from the Black Sea, and much of the time the wind blows from the north as well. Ships waiting for a favorable change in the winds would seek shelter along the eastern coast. According to the standard interpretation, Troy was founded to take advantage of this situation, which allowed it to control traffic going between the two seas. The Hellespont also separated the land masses of Thrace and Anatolia, in other words, Europe and Asia and thus east–west traffic between the two continents. Troy was a hub where both land and sea networks converged.

The Trojans, who played the role of enemy in Homer's *Iliad*, were not the first people to occupy that site. The first Troy was founded in the early third millennium BCE as the fortified stronghold of a local chieftain. Foreign materials including marble, obsidian, and pottery are evident from early times. By the middle of the millennium, the settlement had evolved into Troy II, a much grander place that held a magnificent treasure of gold, silver, and bronze, including 8,750 beads of gold, which were safely buried before the city was overwhelmed by unknown assailants in *c.* 2250 BCE. The source of this wealth, in the standard interpretation, was trade. In one proposed scenario, Anatolian silver was shipped out of Troy and through the Aegean to the Levant in return for Afghan tin. Weapons made from Trojan bronze (copper being easily obtainable in Anatolia) were then channeled into Central Europe. Controlling access to the Black Sea brought Troy a system of contacts that reached to the far edges of the Bronze Age world.

Following Troy II the next few sites were not especially impressive until Troy VI (referred to in Hittite records as Wilusa). According to archaeological evidence, it best fits Homer's description of the place the Achaeans besieged for ten years although the evidence seems to show that Troy VI was knocked down by an earthquake in c. 1275 BCE. It was reoccupied as Troy VIIa, a much less grandiose place that was destroyed by war in c. 1180, the date Greek tradition assigns to the fall of the city. This is an awkward problem for scholars trying to line up Homer's epic poem with historical reality. One possibility is to assume that the collective memory of the various wars and natural disasters Troy suffered was later telescoped into one catastrophic event. In the history of trade, the war itself is important only if commercial issues were involved or if it had a lasting impact on trade patterns.

Modern historians, who tend to be an unromantic lot, generally dismiss the abducted wife explanation as the cause of the war, preferring instead economic and political factors. Troy's strategic position at the crossroads of both sea and land has led to the assumption that this was a commercial war. Were the Trojans interfering with Mycenaean trade in the Black Sea? Were they charging excessive tolls or shutting out the Mycenaeans altogether? Had Troy become too rich for its own good, tempting the war-prone Mycenaeans into one big pirate raid that got out of hand?

In trying to put the archaeological evidence into some context, we turn to Homer to see if the *Iliad* and the *Odyssey* can be of any help. Do they represent long oral traditions in which real historical memories are embedded, or are they simply literary creations? As far as economic activities are concerned, it doesn't seem to matter since there is almost no reference to any productive behavior, only looting, ravaging, and plundering. Only one market is mentioned. This occurs in the *Iliad* during a lull in the fighting when ships from the nearby island of Lemnos unexpectedly show up in the Greek camp with cargoes of wine. First they present 1,000 gallons to the high king Agamemnon as a "gift," apparently for the right to trade with his men, who "now supplied themselves with wine, some in exchange for bronze, some for gleaming iron, others for hides or live cattle, others again for slaves." This was a one-time market, a special event based on barter with no fixed rates of exchange, which did little more than provide the Greeks with the means to stay up all night drinking and partying, hardly an important element in anyone's economy.

Unfortunately, neither the *Iliad* nor the *Odyssey* provides even a hint that the Trojan War had anything to do with commerce. The Homeric attitude toward trade was decidedly negative: it was something that unheroic people like the Phoenicians did. But the *Iliad* and indeed the war itself, like the Troy VI–Troy VIIa conundrum, should not distract historians from the basic issue of trade. In the standard interpretation, Troy VI was a wealthy and prominent city that played a significant role as a regional power and was of strategic economic importance. As the trade of Crete and Mycenaean Greece expanded from the sixteenth century BCE on, so did that of Troy, which anchored the northern end of the Aegean system. Whereas no treasure trove similar to Troy II has been recovered, Troy VI was a great emporium with exotics such as ostrich eggs, hippopotamus ivory, and glass and faience beads coming from the south and amber, raw metals, and slaves from the north. The Trojans themselves produced and exported woolen textiles and probably horses (throughout the *Iliad* the Trojans are referred to as "horse tamers"). Trojan pottery, known as Trojan gray ware, a functional, if not aesthetically pleasing product, was reaching the Levant and Cyprus in modest amounts by the thirteenth century BCE.

The key to Troy's happy condition rested on its pivotal position at the gateway to the northern periphery of the world. Directly north were the untapped riches of the Black Sea; to the east, the mineral-rich Caucasus Mountains; and to the west, the Danubian River valley, which accessed the heartland of Europe. Beyond the Black Sea on what was thought to be the very edge of the earth were the steppe lands that reached from the Carpathian to the Ural Mountains. Troy represented the zone of transition between advanced economies that could produce mass quantities of manufactured goods and more primitive economies that could supply them with the raw materials needed for such production.

The process whereby commodities flowed from the Aegean to the Black Sea is not known. Did ships actually sail through the Hellespont, the Sea of Marmara, and the second strait, the Bosporus, into the Black Sea? Perhaps smaller ships could have managed this although, given the maritime technology and navigation techniques of the time, it is doubtful a vessel even the size of the Uluburun wreck could have made it. The alternative was to offload goods at Troy and ship them overland to a Black Sea port, avoiding the unpleasantries of the straits passage. In any case, Troy would benefit from the tolls it levied, or by providing pilots to guide ships, or by carrying the merchandise overland. At least according to the standard interpretation.

A second school of historians and archaeologists using the same data as those who support the standard interpretation have come to a diametrically opposite conclusion, prompting a new Trojan War, this one spilling as much ink as the first spilled blood. To this second school, who have been labeled as the "Minimalists" by those supporting the standard view, Troy was an insignificant place at the far end of a maritime branch route, hardly grand enough even to be considered a city. Troy had no port (it was actually several miles inland), no traces of a marketplace, no merchant fleet, and didn't produce anything special that anyone else wanted. The Minimalists see no evidence of an east–west trade route running across Anatolia to the Hellespont and into Europe. Most importantly, they not only deny that the Mycenaeans went beyond the Hellespont, they don't believe Troy had any contact with the Black Sea. Currents and winds effectively prevented Bronze Age ships from navigating the Hellespont, and they would have found the Bosporus an even greater challenge. The region around Troy had fertile soil and lots of water and was good for agriculture, stock raising, and fishing, not a bad place to live. But Troy was far away from the real action of the urbanized, commercialized, civilized world, a backwater rather than a gateway. As for the Trojans themselves, they were happy in their bucolic bliss, complacently pursuing, as the Minimalist scholar Denys Page put it, "what seems to have been their favorite occupations, spinning wool and eating shellfish."

So the second Trojan War rages on, which makes it difficult to determine an answer to the question: why was there a first Trojan War? The Minimalists deny that the Mycenaeans comprised a hostile coalition determined to seize control over the Hellespont: why would they want it? And, in any case, the conflict could not have been a trade war since Troy was hardly involved in trade. Their best guess is that Troy became mixed up in larger geopolitical issues involving the Mycenaeans and the Hittite Empire and ended up as one of the convergence points of a greater war. No one disagrees that relations between the Mycenaeans and the Hittites were generally sour, and the Hittites were known to have used trade embargoes as a weapon against the Mycenaeans in other places. But if so, counter advocates of the standard interpretation, why would the two neighborhood heavyweights come to such a third-rate, no-account place to fight it out? Certainly trade or the hope of some form of commercial advantage played a role in this, especially since the trade-happy Mycenaeans were involved.

Whatever caused the war, the fall of Troy sounded the death knell for the Bronze Age, and the victorious Mycenaeans were themselves swept into the dustbin of history in less than a century. If golden Achilles and noble Hector did, indeed, die fighting in a grubby little trade war, it's best not to raise the issue in a world literature class.

Chapter 6

Of purple men and oil merchants

In the eleventh century BCE the coastal Canaanites of the Levant arose from the debris of the Late Bronze Age cataclysm with a vengeance. Henceforth known by the name the Greeks gave them – the Phoenicians – they returned to the sea doing what they did better than anyone of their age: sailing to places hitherto unknown, buying where cheapest, selling where dearest, and making boatloads of money. For a while, they were the master entrepreneurs of the Mediterranean, answering the call for metals by finding new sources and creating new routes to replace those that had been disrupted. They imported raw material, processed it in their workshops, and exported sumptuous luxury products.

As before, the Phoenicians continued to live in independent city states. The ancient port of Byblos revived as a center for the Egyptian trade, but Egypt was not nearly so dominant as before, and the overly conservative merchants of Byblos did not seize on new opportunities. Instead Tyre and Sidon became the chief commercial centers, especially Tyre, which was built on two islands joined together several hundred yards from the mainland. The prophet Isaiah calls Tyre "the merchant of the nations" and "the bestower of crowns whose merchants were princes." Ezekiel concurs, noting, "You satisfied many peoples with your abundant wealth and merchandise, you enriched the kings of the earth." He lists 16 different places in which the Phoenicians traded, from Tarshish in southwestern Spain to Sheba in southwestern Arabia and provides a catalogue of trade goods ranging from precious stones, ivory, ebony, and spices to metals, foodstuffs, livestock, wool, and slaves. For the early centuries of the first millennium BCE, Tyre could justly claim Ugarit's old title of greatest port in the Mediterranean and perhaps the world.

In the tradition of their forefathers, the Phoenicians were excellent sailors who enjoyed certain technical advantages centering on the development of more seaworthy ships capable of long voyages. They were referred to in the Bible as the "Ships of Tarshish," meaning ships capable of sailing from one side of the Mediterranean to the other. They developed the keel, allowing for better control in rough seas, and used adjustable sails. According to Pliny, they "invented observing the stars in sailing" and by using the Pole Star became the first to sail at night beyond the sight of land over the open waters.

Beginning in the ninth century BCE, the Phoenician world became more complicated with the arrival of a new power from the east, the Assyrians. Wisely, the Phoenicians chose to bow to the weight of the ferocious Assyrian war machine, striking a deal under which they paid a large tribute in silver. Tyre lost control over much of its Syrian and Anatolian trade to the Assyrians themselves, but the conquerors did have an important place for the Phoenicians in their overall commercial scheme. Wool, a staple in the Mesopotamian export trade for millennia, was now directed to Phoenician cities where it was woven and dyed purple, then sent to various destinations within the empire, including back to Assyria. The Phoenicians could also help to assure the Assyrians a large and steady supply of metals: gold and silver to power their economy and bronze and iron to equip their armies. Phoenician ports became the Assyrian Empire's window to a new and virtually untapped storehouse of metals, the western Mediterranean.

Despite increasingly exorbitant demands for tribute and not being allowed to trade with Assyria's enemy Egypt, the Phoenician cities generally benefited from their position in the Assyrian system, at least for a while. Assyrian markets were open to Phoenician goods, and the empire provided security and stability. The Canaanite–Phoenicians had always enjoyed a happy balance of palace-based and private sector trade, but under Assyrian control this shifted, reflecting a decline in Phoenician state power. Long-distance overland trade came into the hands of independent merchant houses operating through a system of agents. This system did not endear Phoenician political authorities to Assyrian rule, and in the late eighth and seventh centuries BCE they became party to several unsuccessful attempts at throwing off the imperial yoke. Tyre was not destroyed but was forced to pay an onerous exaction in gold. Sidon, considered as less essential in the Assyrian commercial scheme, paid for a rebellion by being sacked and wasted.

The Assyrian presence helps to explain the most important role the Phoenicians played in the history of trade, their push across the Mediterranean. The collapse of Mycenaean power several centuries earlier had opened the western Mediterranean, but the vacuum had yet to be filled. The need to pay their tribute in silver as well as the opportunity to serve as the connection between the interior of Southwest Asia and the lands ringing the Mediterranean drove the Phoenicians westward to seek new sources of metal. In the end their goal became nothing less than a monopoly over the natural resources of the western Mediterranean. A key strategy in Phoenician trade was to create a demand for a new product, usually a luxury item that would appeal to a local elite, who would then organize production of the commodity the Phoenicians were seeking. Among goods the Phoenicians commonly offered were wine, olive oil, unguents, perfumes, cosmetics, jewelry, trinkets, statuettes, and textiles. The nodes of this network were stations carefully selected as emporia, processing centers, and strongholds for safeguarding vital points along the way. Several were founded with substantial numbers of settlers from the homeland and evolved into independent cities.

Classical authors including Pliny and Strabo claim that the Phoenicians were active in the western Mediterranean in the twelfth century BCE with their earliest outposts at Lixus in Morocco and Gades (Cadiz) in Spain, both beyond the Straits of Gibraltar on the Atlantic side, both founded *c.* 1100 BCE. The archaeological evidence points to the eighth and seventh centuries BCE as the time for such expansion although a recent discovery of Phoenician inscriptions on Sardinia dating to the eleventh or tenth century has rekindled the controversy. Using, perhaps, old Mycenaean routes, the Phoenicians hopped from Cyprus to the Aegean, where they were seeking silver and slaves by the mid-ninth century, and beyond to Sicily, Sardinia, the Balearic Islands, and Spain. Some evidence shows them in the Rabat area of Morocco in the eighth century. They tended to settle their colonies in clusters along the Tunisian and Libyan coasts, on Sicily, and in southeastern Spain. Until the rise of Carthage, the most important was at Gades and beyond in the mysterious land of Tartessia (the Biblical Tarshish) although it is not clear exactly who lived in the latter place, Phoenicians, native Spaniards, or more likely both.

The trip from Tyre to Gades took 3 months, at the end of which a ship had to navigate the Straits of Gibraltar with its treacherous tides and sometimes violent winds. Gades is believed to have been founded in *c.* 770 BCE as the gateway to Tartessia, a place still not archaeologically pinpointed but said to contain so much silver that the inhabitants made furniture from it and ships headed back to Phoenicia used it for ballast. The mining, production, and transport of metals on so large a scale across such a distance were enormous undertakings. The value represented and the profits realized had to be huge to justify the effort. Tartessia became a byword for wealth and remoteness. The early Greeks associated Tartessia with Hades, that is until a Greek merchant named Colaeus was blown off course on his way to Egypt in 638 BCE by a wind so relentless it carried him across the Mediterranean and, according to Herodotus, through Gibraltar to Tartessia: "This trading center was virgin territory at the time, and consequently they came home with the biggest profit any Greek trader we have reliable information about has ever made from his cargo." This amounted to 60 talents, an incredible 3,600 pounds of silver!

In the long run, the richest and most powerful of Punic cities did not prove to be Gades even when combined with Tartessia. Carthage had a spacious natural harbor, commanded a good defensive position, and fronted on a hinterland that proved to be an excellent place to grow grain, olives, grapes, and other fruits. Nearby waters contained the purple-producing murex shellfish. The traditional date for the founding of Carthage is 814 BCE. At first, it was little more than a stopover for traffic en route to Spain, but its position at the narrowest point in the Mediterranean where the North African and Sicilian coasts are only 75 miles apart gave it an unmatched strategic position. The power that controlled both sides could control traffic passing between the eastern and western Mediterranean.

As the mother cities back in Phoenicia slowly declined under the tribute burdens imposed by Assyria, Carthage assumed control over their trade routes. In the late fifth and fourth centuries BCE, Carthage emerged victorious from a series of wars against the Greek cities of Sicily, capturing the trade that had previously flowed through them. Carthage's port had to be refurbished and expanded to accommodate the boom. The metals of Spain and Sardinia were now brought there to be processed, and the city also became famous for other merchandise, especially carpets, pillows, and perfumes. Carthaginian amphorae fashioned in a distinct cigar-shape were shipped around the western Mediterranean, and although the contents are not certain, most indicators point to wine.

Unlike their Roman rivals, the Carthaginians were more concerned with making money than ruling. They had little interest in creating a large land empire stretching out in all directions from their city, and most of the time the Carthaginian gaze was turned toward the sea even when their interest was in Africa. The Phoenicians had sailed into the Atlantic, with their archaeological remains extending as far as Essaouira midway down the Moroccan coast, and they visited Madeira and the Canary Islands. How much farther the Carthaginians went is a matter of speculation. Herodotus has them trading for gold in a version of the silent trade at a location that may have been the mouth of the Senegal River. In another account a fleet under Hanno in 465 BCE is said to have reached a spot between Sierra Leone and the Congo River. The problem in accepting this is that the wind and the current both flow from the north. Hanno may have been able to sail down the West African coast, but neither he nor anyone else of his time had the navigational techniques or the equipment to sail back. This is also a problem in accepting the story of the Phoenicians who circumnavigated Africa under orders from the Pharaoh Necho II.

Pliny mentions Hanno along with a contemporary named Himilco, who was sent to explore the coasts of Europe in what appears to have been a two-pronged assault to bring the lands beyond Gibraltar into the Carthaginian commercial fold. The Tartessians had earlier established trade contact with the "Tin Islands," and Himilco's venture may have been a follow-up on this. Himilco sailed up the coasts of Portugal, northwestern Spain, and France and likely crossed to Britain and Ireland. On the way he reportedly encountered sea monsters and got stuck in a morass of seaweed.

Back in the Phoenician homeland, matters were not getting better. The fall of the Assyrian Empire in the late sixth century BCE brought the rise of a new power in Mesopotamia, the Neo-Babylonian Empire, whose armies besieged Tyre for 13 years. Tyre survived but was exhausted. The Neo-Babylonians didn't last long and soon were replaced by the Persians, under whom the Phoenicians fared somewhat better. The Phoenicians provided the Persian Empire with much of its fleet but, during the Macedonian conquest of Persia, Tyre provoked the wrath of Alexander the Great and was destroyed in 332 BCE. This opened the gate for the last flood of refugees into Carthage and marked the passing of commercial prominence on the eastern shore of the Mediterranean from the cities of the Levant to a new center on the Egyptian coast, Alexandria.

During the heyday of the Phoenicians, their only major commercial rivals in the Mediterranean were the Greeks. The collapse of Mycenaean civilization was so complete that it took the Greeks almost four centuries to recover, a period known as the Dark Ages. The small amount of goods exchanged during this time was through reciprocity rather than commercial trade. Grave goods from Cyprus, the Levant, and Egypt dating from the tenth and ninth centuries BCE have been found at one site, probably carried there by Phoenicians in very casual, sporadic, small-scale trade.

In the Homeric epics, which were composed following the end of the Dark Ages, the attitude toward trade was decidedly negative, which was not a residue from the Mycenaeans, who were enthusiastic traders. Goods might be exchanged on a one-time basis between parties of equal strength, and people who had frequent contact with each other exchanged gifts, but to trade for profit was considered a contemptible vocation. For the Homeric Greeks this was a matter of ethics: it was thought nobler to plunder someone of their goods than to trade for them. In the *Odyssey* Odysseus in disguise visits some Greeks who are holding athletic contests. When he refuses to join in, he is taunted by a brash young man who lays on Odysseus the deepest of insults: "You are more like a skipper of a merchant crew, who spends his life on a hulking tramp, worrying about his outward freight, or keeping a sharp eye on the cargo when he comes home with his extortionate profits. No: one can see you are no athlete."

Beginning in the eighth century BCE, Greece underwent a dramatic change with a population boom amounting to an increase of between 300 and 700 percent over less than a century. The economy changed virtually overnight, with the production of surplus goods, the appearance of an entrepreneurial spirit, the emergence of market forces, and the reestablishment of significant overseas trade. Greece is a relatively small, rocky place with a huge coastline featuring a multitude of natural harbors and bordered by a sea having an abundance of islands and lacking tides. The Greeks returned to this sea with gusto, initially in undecked, broad-bottomed, 20-oared ships but soon in much larger double-banked 50-oared ships up to 80 feet long, the famous pentekontors. The old palace-dominated system of the Minoans and Mycenaeans was not reestablished. Instead profits were the driving force although, taking a lesson from the Phoenicians, Greek merchants often facilitated contact with foreign partners through gift-giving. This long-distance trade would not just focus on securing imports in the form of luxury goods and metals but also on exports, including products manufactured expressly to sell abroad to make a profit.

The initial direction of the new long-distance trade was eastward with old trading partners in the Levant. By 800 BCE Greeks from the island of Euboea were established at Al Mina ("the Port") in northern Syria just up the coast from ancient Ugarit. Al Mina would be used by Greek merchants from various cities for the next four centuries as an emporium for the transfer of goods between the interior of Southwest Asia, the Aegean region, and later the western Mediterranean. Probably the Greeks were seeking metals carried down from Anatolia and Armenia, but later, after they found better sources in the western Mediterranean, they reversed the flow and carried metals, especially iron, into Al Mina. Other goods the Greeks sought from the east included such high-tech products as glass, medicines, and dyes.

The Euboeans also pioneered Greek trade to the west. The common assumption has been that Greek colonization was primarily a matter of overpopulation and land hunger, with surplus people spilling out of Greece to find new places to farm. Whereas this was true in some instances, a closer look at the earliest Greek settlements in the west seems to show most were established as part of a trade-route building process for contact with peoples such as the Etruscans, who lived on the Italian peninsula north of Rome. Even colonies established for agricultural purposes were soon producing surpluses of grain and other products in demand by the folks back home. The earliest of the Euboean colonies in the west was at Pithekoussai ("Ape Island") on the northern rim of the Bay of Naples, a strategic location for contact with the Etruscans but hardly an attractive place to farm. Soon goods were moving from Pithekoussai not just to Greece but as far as Al Mina with stops along the way.

The Euboean Greeks and the Phoenicians were often partners in trade, and part of the population at Pithekoussai was Phoenician. Since the Phoenicians preceded the Greeks in this part of the world, it is unlikely that the Greeks could have entered this market without Phoenician acquiescence. For a time, until the founding of Massilia (Marseilles) in *c.* 600 BCE, the Greeks did not attempt to penetrate farther west into territory that fell under the Phoenician monopoly. In some places Greeks also lived side by side and formed business partnerships with Etruscans. The Greeks did safeguard the entryway into their own area of operation by taking control over the Straits of Messina, the narrow passage separating Italy and Sicily, and various Greek cities set up colonies on both sides, usually where trade prospects looked promising. Soon colonies were founding their own colonies.

The era of peace and partnership, however, did not last indefinitely. By the early sixth century BCE, chronic warfare existed between Greek and Phoenician colonies in Sicily over control of the doorway between the eastern and western

Mediterranean whereas to the north Greeks and Etruscans struggled to determine commercial supremacy in the northwest. The colony of Massilia, which soon became a thriving city, must have been of considerable annoyance to both Etruscans and Phoenicians. Located near the mouth of the Rhone River, it could tap into the huge hinterland of Gaul (France and Belgium).

In Gaul goods moved across well developed exchange networks using river valleys, one running from the Seine to the Saone to the Rhone, another up the Loire to the Rhone. The Greeks of Massilia became middlemen in the flow of goods between northwestern Europe and the eastern Mediterranean. A much desired commodity on this route was tin, some of which came from Brittany on the northwestern coast of Gaul, but the major source was across the English Channel in the British Isles. This system was still active in the first century as noted by the historian Diodorus Siculus, who observed that British tin was transported by packhorse across Brittany by a tribe called the Veneti, who had become very wealthy from this. Along with tin came perishables such as hides, salted meats, grain, slaves, and, from farther north, furs.

The Greeks brought the grape vine and olive tree to southern France, and Massilia sent much of its own wine and oil inland as well as related products such as goblets, cups, jugs, and kraters (bowls used for mixing wine and water). Iron Age princely graves and votive deposits in western and northern Europe contained many elite goods of Greek and Etruscan manufacture, some of which were quite exquisite, including bronze swords; cauldrons and feasting equipment; coral beads, amulets, and brooches; furniture sometimes with ivory inlay; and wheeled carts and wagons. Initially many of the imports were still distributed through prestige chains but, as time went on, more and more entered the nascent market system as exchange moved away from social relationships to profit-making. Economies in the interior became more geared to the production of goods desired in Mediterranean markets in order to obtain Mediterranean goods.

Massilia's interests were not confined to the northern interior. It also came to control the overland trade routes between Spain and Italy and established its own colony at Emporiae (Ampurias) and smaller outposts down the Spanish coast, challenging Carthage's monopoly. One source mentions a maritime route originating in Ireland or Britain, crossing to Brittany, then moving down the Atlantic coast to Tartessia, through Gibraltar and north along the Mediterranean coast to Massilia. This was made possible by the recent introduction of the sail into northwestern Europe, the earliest of which were made of leather. Prior to this, boats had to be paddled or rowed. A trader from Massilia named Pytheas searching for tin claimed to have sailed beyond Britain in the fourth century BCE to a place he called Thule, which modern speculation has as either Iceland, Norway, or the Shetland Islands, then continued on, eventually reaching the Arctic ice. On the way back he picked up a load of amber on an island off Denmark, which must have made the trip worthwhile.

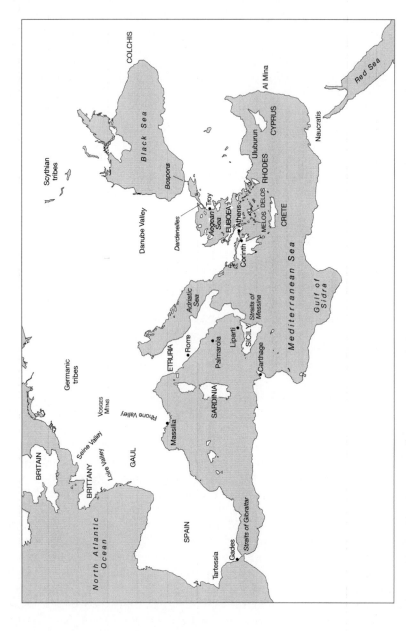

Map 6.1 Mediterranean Basin and Europe 1500 BCE–200 BCE

The Greek diaspora stretched north and south as well as east and west. Greeks settled along the rim of the Black Sea, where there was good agricultural land, particularly on the northern shore and Crimean Peninsula. Soon copious amounts of grain were flowing back to the homeland along with timber, pickled and smoked fish, slaves, horses, hides, furs, honey, wax, amber, gold, and iron. Northern shore cities such as Olbia ("Wealthy"), reputed to be the richest of all Greek colonies, had access to the river system that penetrated far into the Russian interior, and Greek pottery and other products have been found hundreds of miles from the last Greek settlements. On the western shore the Danube River opened the hinterland of eastern and Central Europe, where mountains contained gold and silver, and southern shore cities served as the terminus for land routes running to Iran. Black Sea trade was so crucial for Athens that the Athenians kept careful tabs over the various states that lay along the way, using a combination of diplomacy and threats to keep the grain lifeline open.

Across the Mediterranean to the south in Egypt, the XXVI Dynasty reversed traditional policy and opened Egyptian trade to Greeks and Phoenicians. When Colaeus was blown off course and made his famous detour to Tartessia, he was on his way to Egypt, a trip that apparently was by that time commonplace. Under the XXVI Dynasty Greek ships were required to trade specifically at the delta town of Naucratis, where the government collected rich customs duties. A similar site was assigned to Phoenician merchants, and in both places Egyptians lived side-by-side with the foreigners. Naucratis had four large warehouses and a factory for mass producing faience products, including vases, statuettes, and scarab seals as good luck charms for the Greek market. The main commodities that the Greeks sought from the Egyptians were grain, papyrus, linen, ivory, magic amulets, alabaster, cosmetics, drugs, and semi-precious stones. In return, the Greeks in Naucratis imported from their homeland olive oil and wine and most importantly silver carried as coinage since the Egyptians did not mint their own coins. The merchants of 12 Greek cities were represented at Naucratis, and the relationship they maintained with each other did not involve their home governments.

During the first millennium BCE, the carrying business in the eastern Mediterranean gradually shifted from the Phoenicians to the Greeks, and within the Greek community commercial initiative passed from the Euboeans to Corinth. The Corinthians made much in demand painted pottery vessels that held perfumes and unguents and also assumed a middleman role in re-exporting Egyptian products. Nevertheless, in the mid-sixth century BCE, Corinth's time also passed when the Athenians developed new techniques in pottery-making that allowed them to produce the ultimate in Greek ceramics, known as Athenian black and red figure pottery, a smooth-textured product with brilliant sheen and glossy pigment. Vases in this style were considered so beautiful that they were in demand from Etruria to Syria and Egypt with one found as far as Meroe in Kush (Republic of Sudan).

Initially Greek commerce depended on private shipowners who served as their own captains, raising whatever capital they could for individual voyages. By the fifth century BCE they were renting space on their ships to professional traders. The trading system that was in evidence by the time the Greeks entered their Classical Age was different from earlier luxury-based systems, or even from the Phoenicians, who were essentially middlemen dealing in large-scale commodities such as metals rather than mass consumables. Greek trade reached down the social scale in the production, exchange, and consumption of staple goods such as grain, wine, and olive oil within a mass market context.

Given their soil, topography, and climate, the Greeks could grow olives and grapes much more efficiently than grain, and a modest quantity of oil or wine could return a substantial amount of grain from places such as Egypt, the Black Sea, and Sicily. Such an exchange in bulk goods needed to be transported over water rather than land, again ideally suited for people in the Aegean region. Often it was cheaper for Athens, for example, which imported about two-thirds of the grain it consumed, to buy bulk quantities of grain from Egypt than from parts of Greece less than 100 miles away if that grain had to be brought overland. The Athenians went so far as to legislate which crops could be exported and imported. Athens itself produced the highest quality olive oil, but the best wine came from Ionia, lying across the Aegean on the west coast of Anatolia and nearby islands. The Greeks mixed their wine with water and often added ingredients such as honey, herbs, nuts, lime, and even ashes and goat milk. The quality of Greek wines varied tremendously from excellent vintages to vile swill made palatable only when blended with another strong flavor.

The men that bought and sold these products, the merchants of Athens and similar cities, were often resident foreigners, both Greeks from other city states and non-Greeks. Referred to as "metics," they were frequently encouraged to come to a particular city and allowed to make as much money as they could even though they were relegated to the lower ranks of society and were discriminated against in various ways as, for example, by not being allowed to become citizens or own land. Nevertheless, some metics did very well since in red-hot markets the demand for imported products generally outran the supply, and if a merchant could obtain a desirable product, or even a large quantity of a common product, he could generally sell it for a hefty profit. In large part they were responsible for the great leap into the forefront of international commerce made by the Greeks.

Metics were also involved in the system of banking that developed in Greece since one of the occupations they practiced was that of money-changer. These individuals sat at tables near where ships docked, at city gates, and in the marketplace and took in foreign money, weighed and appraised it, and changed it into local currency for a small fee. At some time they also began to make loans to traders and to broker partnerships for larger ventures. As they had earlier in Mesopotamia, temples were also involved in a basic function of banking by serving as places of deposit since they were considered to be safe under the protection of the temple divinity. The depositor paid a fee for safekeeping unless his deposit, when combined with that of others and the capital of the temple itself, was lent out, in which case he received a portion of the interest. When temples became objects of plunder beginning in the fourth century BCE, the business of accepting deposits for making loans shifted to the class of moneychangers turned moneylenders. Credit was especially important in the grain business. A trader would borrow from a moneylender to purchase a cargo of grain abroad. Rates were high since the cargo served as the only security, and interest was charged by the voyage rather than per annum. The trader then reserved space in which to put his load of exports on a ship headed for a grain-producing region. More often than not, he accompanied the ship as well. On the return home the grain was sold to wholesalers, allowing him to pay off his debt and realize a profit.

The ancient world was turned upside down by the conquests of Alexander the Great, who intended for his empire to be economically integrated. On his early death his political accomplishment broke into pieces, but economic expansion continued. During the Hellenistic period that followed, commerce in the Mediterranean flowered due in part to advances in ship design and construction and improved port facilities. Small-time moneylenders sitting at tables were replaced by large-scale institutions that could transfer funds from city to city through letters of credit. The center of commercial activity shifted from the Greek mainland to transit trade cities on the west coast of Anatolia such as Rhodes, which by the third century BCE had the largest commercial fleet in the Mediterranean.

In matters of trade the most important city in the Mediterranean, particularly as Carthage fell on hard times in its struggle with Rome, was a new one, Alexandria. It exported and imported the same products that had flowed into and out of Egypt for centuries but in vastly expanded quantities. The city's port was an enormous facility with two harbors whose stone quays could reportedly hold up to 1,200 ships at a time. Warehouses lined the shores, but the Pharos lighthouse built on an island three-quarters of a mile offshore was Alexandria's wonder of the ancient world. It was the largest lighthouse in the ancient world, consisting of a tower almost 400 feet high built in three stories with the top functioning as a lantern. There, eight columns supported a cupola under which a huge piece of polished steel served as a convex mirror reflecting sunlight. At night a fire of resinous wood brought up by a lift, possibly powered by hydraulic machinery, guided ships far offshore.

The Hellenistic kings dabbled extensively in trade with the Ptolemies of Egypt, surpassing even their predecessors, the pharaohs, in creating a system in which all economic activity came under state control. With the exception of Alexandria and Naucratis, the king owned all land and virtually all means of production as well as controlled all commerce. The goal was to squeeze as much wealth as possible for the dynasty's use, much of which was then expended on fighting wars with other Hellenistic states. Grain and all other export commodities were taxed several times and attracted compulsory warehouse, lading, and shipping charges. Yet so much grain was produced so efficiently it still undersold all other grain on the Greek market. Imports into Egypt such as timber, metals, oil, wine, and horses were often assessed duties up to 300 percent of their value.

The Hellenistic state-directed commercial model did not completely replace the more free-wheeling system that had emerged under the classical Greeks. Rather, as in earlier times, the two existed side-by-side with the Hellenistic kings themselves often playing the role of entrepreneur on the international market. Trade in the Hellenistic world reached a peak in the mid-third century BCE and declined thereafter due to a series of natural and manmade problems, not the least of which were the results of economic disruption resulting from chronic warfare among Alexander's successors. This did not prove to be a good time for such indulgences. To the west the Second Punic War caused great destruction and economic dislocation, and shortly thereafter Roman armies moved into the eastern Mediterranean, where they dismembered Macedonia, crippled the Seleucid Empire, cowed Ptolemaic Egypt, and reduced the Greek cities. In 146 BCE both Carthage and Corinth were obliterated by the Roman onslaught ostensibly for political reasons although it is hardly coincidental that both were trade rivals of Rome. Other economic powerhouses such as Massilia, Athens, Rhodes, the Greek cities of Sicily and southern Italy, and even Alexandria would eventually be reduced to dependent roles. The Romans extracted a heavy burden in tribute, and wealth flowed out of all other places to the city on the Tiber.

Chapter 7

Shifting cores and peripheries in the Imperial West

The Romans created an empire comprising a complex economic and commercial system or series of overlapping systems that evolved over the centuries. The high point came in the Early Imperial period between the reigns of Augustus and Marcus Aurelius (31 BCE–180 CE), a relatively peaceful time characterized by increased production, trade expansion, capital accumulation, and monetary stability. Long-distance trade existed within the empire and beyond its borders with Roman goods going much farther than Roman merchants. Goods came into the empire sometimes from places so remote that the producers had no idea who the Romans were. In the east, Anatolia and Armenia were gateways into the Parthian Empire of Persia as were Syria and the Levantine coast via Mesopotamia. Beyond lay Afghanistan, Central Asia, and China. Egypt led up the Nile to Nubia, Kush, and Central Africa, and down the Red Sea to Arabia, Axum (Ethiopia), and the Indian Ocean, across which lay India, Ceylon, and Southeast Asia. In another direction Gaul opened northwest to Britain and Ireland and northeast to Germany, Scandinavia, and the Baltic region while the Danubian provinces accessed the Black Sea, southern Russia, and Siberia. The North African provinces were entryways to the oases of the Sahara and the Niger Valley. The possibilities appeared limitless, although the level of commercial activity as it developed was very uneven depending on direction.

Long-distance trade within the empire may be more complicated to reconstruct than the empire's trade beyond its borders. One view is that the empire was a single integrated economic unit, but critics see this as too simple. Another places Italy at the center of the system with peripheral zones extending outward: the core provided mostly finished goods, and the peripheral zones provided raw materials. Critics see this as too contrived. Still another model sees the empire as consisting of autonomous regional economies linked under the imperial political structure, each with its own core and peripheries so that, for example, southern Gaul served as a center not only for the rest of Gaul but for Britain and Spain and for foreign trade into Germany. Critics see this as unnecessarily complicated.

Roman government policy toward commerce varied over the centuries. At times the state appears to have provided little direction except to make certain that it collected as much in customs and taxes as possible and supported whatever strategies were necessary to ensure that the empire's most privileged group, the Roman oligarchy, benefited the most. For reasons related to its military and political needs, the empire did construct and maintain an impressive transportation and communications infrastructure. Roads were built to facilitate the march of armies, but were used by merchants as well. Rivers, chief among them the Tiber, Rhone, Rhine, Danube, Euphrates, Seine, Loire, and Guadalquivir, were also used to transport goods, and canals were dug to connect natural bodies of water. Along the seacoast naval stations were maintained to protect commerce at strategic points, including the Bay of Naples, the northern Adriatic, the southern Aegean, the Syrian coast, and Alexandria. As trade and naval activity increased, ports on the Mediterranean, Black, and Red seas and even the Atlantic were greatly improved, harbors and docks were rebuilt and enlarged, and new harbor basins were put in. The Romans also rebuilt Corinth and Carthage since leaving them abandoned was self-defeating once Roman rule was unchallenged. The Romans recolonized Carthage but initially did not revive its trade in wine and olive oil since these were major Italian exports. Rome, however, needed wheat, and the region around Carthage became one of its breadbaskets. Eventually wine and oil came back to supplement Italian shortfalls, and Carthage also became a center along with Spain for the production of garum, a fish sauce widely used as a condiment.

As was the case in earlier societies, those who engaged in trade and those who benefited most from trade were not necessarily the same people, nor did they form a distinct social class. Merchants could own their own ships, rent space aboard someone else's ship, or serve as agents for goods owned by someone else. Some specialized in only one product such as grain, timber, or slaves. Traders identified as "Roman" could come from anywhere in the empire except the region they were operating in, so, for example, Roman traders in Greece were often Italians, including Greek Italians, but Roman traders in the Indian Ocean trade were more likely to be Syrians or Egyptian Greeks. Italian traders, particularly from the south, did settle in ports around the Mediterranean while others operated in conjunction with Roman armies to secure the spoils generated from plunder. Often they enjoyed privileges that gave them enough advantage to drive their Greek, Levantine, and other competitors out. Several classical authors report that Italian traders had a reputation for greed in dealing with people both in and out of the empire, and in one instance involving Celtic people in the Alps, Italian traders so antagonized the locals that the Roman Senate had to curtail their activities to prevent a war.

The system provided opportunities especially for those well connected, as seen in a story from Petronius in which a merchant who lost five ships loaded with wine in a storm managed to borrow enough capital to replace the ships and cargo and went on to make a fortune. By the Late Republican period, large commercial houses represented politically influential senatorial families who owned latifundias, huge plantation estates worked by gangs of slaves. These produced mass quantities of agricultural products that were transported aboard ships owned by the family and protected by Roman military power. The products were distributed through a network of agents, often family members or slaves, working in conjunction with government officials. It was a very cozy system. On its fringes were small, independent traders who had no political clout and could hope at best to connect up with a great firm through patronage. Small traders tended to form partnerships for indefinite periods not just for specific ventures as was common earlier among the Greeks. Such partners did not need to be from the same place or ethnic group, and often behind them were more prominent people providing capital as silent partners.

Peddler trade became less important with the increase in permanent markets where traders could sell their imports wholesale and pick up exports. In the Late Imperial period a class of middlemen emerged whose activities were not specific to any single product but who sought out opportunities to dabble in whatever might turn a profit in a particular venture. Their interests could vary from luxury to general consumption goods and from caravan to sea trade, and they operated through agents, associates, and partners, whatever worked so long as careful books were kept. Whereas such flexibility appears to be a positive development, it may actually reflect a general decline in business opportunities.

The products traded long distance under the Roman Empire expanded in range and quantity within the basic Mediterranean patterns developed by the Phoenicians and Greeks. The commerce in luxury goods increased in response to demands by the Roman upper classes with Chinese silk and Indian spices the most important new commodities. Trade in cheap mass-produced goods for general consumption such as foodstuffs, pottery, metal products, and textiles had been a major characteristic of the Greek period, and this continued under the Romans. Chief among bulk goods was grain to feed Rome, other cities, and the armies. Imports of grain from outside Italy had become necessary by the second century BCE with the first supplier being Sicily, subsequently joined by North Africa, Spain, Egypt, and occasionally the Black Sea region, and later Gaul. Rome bought grain from conquered peoples at fixed low prices and then provided it free to the urban populace, and there was also private trade controlled by the oligarchy. By the Late Imperial period, the grain trade had moved firmly under the state. Grain ships, particularly those crossing to Egypt, attained enormous sizes capable of carrying hundreds of tons of cargo. Other cheap foodstuffs included garum, meat pastes, preserved fish, and cheese. The range of delicacies was impressive. A small sampling might include bird dainties such as peacock and crane, fish specialties including mussels and oysters, dates and figs from North Africa and Egypt, ham and pickled meats from Gaul, nuts from the Black Sea, and gourmet vinegar from Greece.

Considerable profit could be had from the live-animal market provided the difficulties in transportation could be overcome. The Romans had an appetite for rare and exotic beasts intended for public displays, processions, shows, and circus games. Wild animals included lions, leopards, elephants, ostriches, and even hyenas; animals used for breeding included dogs from Britain and India, cattle from Syria and Africa, horses from Spain and the Eastern Mediterranean, and sheep from various places. Skins, hides, and furs came mostly from northern lands.

The trade in metals, an essential engine in long-distance trade since the beginning of metallurgy, reached a high level of intensity under the Roman Empire. The Romans exploited all mines within their empire and took in whatever was available from the outside, principally to satisfy the needs of their military. They also exported vast amounts of precious metals, particularly silver in the form of coinage, to pay for imports from Asia. The trade in metals was one area of commerce that proved to be less susceptible to periods of economic crisis than other commodities. The empire's construction program also kept quarries active, producing both cheap building material such as cement and more valuable stone such as marble from Greece. Glass from the eastern Mediterranean remained a luxury item with Alexandria exporting exquisite containers; beads from that city have been found as far away as northern France. Later in the Imperial period glass came into more common use. Wood products such as timber, tar, and pitch from Macedonia and cork from Spain also circulated. In textiles many of Rome's needs were satisfied by Italy and Sicily although luxury clothing, carpets, and footwear trickled in from many areas. Although the city of Rome is often pictured as a parasite sucking in a wealth of commodities of every description from around the empire and returning little in the way of material goods, Italy continued to send out exports including craft goods, iron and bronze tools, jewelry, woolen textiles, lamps, building materials, wine, and olive oil.

When the commercial center of gravity shifted to Italy, Greece began a slow if uneven slide. Individual cities did well so long as they were the objects of Roman favor. Rhodes, located off the southwestern tip of Anatolia, rivaled Alexandria for a time as an entrepot for trade. The Rhodians were in the forefront of nautical advances, including better rigging and techniques in navigation, and they devised the first code of maritime law. They also made the most determined effort of any state of their time to combat piracy. Most important to the Romans, Rhodes was an ally in their wars against the Hellenistic empires. But when Rhodes tried to remain neutral in a later war, Rome's favor shifted elsewhere, and Rhodes' halcyon days were over.

The new object of Roman benevolence became the island of Delos 100 miles northwest of Rhodes. In 166 BCE Rome made Delos a free port, meaning that merchants were free from paying duties there. The Romans may have favored Delos, which for centuries was the site of a sacred shrine to Apollo, because it already had a large population of foreign traders, mostly Italians. Once it became a free port, Delos served as a great clearing house for goods coming from the Levant and Egypt to the Aegean and on to Italy. A significant banking industry also developed there. Above all, Delos, the holy island, became the premier entrepot for the trade in slaves provided mostly by pirates operating out of the rocky coasts of southwestern Anatolia, the same pirates Rhodes could no longer contain. Delos, it was reported, could handle up to 10,000 slaves a day, the major consumers being the latifundias of Italy. In the following century, the Romans decided the pirates had to go, and in campaigns led by Pompey they were flushed out of their hideouts and crushed. In the meantime, in a final twist of irony, Delos was sacked in 88 BCE by a general who was allied to the pirates and finally destroyed in 69 BCE by a pirate commander.

Despite the fleeting success of places such as Rhodes and Delos, the great sea arteries no longer originated and terminated in Greek waters. The unification of the Mediterranean basin under one administration created a trans-Mediterranean economy that centered on the Italian peninsula, at least for a while. The Aegean became something of a backwater, its great commercial centers serving the needs of Rome in a secondary capacity.

On the other side of the Italian peninsula new lands were added one by one to the empire, each with its own complement of resources to be exploited, each a potential market for Mediterranean commodities. The integration process was well under way in places such as Gaul long before the Roman army arrived. There the points of entry had been Massilia and Etruria, and the goods had been generally of the high value–low bulk variety. Trade networks running northward were built over earlier routes, some going back to the Bronze and Neolithic ages. Gaul enjoyed very useful south-to-north and east-to-west river systems that proved crucial once commerce expanded beyond the level of luxury goods.

If trade preceded the Roman conquest, a tremendous increase in volume followed it. Maintaining and provisioning the army in itself greatly stimulated commerce by supplying the soldiers with staples. Once peace and security were established, trade was expanded to the local population and eventually trickled down the social scale. Nevertheless, the trade in luxury goods continued to be highly profitable since such commodities served as status symbols for the elite classes. Among products most in demand were wine and items associated with feasting such as bronze and silver drinking and serving vessels, pans, jugs, buckets, and tableware.

A look at the wine trade provides a useful insight into the development of Mediterranean commerce under the Roman Empire. The Greeks had made wine and olive oil, along with their pottery containers, principal exports. Greek colonists brought the arts of wine and olive oil production with them to Sicily and Italy, where both commodities were made in abundance. The homeland Greeks retained their position on the international scene as suppliers of olive oil, and some Greek cities had to pass laws restricting the amount that could be exported in order to ensure an adequate supply for local needs. Wine, however, was a different story. Whereas the very best Greek wines retained their market share and were imported into Rome itself, from the middle of the second century BCE the bulk wine business began to shift away from Greece to Italy and Sicily. The great estates of Italy pumped out massive amounts of wine that commonly circulated from Russia to Nubia. Pliny recounts that in the early days of the Roman Republic wine was so rare that women were not allowed to drink it, and a husband who clubbed his wife to death after catching her imbibing from a vat was acquitted of murder. By Pliny's own time matters had changed so drastically that he counted about 80 different kinds of wine "in the whole world," of which two-thirds came from Italy.

Exactly when Italian wine reached Gaul in significant quantities is uncertain, but a wrecked Italian ship off the coast from the second century BCE contained 15,000–20,000 gallons with the poorer quality stored in the hold and the best on deck. Italian wines were shipped through Massilia to inland distribution centers, and some of it reached as far as the Rhine River. Much depended on overland shipping costs, which tended to limit the flow of cheaper brands. Eventually viticulture was introduced to the soils of Gaul, and by the Late Imperial period some regions including Bordeaux and the Moselle Valley were exporting their own products. Interestingly, the Romans made a major improvement in the packaging and preservation of wine in the Early Imperial period when they borrowed from the Celts the use of metal-hooped wooden casks to replace pottery amphorae.

Caesar reports on one German tribe, the Suebi, whom he describes as "the largest and most warlike of the German nations," as a people who "absolutely forbid the importation of wine, because they think it makes men soft and incapable of enduring hard toil." Fortunately for Italian wine merchants, this was not a prejudice shared by the Gauls. For them wine consumption was especially important at lavish chiefly feasts where huge quantities were quaffed. The Gauls paid for their Roman imports with animal products – Strabo reports flocks of sheep and herds of swine so large "they supply an abundance of cloaks and salt-meat not only to Rome but to most parts of Italy as well." The most important Gaulish export was said to be slaves. Diodorus Siculus reports on a wine-for-slaves trade that appears dreadfully uneven: "They [Italian merchants] transport the wine by boat on the navigable rivers, and by wagon through the plains and receive in return for it an incredibly large price: for a jar of wine they receive in return a slave, a servant in exchange for a drink." Romans were trading for slaves with friendly tribes more than a century before Caesar conquered Gaul, and after Pompey's victory over the pirates Gaul may have become the largest single source of Roman slaves.

Slaves were available and cheap in Gaul because of the ongoing state-building and social-stratification processes. Roman merchants earned fortunes by encouraging warrior communities to expand at the expense of their less organized or militarized neighbors. When the Romans themselves decided to conquer Gaul, slave dealers followed in their wake, depopulating large swaths of the country. As the Gaulish thirst for wine appeared insatiable, so was the Roman need for latifundia slaves. However, slaves had to come from war or from outside the empire. Thus the Roman conquest signaled the beginning of the end of the Gallic slave trade since independent tribes were no longer free to raid and capture each other's people, and rulers were not allowed to enslave their own people once under Roman law.

Gaul's importance in long-distance trade did not fade with the decline of the slave trade. No single product could impact on much larger economic forces at work, which during the Imperial period would see a shift away from Italy to the more peripheral areas of the Aegean–Black Sea frontier in the east and the Gaul–Spain–Britain axis in the west. In Gaul, Roman merchants moved in to elbow aside the chiefly class that had hitherto controlled long-distance exchange. Roman-turned-Gallic merchants assumed the middleman position in trade systems extending to Britain, Germany, and beyond. Cities developed around Roman forts, generating more trade while Roman currency commercialized the Gallic economy down to the village level. Roman products poured into Britain, which would soon join Gaul as part of the empire as did limited sections of Germany.

Not all Roman trade with Germany went through Gaul; some came directly over the Alps or through the Danubian provinces. In border zones a limited market economy developed often using Roman money. Some Roman merchants penetrated into unoccupied Germany to do business at established marketplaces or meet native counterparts bringing goods from farther afield. In this way Roman merchants plugged into the network of commercial contacts that ran through the Germanic world. Some Roman traders were not averse to doing business with groups considered to be unfriendly to the empire although this could be risky since such transactions were not guaranteed by treaties or agreements. At times Roman authorities, including Caesar, used the problems that arose from such dealings as justifications for war. Some German tribes who opposed the Romans refused to trade for Roman goods in the quite perceptive view that a desire for such goods opened the door to Roman economic and cultural influence, which too often led to Roman political domination.

In the border zones, Roman trade goods featured articles for everyday consumption. More luxurious products, including finely made bronze and silver items, jewelry, glass, and gold and silver coins, tended to penetrate much farther into the German hinterland. Somewhere along the line they sometimes ceased being commodities bought and sold through the market economy and entered the older system of elite gift exchange driven by social contacts and political alliances. In Germany, like Gaul at an earlier time, new power structures were developing in which control over prestige goods was an important status symbol. Roman imports from Germany, on the other hand, appear to be something of a hodgepodge with amber still a major item and hides, skins, and leather also arriving in significant quantities. As an interesting comment on Roman society, upper class women were known to decorate their hair with imported blonde curls. Slaves were probably also an important German export. In his commentary on the Suebi, Caesar claims that this tribe traded with foreign merchants "more because they want to sell their booty than because they stand in any need of imports," the booty likely referring to slaves. Among common items consumed in the immediate area, geese and soap are mentioned. In an interesting twist, some Germans exported their agricultural surpluses for use by units of the Roman army, thus helping to support the imperial presence on the other side of their own borders.

After 180 CE the Roman Empire entered a period of recurring crises. One problem was political instability and civil war as the empire turned its military might inward against itself. Even larger economic issues were manifested by out-of-control inflation and ruinous taxation compounded by depopulation. Above all, the empire had one insoluble problem: it couldn't pay for itself. As the empire rotted from within, only the military kept it from collapsing in the face of growing threats from the outside. The army became enormous, stretching across a huge frontier, and eventually it became all powerful, making and unmaking emperors at will. The whole apparatus of imperial government became focused on this one overarching imperative: to pay for the military.

Political upheaval and economic crisis did not create an especially propitious environment for long-distance trade although decline did not occur all at once and varied from region to region. Also it impacted much more strongly on mass-consumption goods such as foodstuffs and handicrafts than on luxury goods. Increasingly local areas satisfied their own immediate needs by producing cheaper goods than could be brought from outside; regional trade replaced imperial trade, and eventually local trade replaced regional trade. The traffic in luxury goods continued to flow at a steady pace unaffected by downturns and crises. Over time the transportation system began to decline as new road and harbor construction ceased and maintenance faded in the face of strained imperial budgets. Customs payments became an increased burden for remaining traffic as the empire attempted to squeeze out whatever money was available to continue its doomed existence. Security diminished, and eventually the roads became largely deserted, their stones ripped up by local folk to recycle for building material.

The Roman state responded by assuming greater control over large sectors of the economy, including trade. The state was foremost concerned with covering its own needs but also with the distribution of primary commodities such as grain, oil, and wine to the urban populace. Products such as metals, building materials, and textiles came under state supervision. The goal was to encourage and protect commerce in the hope of reversing the downward economic trend, but the consequence was to bring bureaucratic regulation and dependency to the mechanism of commerce, which aggravated the situation over the long run.

Modern historians no longer like to talk about the "fall" of the Roman Empire as if at a given time – the two most convenient dates being 410 and 476 CE – a loud ka-boom could be heard off in the distance signaling the collapse of the empire. The newer view is that the empire gradually transitioned into something new, a process more than an event. By most indications, long-distance trade did not benefit during this process. As a growth sector of economy, it shifted to other regions during the following centuries.

Chapter 8

When India was the center of the world

Large bodies of water like the Mediterranean made natural trading zones as under normal conditions trade was generally cheaper and faster by water than overland. And although storms and shipwrecks made sea travel dangerous, land travel had a parallel set of pitfalls, including physical challenges such as deserts and mountains, security-related problems, and if security was guaranteed, a multitude of tolls and tariffs. When a body of water connected with other bodies that served as corridors, as the Mediterranean did with the Aegean and Black seas, or with river systems that acted as branches like the Nile and Rhone, commercial penetration could reach far inland sometimes to another central trade zone.

The Indian Ocean was many times larger than the Mediterranean but not as large as the Pacific, which has become an effective trade zone only recently, and not as turbulent as the Atlantic, which has been tamed only in modern times. Protected by Africa to the west, peninsular and insular Southeast Asia to the east, and the world's most massive mountains to the north, the Indian was the first ocean to become the center of its own commercial zone. Divided by the South Asian subcontinent into two arcs, the Indian Ocean is best seen as a set of interrelated commercial systems, each with overlapping circuits. Merchants did not try to sail from one end to the other. Ships picked up goods on one side of a link and dropped them off on the other where ships from the next link were doing the same. Any given stop could be a terminus as well as a place of transit, and goods could leave the sea routes and enter land systems or vice versa at specific places. More aggressive entrepreneurs often attempted to infringe as far as they could into the next link or skip a link in an effort to cut out rival middlemen. Competition became ever more heated as new elements from the fringes – Egyptians, Greeks, Levantines, and Chinese – joined the Arabs, Indians, and Malays who pioneered the central routes.

By the first century CE some ships were strong enough, their crews had learned enough about sailing conditions, and the rewards had become lucrative enough to make their circuits a full half ocean. Three great corridors, the Red Sea, the Persian Gulf, and the Malacca Straits leading into the South

China Sea connected together East, South, and West Asia and Africa and Europe. As the peoples who lived around the ocean's shore became integrated into this system, many prospered, although not equally. Different parts of the zone experienced fluctuations based on local and regional conditions. Trade balances shifted, opportunities changed as new products became available, and new markets materialized while old ones withered.

Trade among the peoples of the Indian Ocean was well under way by the Neolithic as was trade between the coasts and the interior. Products such as mother-of-pearl, unusual shells, and shell columellae cut into lamps, cups, and beads were much in demand far inland. The first direct long-distance maritime trading system goes back to the Sumerians and Harappans, but longer distance indirect contact also took place. The remains of cloves, which were produced only in the Moluccas Islands of eastern Indonesia on the border of the Pacific Ocean, have been found 5,000 miles to the west, in a pot excavated on the Euphrates River in Mesopotamia dated to 1700–1600 BCE, and peppercorns from India were in the mummy of Pharaoh Ramses II, who died in 1213 BCE.

The core of the Indian Ocean commercial zone was India itself, which constituted a vast internal trade network reaching northward into Central Asia. Following the eclipse of the Harappans, India experienced a period during which the center of gravity shifted to the east and eventually to the south. By the late first millennium BCE, India had reemerged as an economic powerhouse; Strabo called it "the greatest of all nations and the happiest in lot." From west to east five major exporting regions would dominate: the Indus delta, the Gujarat peninsula and Narmada valley, the Malabar coast on the southwest, the Coromandel coast on the southeast, and the Ganges delta in the northeast. The caste system, which was still in the process of developing, would ultimately discourage or even prohibit upper castes, particularly Brahmans, from traveling overseas for fear they would become ritually contaminated. Apparently this proscription was not yet strong enough, however, to dampen the ambitions of many Indians, Brahmans or otherwise, from seeking gain through trade and travel.

Early vessels in the Indian Ocean and its corridors were a mixed lot, and different areas developed different types ranging from small boats barely more seaworthy than riverboats to large ocean-going ships. Two pictures of boats from the Harappan period show one with masts and oar-like rudders and one made from bundles of reeds without a mast. The first Egyptian boats on the Red Sea were made of papyrus. Pliny reports that on the southwest coast of India pepper was brought from producing districts to major ports in canoes made of hollowed tree trunks. Strabo mentions leather boats on the tip of southwestern Arabia, and Pliny tells of Arab pirates using buoyed rafts consisting of a platform held up by inflated skins, often ox bladders. The trip from the Ganges delta across the Bay of Bengal to Ceylon, according to Pliny, was at one time done in reed boats, and Onesicritus, who sailed under orders from Alexander the Great, reports that some ships on this run were "poorly furnished with sails and are constructed without belly-ribs on both sides." Vessels known as sangara used on the tip of southern India were described in the *Periplus Maris Erythraei* as "very big dugout canoes held together by a yoke," the largest of which were two-masted. Pliny puts the size of Bay of Bengal ships at "three thousand barrels" in reference to a system of measurement used in the Mediterranean based on a ship's capacity for holding amphorae wine jars. This would make them about 75 tons. Ships that had to negotiate narrow channels, as in the passage between India and Ceylon, had bows at both ends so they would not have to come about (change directions) when conditions changed.

Most trade goods were carried in craft Western observers referred to as "sewn boats" because their planks were stitched together with ropes made of coir (fiber from coconut husks). In parts of southern India split bamboo was the main form of fastening, but in other places wooden dowels were used to fasten planks. The best wood for shipbuilding was teak, which was hard, durable, and highly resistant to warping, a product of the jungles of India. But the vessels themselves must have had problems with leaking that kept sailors bailing much of the time. Early ports lacked infrastructure, including quays, docks, and warehouses. Any settlement on or near the coast could serve as a port. Ships were simply run onto a beach, or cargo was unloaded onto lighters, small flat-bottom boats used in harbors and roadsteads (places offshore that were less sheltered and enclosed than harbors). Ships hugged the coastlines, risking shoals, reefs, and other hidden dangers, not to mention pirates, to keep the coast in sight so as not to risk getting lost.

Sometime in the first millennium BCE, someone discovered how to navigate across the ocean by using the wind pattern known as the monsoons. That someone may have been the Malays or, coming from the opposite direction, the Arabs, or from the north Indians sailing across the Bay of Bengal, or perhaps all three working independently, although it has been suggested, without any real evidence, that Harappan sailors had this knowledge earlier. A four-month travail inching along the coast became a 40-day ride across open waters using the stars at night and reading signs in the sea and sky to navigate during the day. The Malays traveled east to west across the ocean, settling in Madagascar and probably establishing trading stations at various points along the East African coast to trade in cinnamon, although speculation on the date of this ranges widely. A Malay settlement may have existed on the southwest Arabian coast, which fleets visited periodically, bringing products from Southeast Asia. Indian traders sailed to the "Island of the Black Yavanas" somewhere on the East African coast. Sailors from Ceylon, according to Pliny, developed their own system of open-water navigation: "The Cingalese take no observations of the stars in navigation ... but they carry birds on board with them and at fairly frequent intervals set them free, and follow the course they take as they make for the land."

In the western sector of the ocean the premier maritime traders were the Arabs. Under the Assyrian and neo-Babylonian empires, Arab entrepreneurs managed an ongoing trade in exotic products ranging from aromatic woods to parrots that tied the Persian Gulf to northern India and eastern Africa. Indian vessels, at least from time to time, were prohibited from entering the Bab el-Mandeb into the Red Sea. This may have been the work of Arab rulers in Yemen, or it may have originated with a decree issued by the Persian emperor Darius that favored Arabs over Indians. The result was that Indian ships had to disembark their cargoes in ports along the south Arabian coast. There, Indian goods became mixed with Arab and East African goods so that by the time they reached the Mediterranean they all appeared to come from a single source, which was assumed to be somewhere in southern Arabia, a misconception the Arabs made no attempt to correct.

After the fall of the Persian Empire, the Egyptian side of the Red Sea came under the kings of the Ptolemaic dynasty, who founded ports and established a fleet to patrol against pirates. Egypt-based Greek traders operated to the Bab el-Mandeb although serious trading ventures beyond this did not begin until the late second century BCE. Ptolemaic economic policy was designed to rake in as much revenue as possible to further political and military goals in the Mediterranean. The Ptolemies had little interest in the Indian Ocean and although from time to time they had diplomatic contacts with states in India these resulted in no systematic commercial ties. Ptolemaic officials purchased goods that came both overland on caravan routes running up the western side of Arabia and from ships arriving in their own Red Sea ports. Arab middlemen played a role in this trade, but they paid a heavy price in taxes. In Egyptian territory the government exercised a monopoly over all aromatics and spices, which were manufactured into drugs, ointments, perfumes, and similar products before being re-exported.

In the later years of Ptolemy VIII's reign (145–116 BCE), an Indian sailor, the sole survivor of a shipwreck, was picked up and brought to Alexandria. This fellow, according to Poseidonius, "related that on his voyage from India he by a strange mischance mistook his course and reached Egypt." He offered to serve as guide for the trip back, so the king appointed a certain Eudoxus of Cyzicus to lead an expedition: "So Eudoxus sailed away with presents; and he returned with a cargo of perfumes and precious stones." This was how the sailors of the West learned to ride the monsoons, and soon ships from Egypt were bypassing the Arabs and sailing directly to Indian ports. Poseidonius' account was preserved in Strabo, who was skeptical about it, wondering aloud if "he either invented it himself, or accepted it from others who were its inventors." Strabo notes: "how strange Euergetes' [an honorific name for Ptolemy VIII] scarcity of competent pilots, since the sea in that region was already known by many men." The *Periplus*, on the other hand, ignores Eudoxus but attributes the "discovery" of the monsoons to a Greek ship captain named Hippalos, who lived at about the same time.

Pliny seems to agree and notes that the monsoon wind was henceforth named after Hippalos, and the geographer Claudius Ptolemy named the sea after him as well.

One matter is obvious: neither Hippalos nor Eudoxus discovered the monsoons. Indian Ocean sailors did that long before. Nor did western sailors begin using the monsoons on a significant scale for at least a century or so after Eudoxus and Hippalos. Incidentally, Eudoxus' adventures did not end here. He was sent out on a second trip to India but on his return was blown off course and landed somewhere on the East African coast. The local people provided pilots to help him get back to Egypt, an indication that this route was already well traveled.

The word "monsoon" means seasonal wind resulting from temperature variation between land and sea. Air is either sucked toward the center of the Eurasian land mass during the hot months or shoved out to sea in the cold months. From November to April the monsoon blows from the northeast – a steady, fair-weather, balmy wind – a sailor's delight. From April to October the monsoon turns around and blows from the southwest, bringing high, sometimes ferocious winds, turbulent seas, and frequent storms. At the height of this season in late June, July, and early August, the water was in such an uproar that ports were closed and maritime activity put on hold on the west coast of India. With the wind at their backs, sailors could use the monsoons to push their sails across the seas. But they had to judge their departure times just right to prevent being caught in violent weather or, if they arrived too late, to miss the return wind and suffer a long layover. The full force of the monsoon hit different areas at different times, and bad weather did not prevail in all places during the entire southwest monsoon season. Furthermore, the monsoon arrived and departed in stages, so there were transition periods during which the winds could be variable. Sailors had to determine when the wind was usable, which differed from place to place. Once learned, maritime trade routes were set by the pattern of the winds; it was all a matter of finessing Mother Nature. In the first century BCE only the boldest Mediterranean sailors were pioneering the Indian trade; within a century the mid-ocean had become a highway.

As traders from the Mediterranean were poised to move into the Indian Ocean, the political backdrop was changing as well. During the first century BCE the Eastern Mediterranean came under Roman domination, culminating in the overthrow of the Ptolemies and the conquest of Egypt. The Romans were interested in the Red Sea to Indian Ocean voyage because it was a way around the land routes to the east, now under control of their enemy, the Parthian Empire. Given the preliminary work already done, the Romans were able to plug rather easily into the preexisting trade network. The Romans brought stability, capital resources, and a virtually insatiable new market to the western edge of the Indian Ocean, and the intensity and volume of trade increased accordingly. Henceforth the Roman navy patrolled the Red Sea, and Roman troops guarded and maintained the desert roads between the Nile and Red Sea. This did not come free: tolls were levied and customs duties exacted. In Egypt goods were taxed when they entered and when they exited.

Beginning with the reign of the emperor Augustus (27 BCE–14 CE) embassies from Indian states north and south arrived in Rome to negotiate agreements that included prices and guarantees of protection for Roman merchants. These embassies always carried splendid gifts, doubtless to advertise their wares, although the Romans decided to interpret this as recognition of their position as world power. With the imposition of a 25 percent import duty, the eastern maritime trade became a significant source of income for the state. The Roman government never tried to control commerce in the manner of the Ptolemies, and private enterprise was the general rule, partly because the Roman government was not anxious to assume the risks involved.

Roman Empire traders in Indian waters were referred to collectively by the Indians as "Yavanas." They were rarely Italians, leave aside actual Romans, but they were subjects or citizens of the Roman Empire drawn from the merchant communities of the eastern Mediterranean, principally Greeks (the word "Yavana" derives from "Ionian"), Egyptians (many of whom were ethnic Greeks from Alexandria), Levantines (Syrians and Phoenicians), and Arabs. Behind them providing the capital were investors from all corners of the empire. One document listing parties involved in financing an expedition to the East African coast included men from Rome, Carthage, Sparta, Massilia, southern Italy, and northern Greece. Investors had to be willing to venture capital in what were chancy undertakings that could potentially bring immense returns. Filling up the ships with the kind of merchandise this trade dealt in required substantial capital even though a ship's cargo usually contained consignments from a number of separate traders, merchant families, and consortiums. Although this was all private enterprise, players on the investor side were often connected to the Roman government as officials or as members of the senatorial class. For the Roman elite, who were beginning to feel that they deserved to enjoy the benefits that their superpower status made possible, the Red Sea connection opened the door to luxuries and exotica that their rustic ancestors could not have imagined. Spice warehouses were established in Rome to handle the flow, and supply could hardly keep up with demand despite a steady rise in production and prices.

By the first century CE, construction techniques pioneered in the Mediterranean were being used to build larger, more seaworthy ships in Red Sea and Arabian coast shipyards, in response to the demand for Indian Ocean goods. These ships had planking held together not with coir but by mortise and tenon joints, a much stronger system of construction, and they had reinforced hulls. An increase in quantity matched that of quality. Strabo notes:

"In earlier times not so many as twenty vessels would dare to traverse the [Red Sea] far enough to get a peep outside the straits, but at the present time even large fleets are despatched as far as India." Annual convoys of up to 120 ships, according to Pliny, were involved. And with the Arab monopoly broken, Indian ships began venturing westward again, first to Somalia, then to Red Sea ports, and finally to Egypt itself. Archaeological evidence indicates that Indians and other merchants settled as communities in Roman territory although not as official trading posts or colonies representing their home governments.

Much of the merchandise transported in Indian and Arabian ships was different from that carried in Roman ships. A substantial commerce continued on the coastal route between India, Persia, Arabia, and East Africa involving basic commodities, particularly cotton textiles and foodstuffs such as rice, sesame oil, dates, and sugar cane (used as medicine), along with wood and metals. Horses were exported aboard ship from Persia and northwestern India to central and southern India and as far as Sumatra. Excavations at the Egyptian port of Myos Hormos have produced traces of rice and coconut remains likely originating in India, but this has been interpreted as evidence for the presence of an Indian merchant community rather than as an indication that foodstuffs were among the normal exports from India to Egypt. Roman ships would not waste their hold space on such high-bulk low-value goods. Only the most lucrative of commodities could bear the cost of transportation over such a distance.

The most important imports carried into the Roman Empire from the Indian Ocean fall into a general category of goods that can be divided between basic materials and the products made from them. The former included spices, aromatic woods, and resins; the latter, incense, medicines and drugs, cosmetics, perfumes, unguents, and ointments. Although today a clear distinction is drawn between spices, aromatics, and medicinal drugs, this was not the case two millennia ago – as witnessed by the Chinese, who used the same word to designate all three. Extracts could undergo extensive processing before or after they were transported, and compounds often contained dozens, or in the case of medicines, hundreds of different substances produced from carefully guarded recipes. Whereas peninsular India and the eastern arc of the Indian Ocean constituted the epicenter of the spice trade as did south Arabia and Somalia for aromatic substances, medicines and drugs were sent in all directions with various peoples importing ingredients not available in their own lands while at the same time exporting what they did have. Greece, Egypt, Arabia, Persia, India, Central Asia, and China all had their own traditional pharmacies that together formed a huge international market.

Bodily health was associated with the world of scents. The most popular of all aromatics were frankincense and myrrh, both of which were produced from tree resins harvested from incisions made in the bark of two types of related trees native to different parts of southern Arabia and northern Somalia. The Arabs who controlled their cultivation and trade were successful for a long time in disseminating misinformation about them. Herodotus reports that "every frankincense producing tree is guarded by large numbers of tiny, dappled, winged snakes, and only the smoke of burning storax resin drives them away from the trees." Confusion abounded about the lands that produced frankincense and myrrh. Agatharchides, writing three centuries after Herodotus, claims that "fragrance pervades the whole [south Arabian] coast, providing a pleasure to visitors that is greater than what can be seen or described." He does, however, warn that in the forests of the incense trees lived a purple snake that could leap into the air and whose bite was incurable. The *Periplus*, however, maintains that the production of frankincense was handled only by convicts and slaves: "For the districts are terribly unhealthy, harmful to those sailing by and absolutely fatal to those working there."

The Egyptians had utilized myrrh for embalming at least since the third millennium BCE, but the long-term popularity of both aromatics was due to their use in medicine and perfume, chiefly in incense. This could be used to fumigate one's clothes or body and, when inhaled, was believed to provide relief from the symptoms of certain illnesses and to be an effective treatment for wounds and eye disorders. Health and religion were related, and in many places incense made from frankincense and myrrh was considered to be a magically potent substance. It gave off "a wondrous scent," notes Agatharchides, "so that many come to forget human blessings and think they have tasted ambrosia." This heavenly fragrance led to its use in temples from Rome to China, and frankincense and myrrh were considered divine substances. In Exodus Yahweh instructs Moses to blend "sweet spices with pure frankincense and make an incense ... and put part of it before the testimony in the tent of meeting where I shall meet with you; it shall be for you most holy." The three magi brought frankincense and myrrh as well as gold to the baby Jesus, and Jesus is said to have been buried with myrrh. While Arabia sent much frankincense and myrrh to the Mediterranean, an equally large amount went eastward to India, Central Asia, and China. Arabia also exported other products to the Indian market including wine, figs, dates, and trained slaves, including singing boys and musicians.

Although the demand for frankincense and myrrh was strong, it was not unlimited. Not so for those products of India that are labeled today as spices. The greatest of them, pepper, was available in Athens from at least the fourth century BCE. It was first used for medicinal purposes; Hippocrates recommended mixing pepper with honey and vinegar to treat "feminine disorders." At the height of the Roman Empire, pepper became the cheapest and most plentiful spice. It was shipped in large storage jars, each holding quantities of peppercorns that took up more space in the holds of ships coming from southern India than any other product. India exported three kinds of pepper: long pepper produced from the fruit of a shrub found in northern India; black pepper from the berries of a climbing vine cultivated in southern India; and white pepper made from the same fruit as black pepper but processed differently. While today's palate prefers black pepper, the Romans paid almost four times as much for long pepper, perhaps because it retained its pharmaceutical use longer. Black pepper came to be used principally as a flavoring and secondarily as a meat preservative. Pliny could not understand the pepper craze: "It is remarkable that the use of pepper has come into so much favour ... [since] pepper has nothing to recommend it in either fruit or berry. To think that its only pleasing quality is its pungency and that we will go all the way to India to get this!" Despite Pliny's scolding, pepper became such an important ingredient in the culinary life of respectable Romans that it was not subject to the 25 percent tax, an indication that the Roman authorities considered it less a luxury than a staple – but always a valuable staple. When Alaric and the Visigoths were threatening Rome in 410 CE, among the ransom they demanded was 3,000 pounds of Indian pepper. Over the centuries the demand stimulated tremendous production in Kerala on the southwest tip of India, where hitherto pepper had not been used in traditional vegetarian dishes.

If pepper could be found in many Roman kitchens, this was less true for cinnamon, which was used in medicines, perfumes, unguents, and as a cooking spice albeit at prices that ranged from expensive to astronomical. Actually three different products were involved. True cinnamon, the dried inner bark of the cinnamon tree, a native of Ceylon, has a delicate fragrance and slightly sweet taste. Cassia was the same product from the cassia tree, a native of Burma that was extensively cultivated in southern China. One of the oldest spices, used in China as far back as 2500 BCE, cassia has a flavor that is also sweet but stronger and more aromatic. Malabathrum was made from the leaves of a tree that grew in the Himalayan foothills of northeastern India. All three are closely related members of the evergreen laurel family. The Romans thought cinnamon and cassia were the same product, with cinnamon representing a higher grade (and, indeed, today most cinnamon sold in the United States is actually cassia), but they had no idea that malabathrum was related in any way.

Although cinnamon (actually cassia) had been used in Egypt since at least the mid-second millennium BCE, little was known about it owing to another brilliant campaign of misinformation. In a bizarre report Herodotus recounts the manner in which Arab middlemen claimed to have obtained cinnamon. It was said to have been collected from an unknown source by giant birds and brought back to their nests, which were located on inaccessible escarpments. The Arabs cut the carcasses of oxen and donkeys into large chunks, which they placed below the nests. The birds gathered the chunks but were so greedy they always brought up too much: "The nests break and fall to the ground, where the Arabs come and get what they came for. That is how cinnamon is collected in that part of Arabia, and from there it is sent all over the world."

Giant greedy birds aside, there is some speculation that cassia was first brought westward by Malay sailors who later also carried Ceylon cinnamon over what is referred to as the "Cinnamon Road." This was not a road at all but an all-water route across the Indian Ocean to Madagascar and the East African coast via Ceylon and the Maldive Islands developed sometime in the first millennium BCE. Pliny mentions cinnamon traders who rode the monsoons "from gulf to gulf" on boats he considered to be little more than rafts. From there Arabs carried it north to Somalia where one port handled so much that extra large ships had to be used to carry it up the Red Sea. Ancient writers often referred to Somalia simply as the "Cinnamon Country," and the people of Arabia were said to have had so many rolls of cinnamon and cassia that Agatharchides claimed they used it for firewood. The true sources were concealed so well that when Roman merchants arrived in India, they did not recognize cinnamon trees when they saw them.

Spices and related products accounted for more than half of the goods officially listed by the Roman government as imports from the Indian Ocean and eastern regions. Most lack the name recognition accorded to pepper and cinnamon or even frankincense and myrrh today. One of the most expensive was nard (or spikenard), an aromatic plant that grew high in the Himalayas. From its dried roots and stems, a musky smelling ointment was produced that was used in medicines, perfumes, cosmetics, and cookery. The leaf, according to Pliny, "holds a foremost place among perfumes." He discusses different types of nard, the lowliest being the Gangetic variety, which he calls "putrid, having a poisonous smell." Nevertheless, the demand even for this form of nard was such that it made the journey thousands of miles across land and sea from the roof of the world to the city on the Tiber. The market forces driving the prices of these products remain obscure since not enough information is available to determine how the supply and demand mechanism worked and what additional considerations played a role. For example, costus, a fragrant root from Kashmir used in perfumes and medicine, which appears to have properties similar to nard, cost one-eighth its price. Bdellium, a gum resin obtained from trees similar to myrrh and used in much the same way, cost one-fourth the price of myrrh, which in turn cost a fraction of nard or malabathrum. Frankincense, on the other hand, brought only half the price of myrrh on the Roman market.

Spices, aromatics, resins, and the products made from them were not the only commodities flowing out of the Indian Ocean. India, East Africa, and Southeast Asia were the world's largest exporters of ivory and rhinoceros horn used in the making of a wide variety of artistic and functional products. Powdered rhinoceros horn was also included in the pharmacopoeia of many cultures for prescriptions (none of which had any scientific basis since rhino horn was composed essentially of compressed hair) intended to solve a range of problems from restoring male sexual potency to serving as an antitoxin for snake bites. Other wild animal products included tortoise shell, coming from both tortoises and turtles, which was used for large items such as veneering furniture and doors and for small items such as boxes, plaques, combs, rings, and other jewelry. Tortoise shell was imported into Mesopotamia as early as the Old Babylonian period by the Dilmunites, along with turtle meat and eggs to be eaten in religious rituals, while the eggshells were used in medicines. In some areas of bountiful harvest, these unfortunate creatures were totally exterminated. From the seas of the Indian Ocean also came pearls, which arrived in Greece by the fifth century BCE. Pliny plays the moralist here, devoting a large discussion to pearls and condemning their use as representing unbridled luxury smacking of moral decadence. The Roman populace, however, paid little attention to his railings and instead imported substantial numbers of them from the Persian Gulf, India, and Ceylon. Diving for pearls, according to the *Periplus*, was another job reserved for convicts.

Sometime in the first millennium CE, spices and related products were overtaken as India's most important export, although not as early as the period of Roman trade. Cotton textiles had been produced in India on a large scale as early as the Harappan period, and in the first millennium BCE cotton products from the Deccan, the interior of peninsular India, were being exported in significant quantities through the port of Barygaza. Garments from the region of Bengal in the northeast were considered to be especially fine, but most exports were of the coarser, mass-produced variety intended for common, everyday use and shipped to other ports in the Indian Ocean. This market had significant growth potential, which the Indians would ultimately realize, although not in the Western trade where Egyptian linen and European wool would hold their own for the foreseeable future. Another Indian product that would have a significant impact on the textile industry was indigo (literally "Indian black"), which Pliny informs his readers came from "slime adhering to foam on the reeds." At this time it may have been used more as a drug and a coloring in cosmetics, particularly eye shadow, than as a textile dye.

The textile that Westerners wanted most from India did not originate there but much farther afield at the far side of the Eurasian world. For many centuries China was the world's only producer of silk even though the Chinese themselves did not realize this. Silk came by caravan to Central Asia, where some of it was diverted southward through the high mountains and down the Indus Valley to ports on the Arabian Sea or eastward across the Ganges Valley to the Bay of Bengal and hence to southern India by sea. In the first century this route was made secure by the Kushan Empire, which extended from the border of northwestern China through Central Asia and down into northwestern India. The ancestors of the people who ruled Kushana were old trading partners of the Chinese and remained potential allies against Central Asian nomads. So long as the Chinese and Kushan empires remained strong, tons of silk would flow through India on its way to the Mediterranean to the immense profit of Indian middlemen.

Other exports from India included teak, ebony, and other tropical hardwoods as well as sandalwood originating in Southeast Asia. Indian iron was considered to be of very high quality, some of which went in the form of swords even though the *Arthashastra* called for a prohibition on exporting weapons. Curiously, it also called for a prohibition on the export of gem stones, one of India's oldest commodities. The Deccan was a principal supplier of semi-precious stones, particularly agate and quartz; beryl was mined in Kerala, and carnelian was found in various locations. Rubies and sapphires were products of Ceylon, and other stones passed through India such as Afghan lapis lazuli and Iranian turquoise. Probably most Indians paid as much attention to the *Arthashastra* in these matters as Romans did to Pliny.

Opening the Mediterranean market to Indian Ocean goods created a level of demand that appeared bottomless except that the West wanted such goods more than the East wanted western goods. The frankincense, myrrh, pepper, cinnamon, nard, silk, and other delights of the East had to be paid for, but with what? One of the few Mediterranean products for which there was an ever-present demand in the East was fine wine. This came from three places: Italy, particularly Tuscany; Ionia, the Greek islands and coastal area of western Anatolia; and Laodicea, in northern Syria just south of ancient Ugarit. A visiting Egyptian once quipped that this region "had more wine than water," and Strabo observed that the mountains above Laodicea were "covered with vines almost as far as the summits." The most outstanding of these wines was shipped to both Arabia and India even though Arabia also exported its own wine of less exalted vintage. At Barygaza, the largest and most active port in India for the Roman trade, wine was the most important import.

Other western products for which there was no adequate substitute included colored glass from Alexandria and Syria and murex purple dye. Of more interest is a category of Mediterranean exports for which there were Indian substitutes, but the Indians imported them anyway. For example, India was the gem center of the world, yet one stone was not available. Identified by Agatharchides and Strabo as "topaz," it was actually peridot, a deep yellowish green transparent variety of olivine from the island of Gazirat Zabarjad in the Red Sea. Said to be invisible in the day, this gem supposedly had to be sought out at night when it could be marked for extraction (actually mines existed that went back to the Ptolemaic period). The Indians took as much of it as the Egyptians cared to send. A larger market existed for coral, which had been an early Mediterranean export to northern Europe, the most desirable being very hard and strikingly red in color. Coral was also available in the Red Sea, but it was considered to be of inferior quality.

Roman ships brought plain Egyptian linen to South Arabia and multicolored textiles that were considered an Egyptian specialty to all major

Indian ports, passing on the same docks Indian cotton goods going in the opposite direction. Even stranger was storax, an aromatic resin from a tree found in the Mediterranean basin, used in medicine and for incense. Why nard and costus in India or frankincense and myrrh in Arabia were not considered to be acceptable substitutes is not clear since storax was exported to both India and Arabia. With the many ingredients used in medicines and for pigments coming from the East, the Romans were still able to sell two of their own mineral products to Indian Ocean customers. Realgar (arsenic sulfide) was an orange-red substance found, according to Strabo, in a mountain in Anatolia that was so loaded with it the place was called Mount Realgar. In addition, sulfide of antimony was popular as an eye cosmetic.

The Indians were obviously interested in doing business. The *Arthashastra* proclaims that "Imported goods were to be sold in as many places as possible in order to make them readily available to people in the towns and countryside," and incentives were to be given to encourage the importation of goods. Local merchants who handled foreign goods were to be exempt from taxes, and foreign merchants could not be sued although their local partners could. How many of the specific recommendations in the *Arthashastra* were actually put into effect is unknown. It set profit margins at 10 percent for imported goods, for example, which, given the opportunities made available by this trade, absolutely no one in his right mind would have accepted. But it does convey an attitude that is very positive and probably reflects the business-friendly atmosphere in India. Nevertheless, shiploads of pepper and nard could not be paid for with shiploads of wine and multicolored Egyptian cloth, and there wasn't that much coral in the Mediterranean Sea. A serious balance of trade deficit loomed.

Metals had been a driving force in international trade from early times, and they continued to be in the Mediterranean to Indian Ocean exchanges. If the earlier metals trade involving Mesopotamia, Dilmun, Magan, and Harappan India had some confusing aspects to it, by comparison it is the picture of clarity when set against this later commerce. The Romans are said to have carried tin to East Africa, Arabia, and India. Indeed India was short of tin although there were rich deposits much closer at hand that were being worked in Malaya and Thailand. The Romans also sent copper to Arabia and to both northern and southern India although northern India had its own copper deposits and, according to the *Periplus*, exported copper to Oman and the Persian Gulf. Of course, in the days of ancient Magan this area had been a major copper exporter, and the ore doesn't appear to have been exhausted.

The lead trade is another mystery since the Romans exported it to India, which, again, had its own natural deposits. The iron trade makes some sense since both the Romans and Indians exported it to Somalia and Ethiopia although given the superiority of Indian iron and steel, it is puzzling as to why the Romans enjoyed any share of this market. These matters, however, pale in importance because the really big business was in precious metals, and by the time the Romans were in direct contact with India, the flow was in one direction only. Centuries earlier Herodotus had been told by the Persians that the source of their gold, of which they appeared to have had an abundance, was northern India. This was reportedly extracted in a most peculiar way: giant ants carried it in the sand they brought up from their nests. Indians then collected it, but if detected they were chased by the ants and if caught killed.

The *Periplus* mentions the production of precious metals in a reference to the Ganges delta, where it notes that there were "gold mines in the area" and gold coins being minted. Actually gold could have been panned in the streams and rivers of this area, but there were no mines, and no examples of such coins have survived. Strabo reports "excellent" gold and silver mines in various unnamed mountains but sees a problem with the Indians, who "are inexperienced in mining and smelting; they also do not know what their resources are, and handle the business in a rather simple manner." In fact, deposits were available in India, particularly in the south where gold had been extracted, worked, and shipped by coastal traffic from very ancient times. However, given that India had highly developed political and social systems with ruling classes who had a taste for elite goods as well as advanced religious systems with holy places that needed adornment and sophisticated commercial systems that required some medium of exchange, the country did not have deposits in sufficient quantities to meet its needs.

From early times India's main source of imported gold came from the north. Afghanistan had some in vein and placer deposits often found in association with tin. But the big load was beyond in the mountains of Siberia, which were a major source from which gold flowed west and east as well as south up to the third century BCE when nomadic migration and war disrupted and then destroyed the system. India begged for a new source.

Today Roman gold and silver coins, often with the likeness of early emperors such as Augustus, have been found in substantial numbers in southern India. They were used both as bullion, as a trade good valued by weight, and as currency in areas undergoing rapid commercialization without locally minted coins. Fewer such coins have turned up in northern India, which had its own well-established currency system. There, Roman coins were probably melted down and recycled. Roman merchants simply did not have enough desirable products to cover the Roman demand for Indian products, so the shortfall had to be made up in hard cash. In commenting on which Roman products were in demand in this place or that, the *Periplus* frequently mentions money and in some places such as the Malabar Coast recommends that traders bring "a considerable amount."

The balance of payments problem and its concomitant bullion drain was a source of alarm to some Romans. Pliny mentions it several times, complaining "that in no year does India absorb less than fifty million sesterces of our empire's wealth, sending back merchandise to be sold with us at a hundred times its prime cost" (a sestertius was the principal bronze coin of the Roman Empire valued at a quarter-denarius; the average soldier or working man made about one to two denarii a day). Later he made a more general reckoning as to the cost of trade with the East while fingering the culprits responsible: "By the lowest reckoning India, China and the Arabian peninsula take from our empire 100 million sesterces every year – that is the sum which our luxuries and our women cost us." The emperor Tiberius (14–37 CE) deplored "the ladies and their baubles transferring our money to foreigners," and later the emperor Vespasian (69–79 CE) tried to ban the export of precious metals. All of this did little to deter the Romans from enjoying their imported luxuries, and in any case the Roman government with its huge import tax was one of the main beneficiaries of the trade. The silver drain would cease only when the Romans debased their coinage enough that other people, including the Indians, didn't want it. Gold coins, which were not used for paying soldiers' wages or for other mundane government expenses, suffered less debasement and remained an Indian import.

Chapter 9

Following the *Periplus*

Roman maritime trade with the Indian Ocean began at Alexandria, which served as the Mediterranean's main distribution point for goods coming by sea from Asia and Africa. From Alexandria merchandise was sent up the Nile in riverboats to the port of Koptos located on a bend where the river came closest to the Red Sea. There, goods were offloaded onto camels for the trip across the desert. Roads were usually little more than tracks, but the most important were paved. Strabo notes the great improvement in crossing this leg of the trip: "In earlier times the camel-merchants traveled only by night, looking to the stars for guidance, and, like the mariners, also carried water with them when they traveled; but now they have constructed watering-places, having dug down to a great depth, and, although rain-water is scarce, still they have made cisterns for it."

On the Red Sea coast were a number of ports, the most important being at Myos Hormos ("Mussel Harbor") and Berenice Troglodytica. Berenice had no harbor but was located on an isthmus that provided a number of convenient landing places. Myos Hormos, located farther north, was home to a naval station. In navigating the Red Sea, sailors attempted to shoot straight down the middle. The African coast was mostly barren, the land of the Ichthyophagi ("Fish-Eaters"), self-sufficient communities strung along the shore. According to Agatharchides, some of them lived in huts made from seaweed packed over the rib bones of washed up whales. The Chelonophagi ("Turtle-Eaters"), who inhabited islands south of the Bab el-Mandeb, lived in even stranger dwellings, "under cover of turtle-shells, which are so large that they are used as boats."

The only place that received much traffic before reaching the Bab el-Mandeb was Adulis (Massawa), once a trading post for Arab merchants, later an elephant hunting station for the Ptolemies. The *Periplus Maris Erythraei* calls it "a fair sized village," but it became an important port-of-call as the window on the sea for the inland kingdom of Axum (Ethiopia), high on the Abyssinian plateau, which reached its height of power between the fourth and seventh centuries CE. The kings of Axum took advantage of the country's strategic position between the African interior and the Red Sea to develop a profitable trade. Eventually they opened an overland road to the Nile Valley connecting to Egypt after defeating a number of people and imposing on them the obligation to protect traveling merchants. When a people called the Sarane destroyed a merchant caravan, the greatest of Axumite kings, Ezana, killed or enslaved the whole tribe and three related tribes to set an example.

At the time of the *Periplus*, the Axumites were eager for trade, but their economy was still underdeveloped. Their relationship with both the Mediterranean and India was one of providing exotic raw materials and importing manufactured goods, chief among which were textiles, principally Egyptian linens and Indian cottons, ranging from what the *Periplus* describes as "cloaks of poor quality dyed in colors" to girdles. From the Mediterranean came glass; copper and brass products including utensils, tools, and jewelry; and gold and silver plate for the king. Iron imported from both the Mediterranean and India was made into spears to hunt elephants. Only three exports were in demand: ivory, rhinoceros horn, and tortoise shell. As herds providing the first two were systematically hunted into extinction, the hunting grounds were steadily expanded inland. During the period of the Late Roman Empire, Axum became a principal provider of gold. This was said to come from a place called Sasu, which was reportedly near the source of the Nile. To bargain with the gold miners, the Axumite king sent royal agents who were accompanied by a caravan of private traders numbering about 500. They traded oxen, salt, and iron for nuggets over a period of five days. The round trip took about six months, and the caravan had to be well armed or tribes along the way would plunder it.

If there was little to attract merchant ships to the African coast, there was much to repel them from the central stretches of the Arabian coast, which the *Periplus* describes as "fearsome in every respect." In addition to rocky shores and poor anchorage, it was plagued by pirates and wreckers. However, the southwestern corner of the Arabian peninsula (Yemen) was the key to the whole trade system of the western arc of the Indian Ocean. Agatharchides reports that gold was mined there in such quantities that it was traded for only twice its weight in iron. More valuable were the forests of aromatic trees made luxuriant by extensive irrigation systems. But most important was its strategic position as the linchpin between the Red Sea and the Arabian Sea. During the first millennium BCE the most powerful state in this area was Saba until its collapse in 115 BCE when it was replaced by the Himyarite kingdom. The center of maritime commerce was the port of Eudaimon Arabia (Aden), about 100 miles east of the Bab el-Mandeb, where Indian ships exchanged their cargoes: "No nation seems to be more prosperous than the Sabaeans and [their neighbors] the Gerrhaeans," observed Agatharchides, "since they are the ones who distribute everything from Asia and Europe that is considered valuable."

To get their goods from Eudaimon Arabia to the Mediterranean, the Arabs developed the Incense Road – the most storied trade routes were often known by their most conspicuous product – a caravan track that ran north paralleling the Red Sea. Such a road was made possible by the domestication of the camel in the late second millennium BCE and the rise of caravan cities along the route such as Iathrib (Medina). The Incense Road was exploited by anyone who could muster enough power to threaten it or who controlled vital supplies such as food and well water along the way. Pliny provides a look at how this impacted on the frankincense trade, one of the road's major products. Frankincense was produced east of Saba but had to be conveyed to the Sabaean capital on pain of death to be taxed by the local temple. From there it went north to the country of the Gebbanites, where it was taxed by their king, after which it passed through 65 additional staging posts, each of which levied taxes, fees, and other costs in fixed portions "so that expenses mount up to 688 denarii per camel before the Mediterranean coast is reached; and then again payment is made to the customs officers of our empire." The total trip normally took 70 days. The transporters of these goods may have been a people separate from the Sabaeans and other Arabs whom one scholar, Alessandro de Maigret, has labeled the "Turret-Grave people" from the unique form of burial they practiced. They were thought to be an ancient, autochthonous people who organized and developed the trade system around the Arabian peninsula as early as 3000 BCE.

The area between the northeastern corner of the Red Sea and the Mediterranean came to be controlled by the Nabataeans, sheep herders from the mountains of Jordan turned plunderers turned merchants. The Nabataeans discovered they could accrue more wealth by protecting caravans and providing them with services than by attacking them, so they offered caravaneers food, water, and cool rest areas in the caves of their mountains. When the number of caves proved insufficient, the Nabataeans began carving out their own. In the end they built a caravan city, Petra ("The Rock"), one of the world's truly unique places, a mountain refuge that became a mountain metropolis with facades of colonnaded porticoes sculpted out of the red, pink, and orange sandstone, fronting on rooms that were essentially man-made caverns. A population of 30,000 was supplied by a system of cisterns fed by channels chiseled into the rock, bringing enough spring water to irrigate fruit gardens and wheat fields.

As it turned out, the Nabataeans also had a knack for commerce that made their city one of the richest in the world between the second century BCE and the second century CE. Petra became a hub for routes running in different directions from the Incense Road to Egypt, Mesopotamia, the Levantine ports, and Damascus, beyond which the Incense Road connected to the Silk Road. Strabo notes that Petra was "exceedingly well-governed" and calls the Nabataeans "a sensible people." They had, he observed, two very admirable traits. First, whereas foreign merchants frequently engaged in lawsuits with each other and with the locals, "none of the natives prosecuted one another and in every way kept peace with one another." Profit-making was essentially mandated by law since they "are so much inclined to acquire possessions that they publicly fine anyone who has diminished his possessions and confer honors on anyone who has increased them." The Nabataeans were rivals of Ptolemaic Egypt, but they were wise enough not to challenge the might of Rome when it arrived in the area.

The Roman presence brought changes as well as accelerated trends already present. A Roman army attacked and sacked Eudaimon Arabia, and traffic shifted to Muza on the north side of the Bab el-Mandeb where the Romans exercised better control. During the reign of Augustus the Romans made an attempt to conquer Arabia because, according to Strabo, the Arabs "were very wealthy, and they sold aromatics and the most valuable stones for gold and silver, but never expended with outsiders any part of what they received in exchange; for he [Augustus] expected either to deal with wealthy friends or to master wealthy enemies." However, a Nabataean official serving as guide took the Romans on a wild goose chase for six months, during which at one point they came within two days' journey of reaching the land where myrrh was produced. Finally they turned around and returned to Egypt. The sources of myrrh and frankincense would remain outside imperial control.

Nevertheless, under the new conditions Arab middlemen began to be bypassed, and the long, laborious haul up the Incense Road was used less and less. Petra had offered shelter and protection to caravans, a service the Romans rendered obsolete. Although the Nabataeans controlled two ports on the Red Sea, once maritime trade from Egypt to the Indian Ocean became fully developed, the fortunes of their kingdom began a slow slide. Strabo notes that in his own time, commerce had already shifted from the Petra-to-Phoenicia route to the Red Sea-to-Alexandria route. In 363 CE an earthquake destroyed half of Petra, which lingered on to the seventh century when it was finally abandoned.

The Red Sea ends at the Bab el-Mandeb, where its opposite shores scrunch together almost touching. Ships generally stopped on one side or the other to take on fresh water before heading into the ocean. Some trade took place here, mostly in frankincense, myrrh, and Arabian wine for resale in India. Smaller, lighter ships adapted to Red Sea conditions went no farther. They did circuits, transferring their goods at Arabian and African ports, where they were reloaded onto ocean-going vessels or transshipped to inland caravan routes. Local and Indian goods were picked up for the voyage back to Egypt.

Once ships had passed through the Bab and out into the Gulf of Aden, they could head in three directions: south, along the African coast, turning abruptly at the Promontory of Spices (Cape Guardafui) to cruise down the eastern side of the continent; northeast, paralleling the Arabian coast and eventually to northern India; or due east, across open waters, turning south to catch the tip of southern India. Ships bound on the first course would make for the north Somali coast, which the *Periplus* refers to as "Far-Side

Barbaria." Here were a string of ports where no central government had control. Apparently it was the only area in the western arc where tramping was common. It was also a place where rafts and small craft were much in evidence. Far-Side ports offered ivory and shell but also limited quantities of high-quality myrrh, frankincense and other aromatics, a few "better quality" slaves, and large quantities of cassia. The inhabitants imported mostly staples on a somewhat lower scale than at Adulis, including foodstuffs from India such as rice, ghee (clarified butter), and sesame oil along with wine and unripe olives from the Mediterranean.

Below the Promontory of Spices, Strabo's source can provide no information. However, the *Periplus*, written a century later, has much to say about the shores of East Africa, a land Mediterranean sailors knew as Azania. This was smooth sailing across waters not known for their treacherous conditions or dangerous storms. It was generally safe for craft of all sizes, which meant that small-scale merchants with modest working capital could participate by renting space on what were often flimsy craft, a very different situation than existed on the route to India. The roadsteads and ports that were frequented were not documented, and probably many of them both on the Somali and Azania coasts were little more than seasonal encampments for ships awaiting the change in winds. The major exception was Rhapta ("Sewn," named after the local boats), which is thought to have been near modern Dar es-Salaam in Tanzania although a recent suggestion puts it farther south at Dondo in Mozambique. Despite the lack of archaeological remains, Rhapta must have been a substantial settlement. Claudius Ptolemy rates it as the "metropolis of Barbaria" but puts it "a short distance from the sea." He provides no details of the trade down the coast. Fortunately, the *Periplus* does, reporting that "great quantities" of ivory, horn, and shell were available in Rhapta, probably at bargain prices. And Rhapta was likely a nexus on the Cinnamon Road from Southeast Asia via Madagascar. Rhapta took manufactured goods, including tools, weapons, and glass, and foodstuffs such as grain and wine.

Despite its attractive qualities, the East African coast remained a backwater in the Indian Ocean trade. The coast of East Africa did not serve as an easy avenue for tapping into the wealth of the continent's interior; in penetrating inland, the best routes were far to the south, starting at the Zambezi Valley. The Zambezi led to interior gold deposits that would become a major export centuries later, but at the time of the Periplus gold did not trickle down to coastal areas. Consequently, stops along the coast could offer little more than what was available in their immediate hinterlands. Some archaeological evidence may indicate the existence at this time of an African seafaring culture, referred to as the Tana Tradition, with connections into the interior, but this remains speculative. Ships did not venture south of Rhapta, which remained terra incognita as far as the Periplus was concerned although in Claudius Ptolemy there is some indication that geographical knowledge, presumably obtained from trading voyages, went as far as Madagascar.

If East African trade was limited in potential, it also presented navigational problems for the type of square-rigged ship that Mediterranean sailors used. A round trip between Berenice and Rhapta took a year and a half, which included an 8-month layover in Rhapta. Add six months once back in Berenice to gather a new cargo, and the total amount of time was two years, twice as long as a roundtrip to India. The timing of the monsoon winds was the main problem, particularly the short return trip through the Gulf of Aden. Ships coming from Rhapta on the southwest monsoon had to make a sudden left turn at the Promontory of Spices directly into the wind, which stopped them dead in their tracks until the monsoon changed. On the India trade a ship could sail all the way from Egypt to India and back, stopping only for water and supplies, thus cutting out innumerable middlemen. The East Africa trade, on the other hand, worked better as a series of short, connecting circuits: down the Red Sea to Adulis or the Bab, across the Gulf of Aden to the Promontory, and down the East African slope to Rhapta. It still took goods a long time to reach their destination, but using circuits did not tie up ships, crews, and merchants on long layovers. Most goods reached their destinations in this way although some ships from Egypt did make the complete voyage.

Roman ships not headed for Far-Side ports or Azania were likely to stop at the roadstead of Muza, the principal place to obtain Arabian myrrh: "The whole place teems with Arabs," notes the *Periplus*, "and is astir with commercial activity." For its myrrh Muza took cloth and clothing, wine, grain, and money. In addition, merchants were expected to provide "gifts" to the local ruler in the form of horses, mules, gold, silver, copperware, and expensive clothing. From here some ships headed directly to south India while others cruised up the coast to Kane, the major port of what the *Periplus* calls the "Frankincense-bearing Land," where the same Mediterranean commodities were traded for frankincense. A little past Kane ships left the shoreline and headed across the Arabian Sea to northern India. A few may have made a detour to the island of Dioscarides (Socotra) to take on cargoes of tortoise shell. The trade here was mostly in the hands of Indians, who brought in rice, cloth, and women slaves for the colony of merchants that lived there.

Back on the coast, ships leaving the Arabian peninsula would slide by the entrance to the Persian Gulf, whose sailors had once dominated Indian Ocean commerce. With the Red Sea in ascendancy, the Gulf had slipped into backwater status, but Arab ships from there still brought cargoes of wine, dates, purple dye, slaves, and some gold to India. The major attraction for Roman Empire ships would have been fine-quality pearls. The intervening coastline was another land of Ichthyophagi, where the people built houses from whale bones and oyster shells and there was so much fish and so little else to eat the people are reported to have fed their cattle pounded baked fish meal although the people themselves ate mostly raw fish.

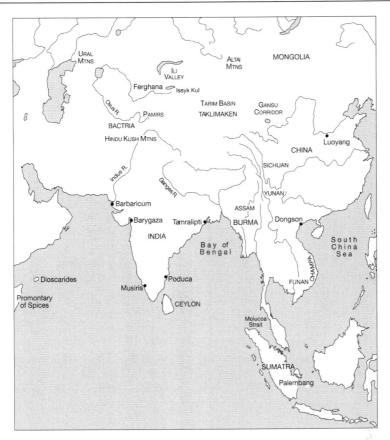

Map 9.1 Asia and the Indian Ocean 500 BCE-700 CE

According to Nearchus, Alexander's admiral who commanded an expedition from the mouth of the Indus to the Persian Gulf, these seas were alive with huge, spouting whales that were so aggressive they had to be kept away from the ships by blowing trumpets.

From just east of Kane to the ports of northern India is 1,200–1,400 miles. For the Roman trade the most important of these were Barbaricum on the Indus delta (near Karachi) and Barygaza (as it was known in Western sources; to the Indians it was Bhrigukachchha; today it is near Bharuch), perched on a steep hill where the Narmada River dividing northern and southern India meets the Gulf of Cambay. Sailors knew they were getting close to the Indian coast, according to the *Periplus*, when they encountered large swarms of snakes "that emerge from the depths to meet them." Nor was this the most disconcerting feature. Mighty tides swept along the northwest coast in some places, roaring into harbors at full and new moons driving ships sideways or capsizing them. The area between Barbaricum and

Barygaza was especially treacherous: in one place shoals and eddies reached beyond the sight of land; in another, rough seas with whirlpools thrashed unwary ships. The entry to Barygaza was so narrow, the current so swift, and the shoals so dangerous the king had to send out pilot boats to escort merchant ships to safe anchorage.

Barbaricum and Barygaza handled much the same merchandise. Leading their exports were spices, aromatics, and resins; long pepper, said to be plentiful but not cheap, nard, costus, and bdellium. Gems from India and nearby countries included turquoise, lapis lazuli, onyx, agate, and carnelian, and India was a major exporter of ivory. Among textiles and related products were locally made cottons and indigo, silk from China, and furs from the Siberian forest. In return, Roman ships brought Italian, Laodicean, and Arabian wines; linen textiles from Egypt, particularly "multicolored girdles eighteen inches wide"; storax, Arabian frankincense, and an unspecified type of "choice" unguent; copper, tin, lead, coral, realgar, sulfide of antimony, peridot, glass, and glassware; at Barygaza certain luxuries for the king such as silverware and high-quality slaves, including musicians and beautiful girls; and last, but perhaps most important, gold and silver coins to compensate for whatever shortfall the barter did not cover. Indian rulers used Roman silver to finance their frequent wars against each other.

Barbaricum, Barygaza, and other ports served as entryways to the subcontinent of India and beyond into the commercial systems of greater Asia. Cargoes offloaded at Barbaricum were forwarded up the Indus River to Purushapura, capital of the Kushan Empire. Barygaza was the major port of another state, the Kingdom of the Shakas, but its commercial hinterland stretched from the Ganges Valley to the Deccan peninsula. Unlike Barbaricum, Barygaza was a manufacturing center noted for its cotton weaving. And whereas foreign trade was in the hands of the royal government at Barbaricum, at Barygaza private enterprise seems to have been the rule.

For the states of India prosperity and power came to depend on control over inland trade routes that brought goods out of the interior to west coast ports. Ox and donkey carts organized into vast wagon trains, pack animals in caravans, and boat traffic running along the Narmada and Ganges rivers connected to arteries running north to south. Some towns that began as administrative centers or pilgrimage sites became important commercial centers if they happened to be located on trade routes while others that started as local markets for the exchange of basic goods extended their wares to include imported prestige items. Local authorities encouraged this as a source of customs revenue. Buddhist monasteries often provided accommodations for travelers, including merchants, and bazaars grew up around them, some of which became established commercial centers.

Roman merchants who wanted to trade with southern India did not generally start at Barbaricum and Barygaza and sail down the coast. Traders could get a shipful of goods at one or both of these ports without further effort or risk, and south of Barygaza pirates were often a nuisance. According to Pliny, ships bound for the Malabar coast of southwestern India headed there once they cleared the Bab el-Mandeb on a fast 40-day ride powered by the southwest monsoon. The trip from Alexandria to southern India could be done in under 100 days' straight travel time, although sailing on the southwest monsoon when it was blowing hardest was a lot more dangerous than cruising the placid waters of East Africa.

The far south of India was the land of the Tamils. There, large-scale external contact helped to stimulate the state-building process and encouraged urbanization as redistributive systems were replaced and gift-giving gave way to commercial trade. According to tradition, one famous chief reportedly defeated a Yavana fleet, which may echo what was actually an early pirating expedition against Roman merchant vessels. Local authorities must soon have realized that they could accumulate more sustainable wealth by peaceful exchange than by piracy. Western traders gathered in Malabar ports such as Musiris, Neleynda, and Bakare, where they may have played a middleman role, unlike at Barygaza, where this was handled by local merchants. However, Roman trade with southern India did not rival in quantity, value, or variety the trade with northern India. The main product was black pepper, available in huge amounts. Other local products included gems and precious stones, ivory, pearls, and cotton textiles. Nard and malabathrum came from the Himalayan region via the Ganges delta, the Bay of Bengal, and the Coromandel Coast of southeastern India, and Chinese silk arrived by the same route. Yavana ships carried a limited selection of their usual products, including wine, glass, copper, tin, and lots of coined silver and gold money.

South of India lay the beautiful, teardrop-shaped island of Ceylon (Sri Lanka; referred to in classical sources as Taprobane). Greeks knew of its existence from at least the third century BCE, but their information was very inaccurate. It was thought to be much larger than it really was – some believed it was the southern hemisphere's equivalent to the Eurasian landmass of the northern hemisphere – and much farther away. Eratosthenes puts it at a seven-day journey from India, and Onesicritus, at 20 days. Strabo has it stretching from south of India toward the East African coast and at a size "not less than Britain." During the reign of the emperor Claudius (41–54 CE), a Roman ship on its way around Arabia was blown off course and eventually landed on Ceylon. After questioning the ship's captain, the local king sent envoys to Rome, who provided a good deal of geographical information about Ceylon and lands to the east, much of which turned out to be inaccurate, even about Ceylon. Nevertheless, contact was established, and direct trade followed. Ceylon produced pearls along with rubies and other gems, cotton garments, and tortoise shell, but its greatest asset proved to be its central location, and by the late fourth century CE it had become the most important maritime commercial center in the Indian Ocean.

East of the Malabar coast and north of Ceylon was the Coromandel coast. Roman Empire ships brought back goods from here, the most important being pearls. Some traffic between the Malabar and Coromandel coasts is known to have come overland by oxcart, and small sea craft also scurried back and forth. But Roman ships rounding Cape Comorin at the tip of India faced contrary winds followed by a narrow strait with dangerous shallows, underwater reefs, and a string of islands whimsically known as Adam's Bridge that served as a barrier to larger ships. Nor was it particularly safe to take the long way around the southern end of Ceylon, where the waters were also dangerous. Nevertheless, preliminary archaeological work at the Coromandel port of Poduca (Arikamedu) unearthed large quantities of Roman remains, including pottery that once held olive oil and garum, not typical items in the Indian diet, indicating a trading station. Coromandel ports faced eastward to the Ganges delta in one direction and to Chryse, the lands of Southeast Asia in the other. Yavana merchants stationed at Poduca would forward incoming goods by land or sea to associates in Musiris and hence on to Alexandria and Rome. More recent excavation, however, has brought closer scrutiny, and now there is some question as to whether eating garum and using olive oil warrants the assumption of a Roman trading station. Whether Greeks or Indians lived at Poduca, it does seem to have occupied a nodal position tying the trade of Southeast Asia and the Bay of Bengal with the Malabar coast and beyond to the Mediterranean from as early as the second century BCE.

Yavana merchants probably didn't go much farther into the Bay of Bengal than Poduca; at least that is what the *Periplus* implies. In explaining where he got his information on India, Strabo states: "as for the merchants who now sail from Egypt ... as far as India, only a small number have sailed as far as the Ganges," which is an indication that at least some of them went that far. Bay of Bengal trade was clearly in the hands of Indian merchants aboard Indian ships. The rapid development of a half dozen or so ports known to have been used on the Coromandel coast peaked in the second century CE as a by-product of the increasing demands of the Mediterranean-to-Indian Ocean system. Development on the east coast was not uniform, and there were long stretches between ports not touched by the new commercial economy. The *Periplus* warns of one such area between the Coromandel coast and the Ganges delta where there were "numerous barbaric peoples, among whom are the Kirradai, a race of wild men with flattened noses, and another people, the Bargysoi, and the Horses Faces, who are said to be cannibals." East coast ports were generally close to river estuaries, the largest being in the Ganges delta, a port the *Periplus* calls simply "Ganges" (actually Tamralipti, modern Tamluk south of Calcutta). Its major exports included nard, malabathrum, Chinese silk, pearls, and a very fine locally made cotton cloth similar to muslin. The only Western export in evidence was Roman money.

To the southeast of Ganges was Chryse. Beyond that, sailing northeast, according to the *Periplus*, "where the sea ends somewhere on the outer fringe," there was a great inland city, Thina (probably from the same root word as China), from which the silk came: "It is not easy to get to this Thina; for rarely do people come from it, and only a few." Although there is no record of Roman ships meeting up with Chinese ships from the opposite direction, Chinese chronicles do report the arrival of a Roman mission in the capital of Luoyang in 166 CE that came by sea. The men claimed to be ambassadors from the emperor Andun (Marcus Aurelius) although apparently they were private merchants, not official envoys. The gifts they presented did not make much of an impression on the Chinese, who, as a result, refused to do business with them. Such a Rome-to-China sea route would have been difficult to maintain, to put it mildly, but this has not stopped many who know of the story from speculating on the possibilities if members of the Chinese court had been more receptive to what has been called a "once in a millennium opportunity." They weren't, leaving the incident as little more than another example of the truism that "what if" history isn't history.

Chapter 10

The all-water route

The gifts of the self-appointed emissaries from Andun that were so cavalierly rejected by the court in Luoyang consisted of ivory, rhinoceros horn, and tortoise shell. The Chinese considered these to be valuable goods, but they suspected, quite correctly, that they came from nearby Southeast Asia. If Romans had really come bearing gifts, they needed to be more exotic than this.

In the West, Southeast Asia was referred to as Chryse. The *Periplus* describes it as "the furthest part of the mainland toward the east" and in a later passage as "an island in the ocean, the furthest extremity towards the east of the inhabited world, lying under the rising sun itself." This begs the question: was it part of the mainland, say Burma (Myanmar), or perhaps the entire Southeast Asian peninsula, or was it an island, probably Sumatra or perhaps the entire Sunda chain of islands (Sumatra, Java, Bali, Timor) or something in between such as the Malay peninsula? As for products, "it supplies the finest tortoise shell of all the places in the Erythreaean Sea." Since Westerners often associated places with their signature products, the name of this place should have had something to do with turtles. But Chryse is from the Greek for "gold" and was also known as the "Golden Chersonese." In Indian literature it was Suvarnadvipa in Sanskrit and Suvannabhumi in Pali, both variations of "Golden Land." As the Indians learned more about this country, they began to specify local areas with names reflecting more realistic expectations, including "Camphor Land," "Cardamom Land," and "Coconut Land."

Claudius Ptolemy's account of Southeast Asia is more extensive than the *Periplus* even if much of his information is problematic. He specifies that Southeast Asia is a peninsula but makes it huge, several times larger than India, extending indefinitely southward, as he does with Africa, to enclose the Indian Ocean. The real Southeast Asia also has islands, large and small, lying to the south and east of the peninsula, and Ptolemy has islands, too, but they are scattered along both sides of the coast. He divides peninsular Southeast Asia into two parts, a western, which he calls "India Beyond the Ganges," and an eastern, referred to as "Sinae." North of both lay Scythia and

Serica. India Beyond the Ganges extended from the Bay of Bengal to the Magnus Sinus ("Great Bay"), which must refer to the region where the peninsula ends and the islands begin, around the Straits of Malacca. The best cinnamon came from here, and some places had much gold.

India Beyond the Ganges lay on the Indian Ocean, but past the Magnus Sinus the land turned and ran south to north along what is now the South China Sea to Ptolemy's Sinae with its port of Kattigata. This was the edge of the world. Ptolemy draws a clear distinction between Sinae and Serica, and although geographically he has them as neighbors, there does not seem to have been any contact between them. Coming from the west, a traveler went to Serica by land and Sinae by sea. Herodotus knew nothing about the Seres, but Roman authors did: it was the land of the Silk people. According to both Pliny and the *Periplus*, north of the Black and Caspian Seas and the Himalayan Mountains was an ocean covering what is actually Siberia, Mongolia, and Manchuria. The Seres could be reached by following its shoreline beyond a land of raging snowstorms, tribes of cannibals, and deserts thronging with wild beasts. The Seres, according to Pliny, had red hair and blue eyes, and "though mild in character, yet resemble wild animals." Exactly which term, "Sinae" or "Serica," equates to the modern China is a bit muddled. Sinae could refer to eastern peninsular Southeast Asia or southern China or both whereas Serica could refer to northern China or Xinjiang and eastern Central Asia or both.

At least some Roman Empire merchants must have visited both India Beyond the Ganges and Sinae, but the frequency, volume, and value of their trade were probably slight. By the time they got there, the Southeast Asians had been engaged in long-distance exchange for many centuries. The earliest involved highland foragers swapping with lowland farmers in reciprocal systems or between inland and coastal peoples, using rivers that flowed from the interior. Exchange was done by barter between communities, and neither specialized traders nor profit-driven trade was involved. They appeared with the arrival of seaborne traders who sought inland and forest products such as ivory, rhinoceros horn, and bird feathers.

Trade also developed in the interior in places such as central Thailand that were endowed with natural resources, particularly copper and tin. In the second millennium BCE exchange involving raw materials and exotic items such as marine shells, marble, volcanic stone, and precious stones was being transacted probably through down-the-line systems. The Iron Age, which began in Southeast Asia in *c.* 500 BCE, greatly stimulated economic growth. Villages of specialized craftsmen began producing products that were marketed at fairs and religious festivals, and soon towns developed as centers for local and long-distance trade. Mortuary goods included precious stones, gold, and glass beads from outside Southeast Asia, and bulk products such as iron along with luxury items such as pearls and coral were traded along the coast. One interesting characteristic of Southeast Asian commerce that likely went far back into the past was the importance of women in trade. In later periods Chinese and Arab observers noted this with surprise and sometimes disdain. Women controlled retail markets in many places and sometimes were key players in wholesale and long-distance commerce.

Out at sea the lanes were dominated from at least the first millennium BCE by the Malays, a term that may refer specifically to the inhabitants of the Malay peninsula but is often applied in a larger, more generic sense to various seafaring peoples who spoke Austronesian languages and lived in parts of Sumatra, Borneo, and other islands as well as on the peninsula. Malay sailors were the earliest long-distance traders in the modern countries of Malaysia and Indonesia, and their activities reached from the South China Sea to the eastern rim of the Indian Ocean. They were skilled mariners with their own advanced nautical technology who may have independently invented the sail. Long before Greek and Roman merchants stepped into Indian Ocean trade, the Malays created commercial networks extending from the Philippines and New Guinea to the east coast of Africa.

Southeast Asia provides an excellent example of what can and cannot be gleaned about early trade routes from tracing artifacts when no written evidence is available. In the seventh century BCE the Dongson culture emerged in the valley of the Red River in northern Vietnam and over the next half millennium developed an advanced bronze-making society that was sea-oriented. Artifacts representative of the Dongson style have been found far beyond Vietnam, the most outstanding of which is known today as Heger I type drums cast in one piece by the lost wax method. They are large, sometimes weighing over 200 pounds and standing 3 feet tall, and squat in shape with a broad flat top, rounded sides, and splayed feet. And they are exquisitely decorated with friezes depicting people engaged in various activities.

Heger I drums appear to have been made from the fifth century BCE to the third century CE. Over 200, some whole, others in fragments, have been recovered in a distribution range extending from Yunnan in south China down the Malay peninsula to Sumatra and across the Sunda Islands to the western tip of New Guinea. Some drums came back into trade networks long after they were first made and exchanged, a process that scattered them farther afield. Chinese observers noted that the people of Southeast Asia used drums as symbols of power and status, and doubtless the function of Heger I drums was ritual or ceremonial. Although they were not likely made and sent out originally with profit in mind, Heger I drums do provide irrefutable evidence of extensive distribution networks extending over thousands of miles prior to the establishment of systems originating in India and China. This funneled not only ceremonial drums but copper, bronze, and iron ornaments and more functional products like tools as well as exotic materials such as glass and beads to the border of the Pacific world.

Eventually trade did come from both India and China, tying Southeast Asia into the larger Eurasian system. For a long time the trade with India was more important than that with China. The motive for such contact usually given in Indian texts is commercial gain: the Indians were out to make a profit, although once goods arrived in Southeast Asia and the initial exchange was made, they were often distributed internally through some mechanism other than strictly commercial-driven trade. The Indians were likely searching for a new source of gold after the Siberian route became defunct, as witnessed by the name they gave to the place. Significant gold deposits existed in central Sumatra, where it was mined in the hills or sieved from river sands, and Champa in central Vietnam, a few places on the southern part of the Malay peninsula, and the island of Sulawesi also had gold although it is difficult to determine how much was being extracted at this time. People of status in the region were noted for wearing jewelry made from a very pure, soft gold. However, Southeast Asia was not the pot at the end of the rainbow, and the early perception of finding a bonanza at the edge of the world was mostly wishful thinking. Nevertheless, once there, the gold seekers found other products, and the trade was on.

Another possibility sees India's link to Southeast Asia as a spin-off of India's tie to the Roman Empire. Southeast Asia contained many of the products the Romans sought in India, including spices, aromatic woods, and resins, and could serve as a reservoir for augmenting Indian supplies. A third possibility also sees the trade as resulting from spin-off but this time from the India-to-China trade in silk. Southeast Asia was a place Indian and Chinese merchants had to pass through to get to each other, and eventually they discovered that it contained valuable commodities and could be developed in its own right as a market for their products. Probably all three proposals played some role although it should be noted that both the second and third suffer to varying degrees from the problem of backward projection, that is, taking the consequence of a historical action and making it the cause. To use proposal three as an example, it is true that what came to be known as the maritime silk route through Southeast Asia eventually became important. But quite a lot of silk was already arriving overland from China into India at the time Indians were venturing into Southeast Asia, and there is no evidence that they were searching for a water passage to China.

Indians may have begun arriving as early as the mid-first millennium BCE. Excavations at an ancient cemetery in western Thailand from a fourth century BCE context have recovered over 3,000 beads, mostly glass, which were made in India for the export market. Six hundred were drilled carnelian and agate beads, including 50 of the etched variety. Other Indian imports were decorated bronze ritual bowls and a carved carnelian lion. Similar products have also been found in sites in coastal Thailand, Burma, and Cambodia. Excavations on the north coast of Bali have unearthed large quantities of Indian goods, including pottery shards from Poduca. Farther afield etched agate beads of a Bengali type have been found in the Philippines, but an even more interesting find from a jar burial in a cave in the Talaud islands in far northeastern Indonesia includes banded agate beads and black beads etched in white, reflecting a style that originated with the Harappans.

The introduction of international trade to an area that had been largely self-contained did have profound social and political impacts not unlike it did in Central and Northern Europe. Some of the societies of Southeast Asia, particularly those that were already producing substantial rice surpluses and were well advanced in metal production, were already on a trajectory leading to stratified class systems, urbanization, and statehood. Large-scale long-distance trade greatly enhanced this process. In other areas where this was not already under way, trade became a primary factor in generating it. Large-scale trade required organization to produce the commodities foreign traders wanted, a function undertaken by traditional leaders. A range of new products became available to elites who used them to enhance their status and power, reinforcing their interest in perpetuating the system. Chiefs, in the process of becoming kings, orchestrated the flow of goods into and out of the areas they controlled. As local areas became absorbed into market networks and their rulers assumed more control over the material wealth it generated, they were able to exercise more power over their people. States emerged.

The earliest states in Southeast Asia developed at strategic commercial locations, one of the most favored being on the northern section of the Malay peninsula at the Isthmus of Kra, the narrowest point on the peninsula at only 35 miles wide. Commercial communities were located here, and valuable resources were nearby, including tin and forest products. As the trade network connection to India took shape, Kra became its linchpin for a while. On the west coast of Kra, cargo was offloaded and shipped by land portage to the Gulf of Thailand, where it was reloaded onto new ships and sent out into the South China Sea. The monsoons determined the schedule. When northeast winds were blowing, ships could sail from India or China to Southeast Asia, where they had to lay over until the winds shifted and the southwest monsoon took them home. Thus ships arrived from both directions at the same time and departed at the same time.

The earliest state in Southeast Asia for which any substantive information is available is known to history by the name the Chinese gave it, Funan. It was not on the Isthmus of Kra but across the Gulf of Thailand on the southern coast of Vietnam in the Mekong delta and upriver in southeastern Cambodia. Nor was it a little city state like those at Kra but rather a country with at least two major cities, a port and a capital. Or at least that is what Chinese sources relate. Modern historians are not so sure, and current speculation is more inclined to see this region as consisting of a series of small, competing principalities scattered along the coast and up the river, with Funan referring either to one particular place that made an impression on the Chinese or to the area in general. Funan's advantage over Kra was that it contained extensive rice lands whereas Kra had mostly forest. Thus Funan could feed without difficulty its own population and the merchants and sailors who had to lay over sometimes up to five months waiting for the monsoons to shift.

Chinese reports on Funan began with the visit of two imperial emissaries who arrived there between 225 and 250 CE likely sent to investigate the opening of an official maritime silk route to India. However, the report they made on their return, or at least what has come down to us, contains relatively little about Funan's trade except that customs taxes were paid in gold, silver, pearls, and perfumes. Other Chinese emissaries followed over the next four centuries as did Funanese embassies to China, conveniently recorded in Chinese imperial archives. The information they convey has been greatly augmented by archaeological excavations carried out at a site in Vietnam called Oc Eo, which must be the place Chinese observers described as Funan's principal port. Oc Eo is a few miles from the coast of the Gulf of Thailand, to which it was linked by a network of canals that also extended to the Mekong River. Cargoes were landed from India bringing carnelian and agate, bronze jewelry and seals, cotton fabrics, pepper, and at least one Buddha head from Gandhara in northwestern India. The same ships carried Roman Empire products, including glassware, gold and silver jewelry, and gold coins, one of which with the likeness of the emperor Antoninus Pius (138–61 CE) was made into a pendant. From China came silk and finely made products such as mirrors and, from closer to home, tin from the Malay peninsula and copper from Thailand.

Over the years Southeast Asian merchants were successful in introducing substitute products at reduced costs for goods passing between Mediterranean and Indian and Chinese markets. Benzoin, a balsamic resin from Sumatra, for example, could be used as a treatment for skin irritations, as a fixative in perfumes, and as incense; it proved to be a good substitute for myrrh. The woods and bark of the camphor tree, also from Sumatra, produced another resin used for incense and as a stimulant in medicines. Agalloch, or aloeswood, from the Malay peninsula, Cambodia, and the highlands of Vietnam was a soft, resinous wood burnt as incense whereas sandalwood, a fragrant, yellowish wood from a parasitic tree found on Timor 1,800 miles east of Funan, was used for furniture, carvings, and containers such as chests and boxes. New spices – cloves, nutmeg, and mace – joined pepper and cinnamon although in much smaller quantities and at much higher prices. Oc Eo was more than just an entrepot; it was also a manufacturing center, at least for jewelry. A range of gems and precious stones, from malachite, jade, and olivine to amethyst, beryl, and rubies, was used along with gold and silver by specialist craftsmen who borrowed Indian and sometimes Roman motifs and styles.

Chinese travelers picked up secondhand information on other trading states located down the Malay peninsula and around the Gulf of Thailand. Referring to the countries of this region, one Chinese report maintains "all the countries beyond the [Chinese] frontier come and go in pursuit of trade," and with regard to one particular Malay port, notes "East and West meet together so that every day great crowds gather there. Precious goods and rare merchandise – these are all there." Ports developed in the Sunda Straits region between the islands of Sumatra and Java, where the king of a place called Zhiayang was said to be importing horses from the Kushan Empire in the mid-third century CE. Thailand was another hotspot of trade. At Khuan Lukpad ("Bead Mound") glass beads were found similar to those of Poduca along with a mutilated Roman coin and two carnelian intaglios done in Roman motifs, one showing the goddess Tyche. Etched beads and other jewelry have also been found in Malaysian sites, including a gold ring with a Hindu design and a carnelian seal with Sanskrit writing. In return for such manufactured products, the people of both areas likely offered tin.

One of the most interesting places to emerge in the early first millennium CE was the kingdom of Champa located up the coast from Funan in what is today central Vietnam. The Cham coast should have been a good place for ships going and coming from China to stop for cargo. The region offered desirable products, which the Chams obtained from trade with the peoples of the interior highlands who needed salt from the coast. These included the usual ivory and rhino horn along with such rare woods as ebony, sandalwood, camphor, aloeswood, and lakawood, a form of black bamboo. Cinnamon, cardamom, lacquer, and kingfisher, peacock, and other rare feathers were also available as were tortoise shell and pearls from the coast. Cham ports were also known to be major slave markets, and herein lay the problem with Cham commerce.

Cham kings exercised only loose control over much of their long coastline, which led to a chronic problem with piracy. The Cham kings themselves did not have a rich agricultural hinterland to tax as did the Funanese to the south and the Vietnamese to the north, so they came to depend on plunder as a major source of state revenue. In the long run such a society was doomed to extinction, which finally came at the hands of the Vietnamese in the fifteenth century. In the shorter run it meant that ships often detoured around the Cham coast, decreasing Cham income from peaceful commerce and further increasing the need to rely on plunder. Champa, which should have been a major partner in Southeast Asian trade, was relegated to a secondary position, which it enjoyed only during more tranquil times.

Champa and Funan were geographically much closer to China than to India, a short sail across the South China Sea, which, however, can be a very turbulent body of water, notorious for its typhoons. Some speculation has put the Chinese on the Malaya peninsula as early as the mid-fourth century BCE and Chinese merchants in India on a limited basis by the first century CE. Third century CE Chinese documentary sources allude to direct sea trade with India, and later in that century contact was said to have been established between the Chinese and a kingdom in the Ganges delta called Tan-Mei (probably Tamralipti). Commercial negotiations may have been carried on in neutral Funan, after which the Indians sent an ambassador to China although Chinese records do not mention this. Notable quantities of artifacts dating from the Han dynasty have started turning up in scattered locations in Thailand, and pottery from the same period has been found in southern Sumatra and Java. Nevertheless, the archaeological record for Chinese contacts with Southeast Asia beyond northern Vietnam is surprisingly meager just as the literary record is vague. In the fifth century CE silk began to be sent in more significant amounts by sea, and stoneware jars made in China appeared as far away as the Persian Gulf, but even for this time the quantity of artifacts is not impressive and would remain so until the Song dynasty at the end of the millennium.

The Chinese were interested in much the same exotic luxury products as the Romans. The Han Shu chronicle notes that in the second century BCE China had become so prosperous "rarities such as luminous pearls, striped shells, lined rhinoceros horn, and kingfisher feathers [were seen] in plenty in the empress's palace." Rhino horn became so popular among Chinese men as an aphrodisiac that rhinoceroses were driven to extinction in Southeast Asia. Birds, especially kingfishers, peacocks, and parrots, were in great demand as were their feathers, which made rather striking fashion statements as witnessed by another passage from the Han Shu describing the emperor "with his back against a screen figured in black and white decked in a coverlet of kingfisher plumes." The Chinese also imported quantities of resins, aromatics, incense, drugs, and spices. Some frankincense and myrrh made it all the way from Arabia, but for the most part the substitute products of Southeast Asia were successfully integrated into the Chinese market. Pepper, cloves, and nutmeg were used more as ingredients in medicine than as flavoring for food. Official trade was carried on through the tribute system, a form of high-level royal gift exchange the Chinese chose to interpret as foreign states sending tribute in token of their submission, for which the Chinese emperor in return bestowed gifts in gracious magnanimity, a conceit the Chinese shared with the pharaonic Egyptians. Records show that the rulers of Funan dispatched 25 missions to China between 226 and 649 CE. Both Funan and Champa sent live elephants – the Cham kings did this a reported 14 times – and Funan also sent a live rhinoceros. In one instance, the Funanese sent a troupe of trained elephants that Chinese authorities considered to be too dangerous and returned.

The Chinese presence was most apparent in northern Vietnam since this was the one place in Southeast Asia that was conquered by an outside power, a process that began in the second century BCE. The class of Chinese–Vietnamese who came to rule over this most distant province of the Han Empire proved to be less interested in setting up an elaborate system of government than in taking advantage of local commercial opportunities. The Vietnamese coast became the passageway between Southeast Asia and south China, offering excellent opportunities for trade, smuggling, and piracy.

Officials were said to have normally extorted from merchants between 20 and 30 percent of goods passing through.

During the first half of the third century CE the Han dynasty fell, and China became divided into north and south. To the west, the Parthian Empire was conquered a few years later, and soon thereafter the Kushan Empire was also invaded and subsequently collapsed. In the far west the Roman Empire struggled into the fourth century with much of its energy sapped. These events profoundly shook the Eurasian overland trading network collectively referred to as the Silk Road and the various arteries that fed into it. Long-distance overland travel became less secure as nomadic peoples moved into the power vacuums created by the fall of the great states. As Chinese trade to the northwest dried up, Chinese trade to the south increased. If overall this was not a good time for long-distance trade, problems on the northern overland route did create opportunities on the southern maritime route.

From the third century CE on, direct Roman commercial activity on the international scene began to recede. In the southeast, focus became increasingly confined to the Red Sea area itself, beyond which Roman commercial contact became more indirect. This had an impact on India, where some cities in the north and west declined. Others, however, prospered as trade shifted rather than collapsed, with the beneficiaries being those cities that were plugged into the Bay of Bengal, Southeast Asian, and Chinese trades. Eventually the Byzantine Empire would replace the Roman, at least for the eastern Mediterranean, and more quickly the Sassanian Empire replaced the Parthian as consumers at the western end of the maritime route. At the eastern end, Southeast Asia seemed to be in the proverbial catbird's seat; with direct links to two systems, it could adjust upward or downward, depending on which side was expanding or contracting. It could also reap the maximum benefit at optimal times when both sides were expanding.

Beginning in the fourth century CE, the highway through Southeast Asia changed, becoming more efficient in response to increased market pressures. Ships began using a new route through the Straits of Malacca between the Malay Peninsula and Sumatra or through the Straits of Sunda between the islands of Sumatra and Java instead of drudging across the overland portage on the Isthmus of Kra. In nautical miles this was a longer trip, but it was all water, making it faster and cheaper. In theory, a ship could leave southeastern India or Ceylon and not touch land until Canton (Guangzhou) in south China although most ships would continue to lay over in Southeast Asia to await the change in winds but now at ports in Sumatra, Java, Borneo, or on the tip of the Malay peninsula rather than at Kra or Funan. Malay sailors are usually credited with engineering this shift, which was gradual if irreversible.

A major factor in the shift to the all-water route was the continued success of substitute products, many of which, like camphor and benzoin, came from the Sumatran forests. Sumatra also became known for its pepper, as did Java, where a new variety with a distinct taste somewhat like allspice was reputed to be effective in treating respiratory problems. The most profitable of these new products, however, came from islands 2,000 miles east of the Malacca Straits. Whereas pepper and cinnamon were available in various places, the so-called "fine spices" – cloves, nutmeg, and mace – came only from a few islands in the Molucca and Banda seas, often referred to collectively as the Spice Islands. If today these spices have been relegated to the back of the spice rack in most kitchens, in the past they were in great demand by those who could afford to pay premium prices. Cloves are sun dried unopened flower buds from the evergreen clove tree. It is a strong spice with a hottish flavor and perfume-like scent. In Europe it was used to flavor meats and sauces while clove oil was used as an anesthetic and breath freshener. Nutmeg and mace are different parts of the same product. Nutmeg is the kernel of the fruit of another evergreen tree used in sweet and savory dishes and considered to be an aid to digestion. It was especially popular in northern India and was later used to flavor beer in Europe. The nutmeg seed is wrapped in a membrane, basically a rind, from which mace is produced. Its flavor is a subtle combination of nutmeg, pepper, and cinnamon, and it was often used in sauces.

The fine spices appear to have entered the long-distance trade network in detectable quantities in the late first millennium BCE. Cloves were being used in China by the third century BCE and reached Rome in time for Pliny to include a discussion on them. The island of Java, more than 1,000 miles from the Molucca and Banda islands, proved crucial to this trade. Javanese ships brought staples, especially rice, which could be grown in abundance on Java, to the Spice Islanders to trade for their valuable products. On the return voyage Javanese ships sailed west on the same winds that took Indian and Chinese ships from Java to their home ports. When winds changed, everyone would go in the opposite direction, meaning that the ships taking these spices to their ultimate destinations were never in Javanese ports at the same time as the ships bringing the spices from the places they originated. Consequently, everyone outside of Java assumed that the spices were produced in Java. On the Spice Islands, large-scale production catapulted the people of these societies from hunter–gatherers into trade states that were soon building their own micro-empires.

With the center of long-distance trade in Southeast Asia shifting southward, new polities arose, intent on protecting, taxing, and controlling the trade. In the seventh century CE a group of ports centering on the city of Palembang in southeastern Sumatra came together to form what was probably a trade-based confederation (although it is often referred to as an "empire") known as Srivijaya. The key to its success was the co-opting of local pirates whose notoriety was a major reason that ships had earlier preferred the Kra portage. The pirates agreed to protect rather than plunder passing ships in return for a cut of the tariff fees. Srivijaya, at times in alliance with a major rice-producing state in Java, dominated long-distance trade in Southeast Asia for the next seven centuries. The big losers in the shift to an all-water route were the Kra and Mekong delta ports and particularly Funan, whose fragile economy depended on ships that no longer arrived by the sixth century CE. When ships going between the Straits and China did stop along the coast, it was to take on products of the hinterland, which could be obtained more cheaply and in larger quantities on the Cham coast provided the local pirates were under control. Eventually Oc Eo was abandoned, and the local center of power moved up the Mekong River into the Cambodian interior.

By the first millennium CE northern Europe was linked to the islands of eastern Indonesia by a series of interconnected routes secured by emporiums all along the way. The Eurasian world had become a unified commercial zone dwarfing all earlier exchange systems. If there was anything that could be considered as the center of the maritime portion of this zone, it was India with the Mediterranean and China anchoring each end. But maritime trade was only half the system; the other half went overland across deserts, mountains, valleys, rivers, steppelands, and forests, in and out of cities, countries, and badlands. The backbone of this overland system was the great Silk Road.

Chapter 11

From the Jade Road to the Silk Road

Of the great civilizations that spanned the agricultural underbelly of Eurasia, China was the most self-sufficient. It was accessible by water from the Indian Ocean, but this required passage around Southeast Asia and across the dangerous South China Sea. Overland was an even greater challenge since separating China from South Asia, West Asia, and the Mediterranean were the highest mountains and some of the worst deserts in the world. In his comments on the Seres, the Late Roman Empire historian Ammianus Marcellinus notes that they "shun intercourse with the rest of mankind. So when strangers cross the river into their country to buy silks or other commodities, they exchange no words with them, but merely intimate by their looks the value of the goods offered for sale; and so abstemious are they that they buy not any foreign products." Of course, this was nonsense, but it is instructive to note that Ammianus Marcellinus is considered as one of the best historians of his time, and by then his countrymen had been trading, albeit indirectly, with the Chinese for four centuries.

Chinese perceptions of the land to the west were not much better but did improve over time. Initially it was viewed as a mythical place of creatures that were part men and part beast, where the Queen Mother of the West rode in a chariot drawn by phoenixes. Somewhat later it was given the name Shizi and was said to be inhabited by devils, spirits, and dragons, that, peculiarly enough, had a commercial bent to them because they traded with the merchants of neighboring countries. The Kingdom of Women played a prominent role in some accounts. Men were said to have lived there, but their activities were confined to military functions: the place was governed by women. The Land of Women also did its fair share of trading with exports that included copper, cinnabar, musk, yaks, horses, and salt. Another story that appeared in a later annal concerns the adventures of a certain Emperor Mu *c*. 1000 BCE. According to modern speculation, this may reflect the actual travels of early Chinese merchants since it contains some real information about geography and trade goods in the form of presents given to Mu, which included jade, horses, leopard skins, and women.

Royal burials for the Shang (*c.* 1600–1050 BCE), the earliest Chinese dynasty for which there is archaeological evidence, contains exotic materials including jade from the west and sea shells from the south. Tortoise shells from as far away as the Malay peninsula were used for royal divination. During the subsequent Zhou period (1050–256 BCE) a system of passable roads was constructed, and the two-humped camel came into general use for transporting goods. The Chinese were known to engage in frontier trade to the north and west, and the Chinese historian, Sima Qian, who lived in the late second to early first centuries BCE, provides a list of commonly traded items, including alcoholic drinks, prepared foodstuffs, silks, hemp, cloth, dyes, hides, furs, lacquerware, copper and iron goods. Silk, the most important Chinese export, was produced from a very early time, and some of it ended up far beyond China's borders. When silk was exported in significant quantities on a large scale is uncertain, although some current thinking puts this as late as the second century BCE. In return, the Chinese imported animal products such as wool, hides, and livestock, including horses, donkeys, camels, cattle, and sheep. Metals, in particular gold, silver, and tin, also came in, as did gemstones and wood.

The most important early import was jade, the common name for two different minerals, jadeite and nephrite, of which only nephrite played a role in early Chinese trade. Nephrite jade washed down from the Kunlun Mountains in Tibet into the Tarim Basin in modern Xinjiang, which at this time was not a part of China. Ranging in color from spinach green to fat white, it is very hard, takes a high polish, and requires considerable effort to grind to shape. The pass through the Gansu Corridor that separated China from the west terminated at a barrier known as the Jade Gate, and early trade routes beyond this are often referred to collectively as the Jade Road. Jade appears in the archaeological record in China as early as *c.* 4000 BCE. It was associated with immortality and often buried with the dead: the tomb of a Shang queen from *c.* 1200 BCE contained over 700 jade pieces, many of which had been made centuries earlier. It was also thought to prolong life and was sometimes ingested. Jade was mostly employed for ritual purposes, but the rich and powerful also owned functional objects made from it such as vases and cups.

Byways such as the Jade Road that brought goods into East Asia from the outside world were mostly in the form of relay and circuit trade trails. One originated in the Ganges Valley and came across Himalayan passes and over the Tibetan Plateau to the Gansu Corridor. What has been called the Fur Road linked Siberia to China and India, bringing not only fur but gold. On the other side of China, the *Periplus* reports on the trade in Himalayan malabathrum that took place in the remote borderlands between Assam (in northeastern India) and Sichuan (in southwestern China) involving a people called the Sesatai. At a given time whole families carrying great packs of leaves went to an appointed spot on the border and held a festival for several days. When they departed they left their packs, which were then retrieved by the people of Thina. What the Sesatai received in return is not mentioned.

The longest and most circuitous of these ancient routes originated in Sichuan and ran south into Yunnan, then through the great gorges of Burma to Assam, then due west into Bengal and up the Ganges Valley into Afghanistan. In some places on this route, goods had to be carried over paths carved into the sides of mountains. The Chinese government had no inkling of this trade until an emissary sent to Central Asia in the second century BCE made a startling discovery: "'When I was in Daxia [Bactria, today northern Afghanistan], I noticed the bamboo staves of Qiong and the cloth of Shu [Sichuan]; when I asked how these had been acquired, the men of Daxia said: "Our merchants go and buy them in the state of Shengdu [northern India]." That state lies some thousands of li [one-third of a mile] southeast of Daxia.'" Of course, Sichuan lay thousands of li beyond Shengdu. When the Chinese emperor learned of this, he dispatched several missions to find this route. All were either attacked and their members killed or became lost before turning around and heading home. The people who controlled this trade wanted no competition, especially from a rival with the resources of the Chinese government. The route faded back into obscurity, where presumably it continued to exist as long as all the parties along the way were able to earn an acceptable profit for their efforts.

Commercial economy in China was given a great boost during the Late Zhou, a time known as the Period of the Warring States (403–221 BCE), when the authority of the central government collapsed and regional states struggled to determine which one would reunify the country. Intense competition among the states stimulated growth, a process aided by the coming of iron technology and the introduction of coinage. Great opportunities became available for large-scale merchants as recounted by Sima Qian: "Lu Buwei was an important merchant from Yangdi. As he traveled about, he bought cheap and sold dear, and his household amassed a fortune." Through his wealth and power Lu Buwei rose to become chief minister of the state of Qin, which eventually emerged as the victor among the warring states. Part of the reason for Qin's success was that it was the westernmost of the states and controlled much of the trade with Central Asia. Once China was reunified, the first emperor, Qin Shihuangdi, introduced a series of centralizing measures, some of which aided commerce, including the improvement of roads and canals; the standardization of weights, measures, and axle widths of wheeled vehicles; and the consolidation of commercial laws.

The Qin dynasty was short-lived (221–206 BCE), being replaced by the much longer lasting Han dynasty (202 BCE–220 CE), whose official ideology became Confucianism. In the *Analects*, Confucius is reported to have said: "The mind of the superior man dwells on righteousness; the mind of a little man dwells on profit." Those who were in a position to set the social canon in China, the aristocracy, saw it convenient to devalue the role of trade and commerce and assign its practitioners to the lowest rung on a four-tier status scale below that of government officials, peasants, and craftsmen. Confucianism is above all a moral doctrine and, from a moral perspective, a merchant's business was seen as being based on greed and selfishness. Long-distance trade was believed unnecessary since the empire was large and varied enough to provide everything that could be needed to carry on a respectable economy. Furthermore, there was nothing positive to be gained from contact with foreigners.

In practice, the government was more ambivalent toward trade and merchants than the prevailing ideology, although such widely held attitudes in high places made it easy to justify heavy commercial taxes or to assume control over trade whenever it appeared advantageous. In theory, the government was supposed to ensure that goods were distributed fairly, and many believed that if a profit was to be made it should go into the public treasury rather than the greedy hands of private merchants. This led the late second century BCE emperor Han Wudi, whose military adventures and expensive foreign policy were "too high for calculation," according to Sima Qian's successor, Ban Gu, to establish monopolies over the production and sale of salt, iron, and alcoholic beverages, industries that had brought vast fortunes to a few well-placed dealers. Subsequently, large-scale grain traffic was also taken over to eliminate speculation in times of need. Monopolies did, however, bring stability to the economy by regulating the prices of basic commodities, and by the waning years of the first millennium BCE, the Chinese economy was highly commercialized. As an occupational group, merchants ranged from the wealthiest of big-time entrepreneurs, who possessed not only vast riches but often political influence despite their social standing, to the most wretched of village peddlers. In a queer twist, the Chinese merchant, so distrusted in his own society, developed a reputation on the international scene for his scrupulous honesty.

The idea that trade with the outside world could be taken or left, that it didn't really matter, did not match reality. The Chinese had a surplus of some goods like silk and lacquerware, and the elite classes had been absorbing imported luxury goods since the first jade arrived. Under the Han, the official attitude toward long-distance trade was more positive than under some other dynasties, not in the least because the state was one of the great beneficiaries reaping substantial income from the various tariffs, taxes, and fees it levied. Sima Qian saw merchants as providers of things people wanted. If they became rich in the process, so much the better; acquisitiveness, so he thought, was natural to humans. In one of his biographical sketches, he details the activities of a chieftain from a friendly nomadic tribe living on the western border of China. This trader–chief swapped horses for silk, which he exchanged with other chieftains for more horses, which he then traded back to the Chinese. Soon his profits were ten times the value of his investment, and he counted his herds by the valleyful.

The Chinese traded with the peoples to their north, south, and east, but their most storied foreign trade was with the west, initially with neighbors like Sima Qian's horse trader and through them with the settled peoples of the oasis cities of Central Asia and beyond to India, Persia, and the Mediterranean. The key to this trade was the nomadic pastoralists who lived on the steppe, that enormous swath of grassland bordered by the taiga forests to the north and high mountains and fierce deserts to the south, which stretched from Hungary in the west to Mongolia in the east. Except in favored locations, most of this land was unsuited to agriculture, being too cold or too dry for crops, but it was a great place to raise animals, particularly horses. The pastoral lifestyle provided a natural training ground for warfare. The skills of horsemanship developed in hunting and the martial adeptness acquired from frequent raiding common among tribesmen, when combined with use of the powerful double curved bow, gave nomadic pastoralists a potency that made them an almost irresistible force in the ancient world. The best way for aspiring leaders to secure loyalty was by redistributing valuable goods, hence the role of trade, tribute, and plunder in steppe politics.

The relationship between nomadic pastoralists and settled communities existed on a continuum with peaceful trade between equal partners representing one extreme and chronic plunder the other. When settled and nomadic peoples lived in proximity, they tended to develop stable relations based on strategies of accommodation. This might include outright tribute payment, tribute disguised as trade, trade disguised as tribute, implied and overt threats and protection guarantees, diplomatic manipulation and negotiated agreements, wall building, limited or sporadic warfare, and temporary alliances usually directed against another nomadic group. Pastoral economies were hardly self-sufficient. They needed a range of items, which made them natural trading partners with settled peoples, and they produced their own surpluses, which they could use in payment. On the most basic level nomads required grain as an essential element in their diet. They also desired products manufactured by the specialist craftsmen and artisans of the cities, ranging from metal goods to medicines. Sometimes the nomads provided the very raw materials that would be returned in the form of manufactured goods in a type of circular trade as, for example, in the case of raw wool to be returned as clothing, carpets, and tapestries. Trade was actually a better way of obtaining luxury goods than raiding and warfare because it was more predictable. Crucial to ongoing trade was the existence of border markets. If these were disrupted, or if settled communities refused to trade, the likely result would be to raid.

The most important items of direct trade between China and the neighboring nomads were silk and horses. Nomadic chiefs used much of the silk they got from the Chinese to attract followers into armies that occasionally became large enough to threaten China. Equally ironic, the most important use for the horses the Chinese obtained from the nomads was in fighting against nomads (not necessarily the same ones the Chinese were trading with, although this did happen). In wars among settled peoples, infantry usually carried the day but woe unto such an army that did not have an adequate cavalry but had to face nomads. In China there was little room for growing grass since farmers had turned most available space into cropland, and whatever horses the Chinese did raise could not begin to satisfy their needs.

While nomads were important as producers and consumers, their most crucial role was as intermediaries between settled peoples in interregional and transcontinental trade. Goods from China that ended up in India, Persia, or Europe often had been passed from group to group in informal relay networks as nomads made their seasonal rounds. Nomads also taxed the professional merchants who traveled across their lands in return for providing services like protection and sometimes guides and transport animals. The liveliest trade often took place at ecotones, transition areas between adjacent ecological regions as, for example, between desert and steppe, steppe and river valley, or steppe and forest. East-to-west nomad networks not only linked the settled societies, they also plugged into north-to-south routes, bringing furs, walrus ivory, gold, and other metals from the Arctic, taiga forest, and Siberian mountains.

Among the earliest horse-breeding steppe nomads that appear in the literature of settled peoples were the Scythians. The Greeks inhabiting the cities on the northern rim of the Black Sea traded directly with the Scythians, exchanging clothing, wine, "and the other things that belong to civilized life," according to Strabo, for slaves, hides, "and such other things as nomads possess." The Black Sea was the entryway into the Russian river system, and Greek goods including, Athenian black figure ware and Ionian wine jars, decorative pieces, mirrors, and weapons have been found in burial tombs far into the interior. This represented a trade in very high-end goods that included sable fur and gold.

The Scythian trade routes ran from the Don to the Volga River, then to the Urals and further on to the Altai ("Golden") Mountains, where most Siberian gold originated. Herodotus indicates that at least some of this was carried on by professional long-distance merchants. In sharing with his readers where he got his information about a people called the Argippaei, he notes that "Scythians sometimes reach these parts, as do Greeks from the trading-center Borysthenes and from other trading-centers on the Euxini [Black] Sea, and it is not hard to get information from them. The Scythians who travel to these tribes conduct their business in seven languages, each requiring its own translator." The Argippaei may have lived in the Ural foothills. Beyond this, Herodotus refers to a poem by a certain Aristeas, who claimed to have traveled to an even more distant people, the Issedones. They told Aristeas that farther on "lives a one-eyed race called the Arimaspians, beyond them is the land of the gold-guarding griffins, and beyond them the

Hyperboreans, all the way to the sea." The Issedones appear to have been intentionally disseminating false information at least with regard to the one-eyed people and the griffins. Herodotus notes only: "I cannot get information from anyone who claims to have firsthand knowledge." Ptolemy follows up on the Issedones by giving them a town, Issedon Scythia, just west of Serica, which means in the general region of Xinjiang. This appears to make Aristeas' Hyperboreans the Chinese.

If the Chinese did not trade directly with Herodotus' Scythians, they did trade with the people of Xinjiang, both nomadic pastoralists and oasis dwellers, who like the Scythians were Indo-European speakers. Other horse-breeding nomadic pastoralists initially lived more to the north of the Chinese, people who were Turkic-Mongolian speakers. They are more difficult to pinpoint in Herodotus' list of peoples, but their importance to both their neighbors on the steppe and to the Chinese would steadily grow from the first millennium BCE on.

In his poem, Aristeas notes that "all these people from the Arimaspians on, except the Hyperboreans, are constantly attacking their neighbors." The consequence of this was usually to dislodge or, less commonly, to absorb or annihilate one's neighbors. The earliest of the nomadic peoples to attempt to create a larger and more stable entity, the first true empire builders on the steppe, were the Xiongnu ("Fierce Slaves," a name given to them by the Chinese), whose homeland is thought to have been Mongolia. The Chinese described them in less than flattering terms: "The Xiongnu live in the desert and grow in the land that produces no food. They are the people who are abandoned by heaven for being good-for-nothing. ... They wear animal skins, eat meat raw, and drink blood. They wander to meet in order to exchange goods."

In the second century BCE the Xiongnu attacked their neighbors, the Yuezhi ("Meat Eaters," another Chinese appellation), an Indo-European group who had lived for some time in the Gansu Corridor and Xinjiang. They had been trading partners with the Chinese across the Jade Road and had provided the Chinese with a buffer against nomadic attacks from the northwest. According to Ban Gu, the Yuezhi had "more than 100,000 trained bowmen and for this reason they relied on their strength and thought lightly of the Xiongnu." This was a mistake; the Yuezhi proved no match for the Xiongnu as Sima Qian reports: "The Xiongnu overcame the king of the Yuezhi and made a drinking vessel out of his skull. The Yuezhi decamped and were hiding somewhere, constantly scheming how to revenge themselves on the Xiongnu."

Following their defeat, the Yuezhi moved first to the Ili River valley far to the northwest (in Kazakhstan), where they were attacked by another tribe, the Wusun, and chased to Lake Issyk Kul (in Kyrgyzstan). From there the Yuezhi moved farther west to the Oxus River valley (Amu Darya in Uzbekistan), then south across the Hindu Kush (through Afghanistan) and finally down the Indus River Valley. In the later stages of this great volkerwanderung, the Yuezhi metamorphosed into a new people and founded their own great empire, the Kushan. Barbaricum became their port on the Indian Ocean and the Roman Empire their new trading partner. On their way across Central Asia, the Yuezhi dislodged another large nomadic group known to Indian sources as the Shakas, actually the local branch of the Scythians, who began their own migration, during which they founded several states, including one in India whose major port was Barygaza.

Dislodging the Yuezhi put the Xiongnu on the doorstep of China. To deal with them, the Chinese developed three different strategies that would prove to be the source of endless debate within their ruling echelons for the next two millennia. The first was exclusion through the building of border fortifications or walls to keep the horsemen out. The earliest wall made of pounded earth had appeared in the seventh century BCE, and during the period of the Warring States others followed. The second strategy was to take the offensive or at least to be proactive in defense. In $c.$ 300 BCE the king of Zhao transformed his army from a traditional infantry into a cavalry complete with nomadic dress, weaponry, and tactics, and other states soon did the same. The third strategy was to attempt peaceful coexistence by promoting trade, employing diplomacy, and, when necessary, acceding to protection payments.

Qin Shihuangdi, the unifier of China, was not a man to prefer peaceful coexistence, and in 215 BCE he sent an army north to clear the Xiongnu out of the border regions. For good measure, Sima Qian reports that he built the first Great Wall by connecting and consolidating the existing walls into a single line and extending it into Gansu. However, when he died and his dynasty collapsed, the Xiongnu reoccupied their old lands and attacked China. The Han dynasty, having come to power under Gaozong, counterattacked in 201 BCE, but was so badly defeated the emperor himself was almost captured. As for the walls, they proved to be less than effective militarily and, by interrupting normal frontier trade, a source of friction. Some trade did continue, funneled to gates where markets occasionally formed, but the existence of the walls exacerbated frustration among those nomads who were interested in peaceful trade, thus provoking further hostilities.

Gaozong's disastrous defeat was followed by a treaty in 198 BCE under which the Chinese agreed to make annual payments in silk, grain, and alcoholic beverages to the Xiongnu. An era of friendly relations was officially proclaimed during which a series of border markets was opened where nomads, farmers, and merchants exchanged goods. The Chinese government did prohibit the sale of iron weapons to the nomads, which some merchants chose to ignore to their profit and risk, and in one instance five hundred of them who violated this ban were publicly executed. But other goods flowed into the steppe over the following decades as never before. Silk came in the form of bolts that the Xiongnu shanyu (paramount chief) redistributed to his supporters. They, in turn, used it as a form of currency to trade for other goods, and eventually some of it passed through Central Asia to the lands farther west and south. In this way, it served as an advertisement that stimulated further demand. As the last link in the Silk Road was being forged, a new emperor came to the throne who was determined to see China and not the nomads as its master.

Chapter 12

The last link

Chinese policy was abruptly reversed during the reign of the emperor Han Wudi (141–87 BCE). He had an interest in foreign lands and their products and no aversion to war, especially when it came to the despised Xiongnu. He intended "to cut off the right arm of the Xiongnu" by separating them from their lucrative trade routes to the west and by seeking allies among other nomads who harbored grudges against them. With this in mind, Wudi sent an emissary named Zhang Qian westward to find the Yuezhi, establish an alliance and trade relations, and gather whatever intelligence he could on the countries he might pass through along the way. Described as "a man of strong physique and of considerable generosity; he inspired the trust of others and the barbarians loved him," Zhang Qian was accompanied by an escort of over 100 men that included a Xiongnu slave named Ganfu, who had been captured by the Chinese but released to serve as guide and interpreter on this most impossible of missions.

Neither Zhang Qian nor Ganfu had any idea where they were going. Shortly after passing into the Gansu Corridor, the entire mission was captured and brought to the shanyu in western Mongolia. Zhang Qian told the shanyu part of the truth, that he had been sent on a mission to the Yuezhi: "The Shanyu said: 'The Yuezhi lie to the north of us; how may Han send its envoys there? If I wished to send envoys to Yueh [an independent state encompassing part of southeastern China and northern Vietnam], would Han be willing to let me?'" Zhang Qian and his men were enslaved, and he spent the next ten years tending cattle and sheep, during which he married another slave. One day he was part of a group who escaped. They headed west since their pursuers were coming from the east, skirting deserts and crossing mountains that took them first to the Ili Valley, then past the Issyk Kul into the land of Ferghana. They were trying to catch up to the Yuezhi, who were also on the move, attempting to put as much distance as they could between themselves and the Xiongnu. With help along the way from the Wusun, who, according to Ban Gu, "had heard of Han's abundant wealth and had wished to establish contact but had not been able to do so," Zhang Qian finally caught up to the Yuezhi in Bactria. Unfortunately, as Sima Qian put it, the Yuezhi had "decided to enjoy this life of peace. Moreover, since they considered themselves too far away from China, they no longer wanted to revenge themselves on the Xiongnu." For a year Zhang Qian waited unsuccessfully for the Yuezhi to change their mind before beginning his return trip home. Since he had previously experienced so much trouble coming across the northern route, he returned by the south through the Kunlun Mountains. Nevertheless, he was captured, enslaved, and escaped again, this time after only a year. Thirteen years after he set out, Zhang Qian, his wife, and Ganfu straggled back into China.

The emperor was most pleased. Zhang Qian was rewarded, promoted, and sent back on two subsequent missions, the more important of which in 115 BCE was to the Wusun in the Ili Valley, who some modern scholars surmise to be Herodotus' Issedones. Wudi hoped to replace the Yuezhi with the Wusun as allies, so Zhang Qian was provided with gold, silk, and other valuables that, according to Sima Qian, were "worth millions," and was accompanied by a large number of deputy envoys that were to be sent on to neighboring states. The gifts were really exchange items for which the Chinese expected to receive adequate compensation. Zhang Qian had no trouble reaching the Wusun, but he found them no more anxious to be drawn into a war with the Xiongnu than had the Yuezhi. However, he was given fine horses to take back as a present. About a year after his return, his deputy envoys began arriving, sometimes accompanied by embassies from the various places they had visited.

From the accounts of Zhang Qian and his deputy envoys, the emperor learned much about the products and economies of the countries to the west. Other missions were sent with additional gifts, and new gifts arrived: "The Son of Heaven heard that [places] such as Ferghana as well as Bactria and Persia were all large states with many rare goods; that the people were attached to the land [i.e., they were not nomads]; and that their way of life was rather similar to that of China; however, their forces were weak, and they prized Han wealth and goods." Beyond such lands were even more exotic places like Shengdu, Tiaozhi (Mesopotamia), and Lijian (the Roman Empire). Most of these places were already using Chinese products in varying amounts, particularly silk, and even trading it among themselves.

Han Wudi was not a man of moderation, and soon missions were being dispatched en masse. Unfortunately, the economies of the various peoples now being visited by Chinese envoys were not prepared to absorb the flood of Chinese goods that quickly inundated them, nor were China's new partners prepared to meet demands for the specific items the Chinese wanted. Eventually the peoples of Central Asia would come to realize the tremendous potential their position gave them as middlemen in passing Chinese products to the west and south. But for the moment, they were saturated. The emperor would have to learn the limits of royal gift exchange.

Of all the products of Central Asia, Wudi desired horses the most. The horses the Chinese usually obtained from the nomads on their northern border were of the small, shaggy, pony-like variety, and Wudi's ongoing war with the Xiongnu had severely depleted their stock. Zhang Qian had reported seeing special breeds of horses – large, muscular, swift, sleek, beautiful, and superior in every way – in the Ili Valley and Ferghana. The surplus from these herds was normally sent south into India, but the local people kept the best for themselves. On request, the chief of the Wusun twice sent gifts of 1,000 horses from the Ili Valley, but Chinese envoys to Ferghana learned that the people there had a small number of horses that were so special they were kept hidden whenever Chinese envoys came around. Wudi, who was becoming increasingly obsessed with obtaining horses, was familiar with a passage from a divination text predicting that "supernatural horses" would come from the northwest. The horses of Ferghana, so Zhang Qian had been told, "were descended from the Heavenly Horses," and they sweated blood as a manifestation of their special nature. Apparently these horses exuded a reddish lather that has never been explained to everyone's satisfaction, one suggestion being that this resulted from a particular parasite that afflicted them. The Chinese believed that heavenly horses emerged from a mystical river that was also the home of a dragon, and like dragons these horses had magical powers, including the ability to fly. On his death, the emperor would be carried into heaven by such horses.

In 107–106 BCE, Wudi sent a mission to Ferghana carrying 1,000 pieces of gold and the statue of a horse (size unknown) made of pure gold in exchange for some of the heavenly horses. However, the request was denied, the Ferghanans reasoning: "China is far off and the road is long; travelers lack both fodder and water. ... How could an army reach us? China can do nothing to harm us. The inestimable horses ... shall remain the horses of Ferghana." The envoys, realizing that they would be in very hot water if they returned empty handed, "spoke in anger and without restraint, and went away after smashing the golden horse." This was taken as a deep insult by the Ferghanans, who had the envoys murdered in retaliation soon after they departed.

When word of this debacle reached Wudi he was furious, and his appetite for the horses now became whetted to a ravenous pitch. In 104 BCE he dispatched an army on a 2,500 mile journey that included crossing the Taklamakan, one of the most formidable deserts in the world, and going over the Pamirs, one of the highest mountain ranges in the world. The army, described by Ban Gu as consisting of "some tens of thousands of ill-disciplined young men," tried to live off the land it traveled through, provoking hostility along the way. After two disastrous years, an estimated 10–20 percent of the original force straggled back to the Jade Gate, having never reached the capital of Ferghana. Wudi was so angry he ordered the gate closed, locking the survivors out.

In 103 BCE a second expedition, this time consisting of 100,000 men (or 60,000; the sources are at variance) accompanied by bountiful supplies returned. It reached Ferghana and besieged its capital for over 40 days. The nobles inside decided to blame the whole matter on the king and murdered him, sending his head to the Chinese general with a proposal: "'If the Han will not attack us, we will bring out all the fine horses. Han may choose what it likes, and we will supply the Han army with provisions. If Han does not listen to us, we will kill all the fine horses.'" The Chinese agreed, and the war ended. The Chinese were given 30 heavenly horses and 3,000 of lesser stock, of which about 1,000 survived the trip back to China. Subsequently the new king of Ferghana agreed to send two heavenly horses a year to the emperor. Wudi was so inspired when the horses arrived he wrote a hymn of celebration entitled "The Heavenly Horses Are Coming," which concludes:

> The Heavenly Horses have come
> And the Dragon will follow in their wake.
> I shall reach the Gates of Heaven
> I shall see the Palace of God.

The chastising of Ferghana was not Wudi's only military success. Beginning in 133 BCE he sent a number of expeditions against the Xiongnu in which his armies, numbering in the hundreds of thousands and led by a cavalry steeped in Xiongnu tactics, captured herds of horses and flocks of sheep and cut traditional trade connections, disrupting the Xiongnu economy. Following a battle in 121 BCE in which the Chinese reportedly killed "men by the ten thousand," the Xiongnu were expelled from the Gansu Corridor, and the Jade Gate was opened. Continuing Chinese success on the battlefield led to internal dissension within the Xiongnu, which split in two in the middle of the first century BCE. The Eastern (or Southern) Confederation submitted to the emperor and became allies of the Chinese while the Western (or Northern) Confederation continued the struggle. Modern historians long believed the Western Xiongnu eventually moved farther west, becoming the Huns of Roman history, a theory that has recently been challenged.

With the Xiongnu humbled, the Chinese could extend their power across the Tarim Basin, lying between the Gansu Corridor and Ferghana. In the heart of the Tarim Basin was the Taklamakan Desert, where oasis city states had long paid tribute to the Xiongnu. These cities owed their existence to trade and generally bent with the wind in political matters, which was now blowing from China. In the years that followed, a system of protectorates and alliances was established and military commanderies and agricultural colonies set up. For a while Chinese power dominated Central Asia as far as modern Uzbekistan. An official mission was dispatched to Persia, where it was greeted at the border by the king at the head of 20,000 cavalry. Into China "wonderful goods of diverse climes were brought from the four quarters of the world." For the Chinese, long-distance trade was seen as more than just a way of obtaining exotic goods: it was an extension of imperial foreign policy. One high-ranking official put it this way:

> A piece of Chinese plain silk can be exchanged with the Xiongnu for articles worth several pieces of gold and thereby reduce the resources of our enemy. Mules, donkeys, and camels enter the frontier in unbroken lines; horses, dapples and bays and prancing mounts, come into our possession. The furs of sables, marmots, foxes and badgers, colored rugs and decorated carpets fill the imperial treasury, while jade and auspicious stones, corals and crystals become national treasures.

The long and involved story of Zhang Qian, Wudi's obsession with the Heavenly Horses, the expedition to Ferghana, and the Han war with the Xiongnu are important to the history of long-distance trade because the Chinese credit these events as directly leading to the opening of the Silk Road and thus the establishment of commercial relations with the rest of Eurasia. As Ban Gu puts it: "For the first time the states of the north [more the west] then came into communication with Han. It was Zhang Qian who had pioneered the way." Critics of this view find it oversimplified, misleading, and terribly Sinocentric. The events of Wudi's reign may have symbolic value in Chinese historiography, they concede, but the creation of the Silk Road was a long, laborious historical process, not a single event attributable to one or several individuals who did something at a specific time. The actions of Zhang Qian and Wudi at most represent China's entrance into an already established system that had been operational for millennia. Even this, however, may be problematic because the Chinese can be seen as having been a part of this system since at least the beginning of the Jade Road. And the Jade Road itself was one part of a much larger system that has been called the Proto-Silk Road, a chain of relays or circuit links.

Some speculation puts the origin of the Proto-Silk Road in routes going back to the Neolithic period, but the date of 2000 BCE is often used as a convenience for designating a chronological point at which elements of these ancient interconnections were functioning as an identifiable system. On its western side lapis lazuli from Afghanistan had been reaching Mesopotamia for some time, and copper seals of a particular style from Central Asia have been found from Shahr-i-Sokhta in Iran to the Ordos region that separates China and Mongolia. What has been proposed as the "Middle Asian Interaction Sphere" tied Mesopotamia, the Indus River Valley, and Central Asia through a network of overland connections funneling commerce in luxury goods between *c.* 2600 and 2000 BCE. On the eastern side, Chinese silk has been found in an excavation in Bactria from *c.* 1500 BCE and vases dating from *c.* 1200 BCE tie Shanxi in northern China with the land of Sogdiana (in Uzbekistan) that lay west of Ferghana. The earliest known embroidered silk dated at *c.* 1100 BCE has been discovered not in China proper but in a tomb from Xinjiang.

The discovery of silk in isolated second-millennium BCE finds from outside China, however, can hardly be considered as an indication of consistent trade patterns. Neither the Jade Road nor the Proto-Silk Road were the Silk Road, especially if silk did not achieve its great prominence on the international scene until the second and first centuries BCE as is now proposed. And, incidentally, the Romans did not coin the term "Silk Road," contrary to some textbooks; that was the brainchild of a German explorer, Baron Ferdinand von Richthofen, in 1877. The Silk Road begins with sericulture, the production of silk by raising silkworms. Indications are that the Chinese were practicing sericulture as early as the fifth millennium BCE with the oldest piece of surviving cloth dated at 3630 BCE. The Chinese would keep the secrets of silk making as well as the domestic silkworms to themselves until the sixth century CE.

Silk is made by unwinding the filament from the cocoon of the silkworm caterpillar (*Bombyx mori*), which comes as one very long unbroken thread, usually between 500 and 1,200 yards, but sometimes up to 2,000 yards. Between five and ten filaments are then twisted together to form a single thread of silk that is woven into cloth. The unusual length of the filament accounts for the exceptional strength of silk. It is also smooth, supple, lustrous, and shiny. It holds dye better, is softer and more comfortable to wear, and is more beautiful than any other natural fiber. Under the Qin and Han, government workshops produced silk as did thousands of private producers from whom the government collected taxes in silk. It also paid its officials and sometimes its soldiers in bolts of silk.

Silk clothing, albeit at a low level of quality, was common in China, hemp being the only other principal material used for clothing. Silk exchanged for jade with the Yuezhi was sometimes passed westward again over the Proto-Silk Road or along the Scythian steppe route described in Herodotus. How far west Chinese silk came is evidenced by threads found in a Hallstatt princely grave dated from the sixth to fifth centuries BCE in southern Germany. Later, when the Xiongnu were extorting silk from the Chinese government, it reached the Mediterranean in ever larger quantities.

It is at this point that Zhang Qian and the emperor Wudi entered the scene. Zhang Qian's protracted, high-profile adventures across Central Asia followed by Wudi's armies gave notice that the Chinese had arrived and were open for business. As Sima Qian notes: "After the Han had sent its envoy to open up communications with the state of Daxia all the barbarians of the distant West craned their necks to the East and longed to catch a glimpse of China." The domination of routes through Central Asia passed from nomadic pastoralists to the settled empires: the Chinese in the east, the Kushans in the south, and the Persians in the west. To the peoples of Central Asia, the door to a treasure house of opportunity went from being ajar to sprung wide open. Silk became the first Chinese commodity to reach the Far West on a large scale.

The Chinese and the Romans became aware of the existence of each other at about the same time. In the *History of the Later Han*, Rome was described as well governed under an elected monarchy, a wealthy place with honest merchants, some of whom made profits of 1,000 percent from Indian Ocean trade. They were said to have dealt in gold, silver, coral, amber, jasper, lapis lazuli, cloth, and perfumes, all of which were actual products that reached China from the far side of the Silk Road. The Chinese also claimed to have obtained some very strange products from there: a "ring that shines at night," "moon-bright pearls," the "rhinoceros that frightens chickens" (?), and an "ointment which makes gold."

Roman sources mention almost nothing about Chinese merchants and not much about what the Romans used to pay for Chinese products. But they were interested in silk, which became quite popular in the Roman Empire. Pliny maintains that the Seres got their silk from trees. Following him, with one exception – a second century writer named Pausanias, who claimed that silk was produced by an insect resembling a huge spider – the Romans continued to believe for over five centuries that silk came from a plant rather than an animal. Nor did they have any idea as to how the silk came to them. The import of silk was not universally welcomed and not just because of its impact on the balance of payments problem as in the case of pepper. The dour republican rhetorician Seneca the Elder (54 BCE–39 CE) considered the wearing of sheer, bordering on the transparent, garments indicative of the moral decline his country was slipping into: "Wretched flocks of maids labor [in making silk clothes] so that the adulteress may be visible through her thin dress, so that her husband has no more acquaintance than any outsider or foreigner with his wife's body."

Apparently Seneca the Elder did not appreciate the larger picture. Roman women wearing Chinese silks represented the last link in a world system that had been in the works for millennia. In this the addition of China was crucial. It didn't just connect a new region; it opened a new world that offered new products and new markets, a world that had its own fully developed complex of circuits and routes, emporiums, transit points and termini, cores and peripheries. The cultural and technological impact in both directions will remain an endless source of speculation and debate among historians, but the economic consequence is much more straightforward. With China connected to Central Asia, interlocking routes now ran from one side of the Eurasian landmass to the other. By the early years of the first millennium CE, the sustained, systematic, large-scale movement of goods across a fully integrated land system and a parallel sea system had become a reality.

Epilogue

The premodern Afro–Eurasian world system was the product of developments that are best understood by relating them to the basic questions mentioned in the Preface. First, who and why: exchange began as reciprocal gift-giving under the control of institutional authorities but over time gave way to the entrepreneurial, profit-driven activity of private individuals. Second, what and why: the earliest exchange goods were of the luxury variety and had some social value attached. This was followed by the earliest mass-produced goods, which were metals, and the earliest large-scale consumer goods, which were textiles. Third, how and what: trade was conducted by land and water evolving from unsystematic trickle trade in the prehistoric period to directional trade and finally to grids of exchange that coalesced into a single whole by the first millennium CE. As the transactions became more complex, simple barter came to be replaced by the use of mediums of exchange, that is, money. And finally, so what: the impact of long-distance trade was not just economic; it was a major component in the formation and development of political and social systems.

For almost a millennium and a half, the Afro–Eurasian trade zone, the "world system," maintained its basic structure and systemic integration. It experienced periods of vigor and regression, but the accompanying changes did not transform its essential character. The ebbs and flows of the overland system were determined mostly by considerations relating to security and stability. On the sea lanes much depended on security but also on improvements in ship construction and navigation techniques. As a result, there was less change on land than at sea. Underlying shifts in trade were basic considerations involving agricultural productivity, demographic pressures, and ultimately climatic change. The disruption of trade usually did not impact equally on all parts of the system. Trade continued so long as the demand for certain goods held the promise of profits and the basic commercial infrastructure remained intact.

The period of expansion that finally linked Eurasia together was followed by a period of crisis. Between the third and fifth centuries CE, empires across the civilized underbelly disintegrated, and people from the nomadic fringes poured in. China lost control over Central Asia; indeed, China itself lacked a central government between 220 and 581. On the opposite side of the land mass, the basic structure of Western European society was so disrupted that the region remained a backwater for trade and commerce for many centuries, skipping the next up cycle completely. India was also out of sync but in a different way, enjoying an upsurge under the Gupta Empire (320–550) in a period of general downturn, then experiencing a downturn in overland traffic to the north when other regions were experiencing a recovery. Southwest Asia and China were in sync, enjoying a great period of commercial prosperity from the seventh to ninth centuries under the early Abbasid dynasty (749–1258) in Baghdad and the Tang dynasty (618–907) in China. The revival of long-distance Chinese trade is especially impressive since the knowledge of sericulture, along with the silkworms themselves, was smuggled out of China in the sixth century and silk industries established in the Byzantine Empire and Persia. Nevertheless, Chinese silk continued to be a major export joined by hand-glaze ceramics in the form of porcelain and stoneware.

The most important addition to the Afro–Eurasian world system in the late first millennium CE was the complex of routes known collectively as the Trans-Saharan, which made it possible for the commodities grown, mined, and manufactured on one side of the largest desert in the world to get to the other side. In doing so, it tapped into the commerce of a whole new part of the world, Sub-Sahara Africa. Products had reached West and Central Africa from North Africa and vice versa since the prehistoric period through trickle trade and relay networks between oases and nomadic tribes. This willy-nilly process would become a viable commercial enterprise only with the coming of the camel (dromedary), which, for reasons that are not readily apparent, took an inordinately long time to become fully integrated into Saharan commerce given its usefulness much earlier on the Incense Road in not-too-distant western Arabia.

The Trans-Saharan system was built by Berber merchants beginning in the eighth century. It was not a single highway but rather three major routes running southward from commercial centers in North Africa, one starting in western Morocco and running parallel to the coast, a second crossing the heart of the desert in modern Algeria, and a third connecting Tripoli with Lake Chad. They were not just unpaved and unmarked but sometimes not even beaten into paths, and they changed over time according to conditions. At the southern edge of the desert, they connected into another system, the Trans-Sudanic, which ran across the grasslands and into the tropical forests of West and Central Africa and was operated by a class of African merchants known as the Wangara. The connecting points of these two systems were cities like Awdaghust and Tadmekka in the early centuries and later Timbuktu. Caravans, the largest of which were reportedly up to 10,000 camels, brought metal goods, textiles, and an enormous variety of other products from across North Africa, Europe, and Asia to be joined by salt from mines located in the northern Sahara. These were exchanged for the special products of West and Central Africa: skins, ivory, civet (a secretion from the wild civet cat used in perfumes), luxury slaves (women, eunuchs, and bodyguards), and later kola nuts, malaguette pepper, and ostrich feathers. But the product that drove Berber merchants southward and Wangara merchants northward was gold, which came from three different gold fields scattered around West Africa that were exploited in succession. By the fourteenth century, West Africa was the largest producer of gold in the world and would remain so until the discovery of the Americas.

In East Asia in the centuries following the fall of the Tang, the fortunes of the Silk Road continued to oscillate in response to the risings and fallings of various nomadic groups. The greatest of these, representing the culmination of empire building on the steppe, came under the Mongol Empire of the thirteenth and fourteenth centuries. The creation of this empire was a horribly destructive process, which included the obliteration of some trade cities and significant damage to the commercial infrastructure in certain places. However, the Mongols, who were not a mercantile people themselves, were not anti-trade or anti-merchant; quite the contrary. Nomads had always depended on traders and usually appreciated their role more than most settled folks. Under their empire merchants from many different lands supplied the Mongols in their newly conquered cities with luxuries and staples and in the process helped dispose of their war booty. For a while, the largest land empire in history became a vast trade zone although the major trans-Asian routes shifted to the open steppeland north of the old Silk Road.

The halcyon days of Mongol trade lasted only about a century before the empire split into rival khanates that were frequently in conflict with each other. Under such conditions Central Asia again became a barrier rather than a corridor for Chinese contact with the west. Towns along the Silk Road decayed, and some ceased to exist. In the fourteenth century the Black Death, an enormous demographic and economic catastrophe, traveled across the old land routes further dislocating an already reeling commercial system. Areas like Southwest Asia, parts of which had not recovered from the Mongol devastation, suffered increased impoverishment and economic stagnation. Mesopotamia, the first great core of long-distance trade and for four millennia a major player, faded into periphery status.

In the past when conditions on the land route took a turn for the worse, the parallel sea route usually picked up the slack. Although they both carried goods between one side of Eurasia and the other, the Silk Road and the Indian Ocean maritime system were never locked in head-to-head competition. Rather they tended to complement each other, and in good times both prospered without any appreciable damage to the other. In the first half of the second millennium, however, the dynamics of both systems changed, sending them down different paths. If the land route enjoyed one really good period under the Mongols, the maritime route boomed for the better part of five centuries. Innovations in Chinese shipbuilding and maritime technology allowed for the construction of larger, faster ships culminating in huge, ocean-going junks equipped with new devices like magnetic compasses and safety improvements like watertight compartments. The volume of traffic increased many fold, led by mass-consumption bulk goods, including rice and other foodstuffs, cotton textiles, and timber. The price of spices, at least for the peoples of the Indian Ocean, dropped to a level where pepper became a common staple. Chinese porcelain, a heavy but at the same time delicate item for camel and donkey transport, became a standard commodity aboard Indian Ocean ships. India prospered, and the trade up the Red Sea to the Mediterranean flourished. Small commercial states thrived on the ocean rim from East Africa to Southeast Asia in a system of competitive free trade.

The big engine for this boom was China, which during the Song, Yuan (Mongol), and early Ming dynasties (960–1433) experienced its greatest expansion in maritime trade for the entire premodern period. The Song and Yuan encouraged trade as a source of revenue, leaving it largely in private hands while carefully watching and regulating as well as heavily taxing it. The founder of the Ming dynasty, however, was so suspicious of private foreign trade that he forbade it. He and his immediate successors did favor a revival of the ancient tribute system, channeling all foreign trade through the government. In this vein the third Ming emperor inaugurated a series of seven grand expeditions between 1405 and 1433. Under admiral Zheng He, fleets of up to 60 ships carrying as many as 28,000 men were sent south and west, some reaching the coast of East Africa and the Persian Gulf. The largest of these so-called "treasure ships" was up to 400 feet long (Columbus' Santa Maria was 85 feet) and contained nine masts. The goal of the treasure fleets was to seek symbolic submission and official acknowledgment of China's suzerainty from the various maritime states of Southeast Asia and the Indian Ocean. In the process vast quantities of goods were exchanged, but the objective was not to make a profit, which, given the huge expenses involved, these missions most certainly did not. No trading posts, forts, or long-term exchange networks were established: the treasure ships came and went as phantoms in the night, leaving nothing tangible behind.

After 1433 the voyages stopped. Political infighting within the Chinese court ultimately led to the rise of a faction of Confucianists who were set against overseas trade in part because their defeated rivals, a faction of court eunuchs, were very much in favor of it since some of them had made vast fortunes in often very shady dealings. Among the Confucianists, anti-foreign and anti-commercial strains blended. They saw the treasure fleets as a wasteful expense of funds better spent on defending China's northern border, and they dismissed the idea that trade could be profitable and beneficial for both state and society. Shipyards were closed, and over time the knowledge of how to build such magnificent vessels faded. An edict of 1525 ordered all ocean-going ships to be destroyed, and another in 1551 made it a crime to go to sea in a ship equipped with multiple masts. Merchants on the high seas were assumed to be pirates and treated as such. When the Ming were replaced by the Qing (Manchus), maritime China remained closed, foreign trade being officially forbidden in 1655. Thus China disengaged from the maritime system at almost exactly the same time the Europeans, coming from the opposite end, were entering it.

For trade, the transition into the modern world was a two-step process beginning in the sixteenth and culminating in the eighteenth and nineteenth centuries. The relative importance of these steps remains the source of a howling debate with partisans insisting that one or the other was the real beginning of the world as we know it today. In fact, once again, modernization was a process rather than an event, one that was rather drawn out with something of a pause, in the form of the seventeenth century, in between. There can be no doubt the trajectory of world trade experienced a radical turn, beginning in 1492 when Columbus pioneered the extension of Old World trade networks to the New World. This was followed in 1497–99 by Vasco da Gama's forging of a direct maritime link between the Atlantic and Indian oceans and in 1519–22 when Ferdinand Magellan and Sebastian del Canto completed the global connection by circumnavigating the globe. A true worldwide system of exchange became possible.

Under the new conditions, the Atlantic coast of Eurasia, which during most of its history was no more than a periphery and sometimes the fringe of a periphery, quickly assumed the role of nexus, becoming the core of its own system embracing the Americas and Atlantic Africa. Patterns of long-distance trade became greatly altered, centers of capital accumulation shifted, and a new commercial order began to take shape. Changes in technology underlay much of the European upsurge. For some time Europeans had been experimenting, often using ideas borrowed from others, with innovations in maritime transportation. This process greatly accelerated, producing ever larger and better designed vessels, more effective instrumentation, and greater overall efficiency.

Changes produced their own changes. The invasion of the Americas led to the looting of the Americas, which resulted in a large injection of bullion, particularly silver, into exchange networks across the Old World. This eventually penetrated even into China, where it helped in the commercialization of the economy to the general dismay of the Confucianists. In Europe widespread monetization provided a foundation for the further development of capitalism. Europeans also used the windfall in an attempt to gain control over areas not in their system such as the Indian Ocean. However, here the pace of change slowed down. Old history books liked to portray Portuguese fleets sailing around the Indian Ocean having their way with the commerce there when, in fact, changes outside of the new European core zone often came slowly or remained incomplete for a long time. The Portuguese had an impact on Indian Ocean commerce but never achieved a monopoly, and while Europeans did come from time to time to control markets in certain commodities, they never came close to dominating Indian Ocean trade before the eighteenth century.

During the sixteenth and seventeenth centuries, the total trade of the Indian Ocean increased for everyone involved, Portuguese and Asians alike. India and China still led the world in manufacturing and in volume of exchange even though much of Chinese external trade was stifled or had to come from smuggling. This was a period of particular strength for Indian trade; the Indians dominated the textile business, for example, more completely than the Portuguese dominated any trade. When the Portuguese became too greedy and interfered too much with the trade of others, those people simply readjusted and redeployed, bypassing whatever problem the Portuguese were causing. As a result the old spice route up the Red Sea to Egypt did not collapse in the sixteenth century but rather prospered. The Portuguese, in fact, had ambitions beyond their capacities. Their successors, the Dutch and English, had considerably more capacity and proved to be more efficient and relentless. In the seventeenth century they came much closer to imposing monopolies over their own parts of the trade, and in the following century the great age of Indian shipping ended with a resounding thud. This heralded much larger changes for the world of the eighteenth century in manufacturing, where Europe challenged and then quickly surpassed Asia.

Indeed, the final passing of the premodern world concluded in the eighteenth century with the advent of industrialization. Whether the modern capitalist system, which sets everything that came before it apart from everything that came after it, can be traced to around the sixteenth century, as one school of scholars maintains, or can be seen as having been in the process of development since the fourth millennium BCE, as their opponents claim, no one can deny the transformative role of the industrial revolution. It represents the second step, the final maturation of the world system, by inaugurating a new kind of economy and concomitantly an essentially different kind of society. The mechanization of production and the harnessing of science and technology unleashed hitherto unimaginable forces for the production of goods. This was accompanied by a quantum shift in the scale of distribution, exchange, and consumption and the final triumph of price-setting markets and techniques of cost efficiency. Mercantile elites assumed control within their states, and commercial states soon marginalized their more traditional (and less "modernized") rivals. What has been called the "historical center of gravity" shifted away from its ancient cores. In the nineteenth century sails passed to steam and carts gave way to railroads. All older systems, world, regional, or otherwise, were subsumed as networks merged into a truly global system. That time and place we know as the modern world had finally arrived.

If the divide between the premodern and modern worlds is very real, we must not forget that history is an organic rather than a mechanical process and what exists in history has always come out of what had existed before it. Modern patterns and methodologies of trade have their origins in the exchange of seashells and obsidian and later in the Sumerian maritime link with Dilmun and Melukha and the old Assyrian overland route to Kanesh. If modern tankers carry petroleum rather than olive oil and textiles now tend to be exported from peripheries to cores rather than vice versa, these are variations and adaptations developed from an existing theme. And just as the Silk Road, the Incense Road, and the Trans-Saharan went the way of the Amber Route, the Kra portage, and the Jade Road, so will modern systems evolve into new forms. While scientists mapping the human genome may never isolate the gene for commerce, the driving force to trade will continue to lie deep in the human psyche.

Select bibliography in English

Primary sources

Ammianus Marcellinus (1985) *The Later Roman Empire (A.D. 354–378)*, trans. J.C. Rolfe, Cambridge, MA: Harvard University Press.
Breasted, James Henry (ed. and trans.) (1906–7) *Ancient Records of Egypt, Historical Documents*, 5 vols., Chicago: University of Chicago Press.
Burstein, Stanley M. (ed. and trans.) (1989) *Agatharchides of Cnidus: On the Erythraean Sea*, London: Hakluyt Society.
Casson, Lionel (1989) *The Periplus Maris Erythraei: Text with Introduction, Translation, and Commentary*, Princeton: Princeton University Press.
Claudius Ptolemy (1991) *The Geography*, trans. Edward Luther Stevenson, New York: Dover.
Diodorus Siculus (1933–67) *Library of History*, 12 vols., trans. C.H. Oldfather, Cambridge, MA: Harvard University Press.
Herodotus (1998) *The Histories*, trans. Robin Waterfield, Oxford: Oxford University Press.
Hulsewé, A.F.P. (1979) *China in Central Asia, The Early Stage: 125 B.C.–A.D. 23: An Annotated Translation of Chapters 61 and 96 of the History of the Former Han Dynasty*, Leiden: E.J. Brill.
Julius Caesar (1982) *The Conquest of Gaul*, trans. S.A. Handford, New York: Penguin Books.
Kautilya (1992) *The Arthashastra*, ed. and trans. L.N. Rangarajan, New Delhi: Penguin Books India.
Kramer, S.N. (1952) *Enmerkar and the Lord of Aratta*, Philadelphia: University Museum.
Leslie, D.D. and Gardiner, K.H.J. (1996) *The Roman Empire in Chinese Sources*, Rome: Bardi.
Pliny (Gaius Plinius Secundus) (1938) *Natural History*, 10 vols., trans. H. Rackham, Cambridge, MA: Harvard University Press.
Strabo (1917) *Geography*, 8 vols., trans. Horace Leonard Jones, Cambridge, MA: Harvard University Press.
Tacitus (1973) *Agricola and Germania*, trans. H. Mattingly, rev. S.A. Handford, New York: Penguin Books.
Waley, Arthur (1955) "The Heavenly Horses of Ferghana: a new view," *History Today*, 5: 95–103.
Watson, Burton (1961) *Records of the Grand Historian of China translated from the Shih chi of Ssu-ma Ch'ien*, 2 vols., New York: Columbia University Press.

Secondary sources

Adams, Robert McC. (1974) "Anthropological Perspectives on Ancient Trade," *Current Anthropology*, 15(3): 239–58.

Algaze, Guillermo (1993) *The Uruk World System*, Chicago: University of Chicago Press.
Anderson, J.L. (1991) *Explaining Long-Term Economic Change*, Cambridge: Cambridge University Press.
Appadurai, Arjun (ed.) (1986) *The Social Life of Things: Commodities in Cultural Perspective*, Cambridge: Cambridge University Press.
Aubet, Maria Eugenia (1993) *The Phoenicians and the West: Politics, Colonies and Trade*, trans. Mary Turton, Cambridge: Cambridge University Press.
Bass, George (1987) "Oldest Known Shipwreck Reveals Splendors of the Bronze Age," *National Geographic*, 172(6): 693–734.
——, Pulak, C., Collon, D., and Weinstein, J. (1989) "The Bronze Age Shipwreck at Ulu Burun: 1986 Campaign," *American Journal of Archaeology*, 93: 1–29.
Beagon, Mary (1992) *Roman Nature: The Thought of Pliny the Elder*, Oxford: Oxford University Press.
Beaujard, Philippe (2005) "The Indian Ocean in Eurasian and African World-Systems before the Sixteenth Century," *Journal of World History*, 16(4): 411–65.
Begley, Vimala and De Puma, Richard Daniel (eds) (1992) *Rome and India: The Ancient Sea Trade*, Oxford: Oxford University Press.
Bellwood, Peter (1997) *Prehistory of the Indo–Malaysian Archipelago*, rev. edn, Honolulu: University of Hawaii Press.
Bentley, Jerry H. (1993) *Old World Encounters: Cross Cultural Contacts and Exchanges in Pre-Modern Times*, New York: Oxford University Press.
Boardman, John (1964) *The Greeks Overseas*, Baltimore: Penguin Books.
Boussac, M.F. and Salles, Jean-Francois (eds) (1995) *Athens, Aden, Arikamedu: Essays on the Interrelations between India, Arabia and the Eastern Mediterranean*, New Delhi: Manohar.
Bradbury, Louise (1988) "Reflections on Travelling to 'Gods Land' and Punt in the Middle Kingdom," *Journal of the American Research Center in Egypt*, 25: 127–56.
Burstein, Stanley (ed.) (1998) *Ancient African Civilizations: Kush and Axum*, Princeton: Markus Wiener.
Cappers, Rene T.J. (2003) "Exotic Imports of the Roman Empire: An Exploratory Study of Potential Vegetal Products from Asia" in Katharina Neumann, Ann Butler, and Stefanie Kahlheber (eds) *Food, Fuel and Fields: Progress in African Archaeobotany*, Cologne: Heinrich Barth Institut.
Casson, Lionel (1994) *Ships and Seafaring in Ancient Times*, Austin: University of Texas Press.
Castleden, Rodney (1993) *Minoans: Life in Bronze Age Crete*, London: Routledge.
Chakrabarti, Dilip K. (1990) *The External Trade of the Indus Civilisation*, New Delhi: Munshiram Manoharlal.
Chaliand, Gerard (2004) *Nomadic Empires: From Mongolia to the Danube*, trans. A.M. Berrett, New Brunswick: Transaction.
Chaniotis, Angleos (ed.) (1999) *From Minoan Farmers to Roman Traders*, Stuttgart: Franz Steiner.
Chase-Dunn, Christopher and Anderson, Eugene N. (eds) (2004) *The Historical Evolution of World Systems*, New York: Palgrave Macmillan.
Chattopadhyaya, Brajadulal (ed.) (1987) *Essays in Ancient Indian Economic History*, New Delhi: Munshiram Manoharlal.
Chaudhuri, K.N. (1991) *Asia Before Europe: Economy and Civilisation of the Indian Ocean from the Rise of Islam to 1750*, Cambridge: Cambridge University Press.
Christian, David (2000) "Silk Roads or Steppe Roads? The Silk Roads in World History," *Journal of World History*, 21(1): 1–25.

—— and Benjamin, Craig (eds) (1998) *Silk Road Studies II: Worlds of the Silk Roads: Ancient and Modern*, Turnhout: Brepols.

Clarke, Katherine (1999) *Between Geography and History: Hellenistic Constructions of the Roman World*, Oxford: Clarendon Press.

Cline, Eric H. (1994) *Sailing the Wine-Dark Sea: International Trade and the Late Bronze Age Aegean*, Oxford: Tempus Reparatum.

Crawford, Harriet (1991) *Sumer and the Sumerians*, Cambridge: Cambridge University Press.

Curtin, Philip D. (1984) *Cross-Cultural Trade in World History*, Cambridge: Cambridge University Press.

Davies, Glyn (2002) *A History of Money: From Ancient Times to the Present Day*, 3rd edn, Cardiff: University of Wales Press.

Davies, W. Vivian and Schofield, Louise (eds) (1995) *Egypt, the Aegean and the Levant: Interconnections in the Second Millennium B.C.*, London: British Museum Press.

Denemark, Robert A., Friedman, J., Gills, B.K., and Modelski, G. (eds) (2000) *World System History: The Social Science of Long Term Change*, London: Routledge.

Dercksen, Jan Gerrit (1996) *The Old Assyrian Copper Trade in Anatolia*, Leiden: Nederlands Instit voor het Nabije Oosten.

DeRomanis, F. and Tchernia, A. (eds) (1997) *Crossings: Early Mediterranean Contacts with India*, New Delhi: Manohar.

Derow, Peter and Parker, Peter (eds) (2003) *Herodotus and His World*, Oxford: Oxford University Press.

Di Cosmo, Nicola. (1994) "Ancient Inner Asian Nomads: Their Economic Basis and its Significance in Chinese History," *Journal of Asian Studies*, 53(4): 1092–1126.

Dickinson, Oliver (1994) *The Aegean Bronze Age*, Cambridge: Cambridge University Press.

Dixon, J.E., Cann, J.R., and Renfrew, Colin (1968) "Obsidian and the Origins of Trade," *Scientific American*, 218(3): 38–46.

Dueck, Daniela (2000) *Strabo of Amasia: A Greek Man of Letters in Augustan Rome*, London: Routledge.

Earle, Timothy K. and Ericson, Jonathon E. (eds) (1977) *Exchange Systems in Prehistory*, New York: Academic Press.

Easton, D.F., Hawkins, J.D., Sherratt, A.G., and Sherratt, E.S. (2002) "Troy in Recent Perspective," *Anatolian Studies*, 52: 75–109.

Ericson, Jonathan E. and Timothy K. Earle (eds) (1982) *Contexts for Prehistoric Exchange*, New York: Academic Press.

Fattovich, Rodolfo (1993) "Punt: The Archaeological Perspective" in *Sesto congresso internazionale de egittologia*, 2: 399–405, Gian Maria Zaccone and Tomaso Ricardi di Netro (eds), Torino: Italgas.

Finley, M.I. (1965) *The World of Odysseus*, 2nd edn, New York: Penguin Books.

Franck, Irene and Brownstone, David M. (1986) *The Silk Road: A History*, New York: Facts on File.

Frank, Andre Gunder (1996) "The Centrality of Central Asia," *Bulletin of Concerned Asian Scholars*, 24(2): 50–74.

—— and Gills, Barry K. (eds) (1993) *The World System: Five Hundred Years or Five Thousand?*, London: Routledge.

—— and Thompson, William R. (2005) "Afro–Eurasian Bronze Age Economic Expansion and Contraction Revisited," *Journal of World History*, 16(2): 115–72.

Gilbert, Erik and Reynolds, Jonathan (2006) *Trading Tastes: Commodity and Culture Exchange to 1750*, Upper Saddle River: Pearson/Prentice Hall.

Gill, Sandrine (1999) "Mahasthangarh: A Riverine Port in Ancient Bengal," 154–72, in Himanshu Prabha Ray (ed.) (1999) *Archaeology of Seafaring: The Indian Ocean in the Ancient Period*, Delhi: Pragati.

Gould, John (2000) *Herodotus*, New York: St. Martin's.

Harding, A.F. (1984) *The Mycenaeans and Europe*, London: Academic Press.

Harmatta, Janos (ed.) (1999) *History of Civilizations of Central Asia: The Development of Sedentary and Nomadic Civilizations 700 B.C. to A.D. 250*, vol. 2, Delphi: Motilal Banarsidass.

Heichelheim, Fritz M. (1958) *An Ancient Economic History*, 3 vols., trans. Joyce Stevens, Leiden: A.W. Sijthoff's Uitgeversmaatschappij.

Herrmann, Georgina (1968) "Lapis Lazuli: The Early Phases of its Trade," *Iraq*, 30: 21–57.

Higham, Charles (2001) *The Civilization of Angkor*, London: Phoenix.

Hutterer, Karl (1977) *Economic Exchange and Social Interaction in Southeast Asia: Perspectives from Prehistory, History, and Ethnography*, Ann Arbor: University of Michigan Press.

Jablonka, Peter and Rose, C. Brian (2004) "Late Bronze Age Troy: A Response to Frank Kolb," *American Journal of Archaeology*, 108: 615–30.

Johnstone, Paul (1980) *The Sea-craft of Prehistory*, London: Routledge.

Kardulias, Nick (ed.) (1999) *World-Systems Theory in Practice: Leadership, Production and Exchange*, Lantham: Rowman and Littlefield.

Kenoyer, Jonathan Mark (1998) *Ancient Cities of the Indus Valley Civilization*, Oxford: Oxford University Press.

Kindleberger, Charles P. (1962) *Foreign Trade and the National Economy*, New Haven: Yale University Press.

Kipp, Rita Smith and Schortman, Edward M. (1989) "The Political Impact of Trade in Chiefdoms," *American Anthropologist*, 91: 370–85.

Kitchen, Kenneth Anderson (1971) "Punt and How to Get There," *Orientalia*, 40 (new series): 184–207.

Kohl, Philip L. (1978) "The Balance of Trade in Southwestern Asia in the Mid-Third Millennium B.C.," *Current Anthropology*, 19(3): 463–92.

Kristiansen, Kristian (1987) "From Stone to Bronze – The Evolution of Social Complexity in Northern Europe, 2300–1200 B.C." in Elizabeth M. Brumfiel and Timothy K. Earle (eds) (1987) *Specialization, Exchange, and Complex Societies*, Cambridge: Cambridge University Press.

LaBianca, Oystein S. and Schum, Sandra (eds) (2004) *Connectivity in Antiquity: Globalization as Long-Term Historical Process*, New York: Continuum.

Liu, Xinru (2001) "Migration and Settlement of the Yuezhi–Kushan: Interaction and Interdependence of Nomadic and Sedentary Societies," *Journal of World History*, 12(2): 261–92.

—— and Shaffer, Lynda Norene (2007) *Connections Across Eurasia: Transportation, Communication, and Cultural Exchange on the Silk Roads*, Boston: McGraw Hill.

Loewe, Michael (1968) *Everyday Life in Early Imperial China during the Han Period 202 BC–AD 220*, New York: Dorset.

—— and Shaughnessy, Edward L. (eds) (1999) *The Cambridge History of Ancient China: From the Origins of Civilization to 221 B.C.*, Cambridge: Cambridge University Press.

Mark, Samuel (1997) *From Egypt to Mesopotamia: A Study of Predynastic Trade Routes*, College Station, TX: Texas A & M University Press.

Markoe, Glenn (2000) *Phoenicians*, Berkeley: University of California Press.

Milisauskas, Sarunas and Kruk, Janusz (1989) "Neolithic Economy in Central Europe," *Journal of World Prehistory*, 3(4): 403–46.

Miller, J. I. (1998) *The Spice Trade of the Roman Empire*, Oxford: Clarendon Press.

Muckelroy, K. (1981) "Middle Bronze Age Trade between Britain and Europe: A Maritime Perspective," *Proceedings of the Prehistoric Society*, 47: 275–97.

Nelson, Sarah M. (ed.) (1995) *The Archaeology of Northeast China: Beyond the Great Wall*, New York: Routledge.

Oppenheim, A.L. (1954) "The Seafaring Merchants of Ur," *Journal of the American Oriental Society*, 74(1): 6–17.

Ormerod, Henry A. (1997) *Piracy in the Ancient World: An Essay in Mediterranean History*, Baltimore: The Johns Hopkins University Press.

Page, Denys (1966) *History and the Homeric Iliad*, Berkeley: University of California Press.

Pollock, Susan (1992) "Bureaucrats and Managers, Peasants and Pastoralists, Imperialists and Traders: Research on the Uruk and Jemdet Nasr Periods in Mesopotamia," *Journal of World Prehistory*, 6(3): 297–336.

Polanyi, K., Arensberg, C., and Pearson, H.W. (eds) (1957) *Trade and Market in the Early Empires*, Glencoe, IL: Free Press.

Possehl, G.L. (ed.) (1993) *Harappan Civilization: A Recent Perspective*, 2nd edn, New Delhi: Oxford University Press.

Postgate, J.N. (1992) *Early Mesopotamia: Society and Economy at the Dawn of History*, London: Routledge.

Potts, Timothy (1994) *Mesopotamia and the East: An Archaeological and Historical Study of Foreign Relations c. 3400–2000 B.C.*, Oxford: Oxbow Books.

Ratnagar, Shereen (1981) *Encounters: The Westerly Trade of the Harappa Civilization*, Oxford: Oxford University Press.

Ray, Himanshu Prabha (1987–88) "Early Trade in the Bay of Bengal," *Indian Historical Review*, 14(1–2): 79–89.

——(1994) "The Western Indian Ocean and the Early Maritime Links of the India Subcontinent," *The Indian Economic and Social History Review*, 31(1): 65–88.

——and Salles, Jean-Francois (ed.) (1996) *Tradition and Archaeology: Early Maritime Contacts in the Indian Ocean*, New Delhi: Manohar.

Raychaudhuri, Tapan and Habib, Irfan (eds) (1982) *The Cambridge Economic History of India*, vol. 1, Cambridge: Cambridge University Press.

Reade, Julian (ed.) (1996) *The Indian Ocean in Antiquity*, London: Kegan Paul International.

Renfrew, Colin, Dixon, J.E., and Cann, J.R. (1966) "Obsidian and Early Cultural Contact in the Near East," *Proceedings of the Prehistoric Society*, 32: 30–72.

——and Shennan, Stephen (eds) (1982) *Ranking, Resource and Exchange: Aspects of the Archaeology of Early European Society*, Cambridge: Cambridge University Press.

Rowlands, Michael, Larsen, Mogens, and Kristiansen, Kristian (eds) (1987) *Centre and Periphery in the Ancient World*, Cambridge: Cambridge University Press.

Sabloff, Jeremy A. and Lamberg-Karlovsky, C.C. (eds) (1975) *Ancient Civilization and Trade*, Albuquerque: University of New Mexico Press.

Saggs, H.W.F. (1989) *Civilization Before Greece and Rome*, New Haven: Yale University Press.

Scarre, Chris and Healy, Frances (eds) (1993) *Trade and Exchange in Prehistoric Europe*, Oxford: Oxbow Books.

Seaman, Gary (ed.) (1990) *Ecology and Empire: Nomads in the Cultural Evolution of the Old World*, vol. 1, Los Angeles: Ethnographics/USC.

Shaffer, Lynda Norene (1996) *Maritime Southeast Asia to 1500*, Armonk, NY: M.E. Sharpe.

Sidebotham, Steven E. (1986) *Roman Economic Policy in the Erythra Thalassa* Leiden: E.J. Brill.

Sinor, Denis (ed.) (1990) *Cambridge History of Early Inner Asia*, Cambridge: Cambridge University Press.

Soren, David, Khader, Aicha ben Abed ben, and Slim, Hedi (1990) *Carthage: Uncovering the Mysteries and Splendors of Ancient Tunisia*, New York: Simon and Schuster.
Stech, Tamara and Pigott, Vincent C. (1986) "The Metals Trade in Southwest Asia in the Third Millennium B.C.," *Iraq*, 48: 39–64.
Stein, Gil J. (1999) *Rethinking World Systems: Diasporas, Colonies, and Interaction in Uruk Mesopotamia*, Tucson: University of Arizona Press.
—— and Rothman, Mitchell S. (eds) (1994) *Chiefdoms and Early States in the Near East: The Organizational Dynamics of Complexity*, Madison, WI: Prehistoric Press.
Tandy, David W. (1997) *Warriors into Traders: The Power of the Market in Early Greece*, Berkeley: University of California Press.
Tarling, Nicholas (ed.) (1992) *Cambridge History of Southeast Asia From Early Times to c. 1800*, vol. 1, Cambridge: Cambridge University Press.
Tarn, W.W. (1952) *Hellenistic Civilization*, 3rd edn, Cleveland: The World Publishing Company.
Taylor, Keith Weller (1983) *The Birth of Vietnam*, Berkeley: University of California Press.
Thapar, Romila (2002) *Early India: From the Origins to AD 1300*, Berkeley: University of California Press.
Torrence, Robin (1986) *Production and Exchange of Stone Tools: Prehistoric Obsidian in the Aegean*, Cambridge: Cambridge University Press.
Trigger, B.G., Kemp, B.J., O'Connor, D., and Lloyd, A.B. (1983) *Ancient Egypt: A Social History*, Cambridge: Cambridge University Press.
Van Seters, John (1980) "What is Trade: The Nature of Egyptian Trade in the Eastern Mediterranean During the Second Millennium B.C.," *Archaeology News*, 8: 137–39.
Veenhof, K.R. (1972) *Aspects of Old Assyrian Trade and its Terminology*, Leiden: E.J. Brill.
Wallerstein, Immanuel (1974) *The Modern World System*, New York: Academic Press.
Warmington, E. H. (1974 reprint) *The Commerce Between the Roman Empire and India*, Richmond, UK: Curzon Press.
Watson, Burton (1958) *Ssu-ma Ch'ien: Grand Historian of China*, New York: Columbia University Press.
Weiks, Robert S. (1992) *Money, Markets and Trade in Early Southeast Asia*, Ithaca: Cornell University Press.
White, Randall (1982) "Rethinking the Middle/Upper Paleolithic Transition," *Current Anthropology*, 23(2): 169–92.
Whitfield, Susan (1999) *Life Along the Silk Road*, Berkeley: University of California Press.
Wills, John E. Jr. (1994) *Mountain of Fame: Portraits in Chinese History*, Princeton: Princeton University Press.
Wolters, O.W. (1967) *Early Indonesian Commerce: A Study in the Origins of Srivijaya*, Ithaca, NY: Cornell University Press.
Wood, Frances (2002) *The Silk Road: Two Thousand Years in the Heart of Asia*, Berkeley: University of California Press.
Yamauchi, Edwin M. (2007) "Historic Homer: Did it Happen?," *Biblical Archaeology Review*, 33(2): 29–37.
Ying-shih Yu (1967) *Trade and Expansion in Han China: A Study in the Structure of Sino-barbarian Economic Relations*, Berkeley: University of California Press.
Zagarell, Allen (1986) "Trade, Women, Class, and Society in Ancient Western Asia," *Current Anthropology*, 27(5): 415–30.

Index

Abbasid dynasty 138
Achaeans *see* Troy and Trojan War
Achilles 62
Adam's Bridge 108
Aden, Gulf of 46, 102, 104
Adulis (Massawa) 99, 104
Aegean Sea 54, 84; amber 22; Hellespont 59; Levant and Egypt 55; obsidian 20; Roman Empire 79, 81
Aestil 22
Afghanistan 34, 41, 58, 75, 123, 127; gold source 97; lapis lazuli source 37, 134; tin source 25, 30
Africa: Central 75, 138–39; circumnavigated 50; East 9, 28, 46, 86–90, 93, 96, 102–4, 107, 112, 140; Indian Ocean 84–85; interior 6, 19, 40, 42, 99, 103; North 75,77; on Ptolemy's map 110; Roman trade 99, West 138–39, 141
Agamemnon 60
agate 37, 95, 106, 114–15
Agatharchides 10, 91, 93, 95, 99–100
Akkadian Empire 28, 33, 39–40
alcoholic beverages 122, 124, 128; *see also* wine, beer
Alexander the Great 67, 73, 86
Alexandria 10–11, 76, 89; rise of 67, 73–74; glass exports 78, 95; Indian Ocean 99, 107–8
Algeria 14, 138
Al-Mina 68
aloeswood 115–16
Altai Mountains 126
amazonite 34
amber 19, 54, 61, 136, 143; Baltic source 21–22; demand for 23, 58, 82
Americas 141
amethyst 42, 57, 115
Ammianus Marcellinus 121

Anatolia (Turkey) 7, 40, 41, 55, 75; Catal Huyuk 15; metals source 19, 25–26, 28, 30, 68; obsidian source 20; pirates 79; Troy 59–60, 62
Antoninus Pius 115
aphanite 16
Arabia and Arabs 63, 84, 86–87, 89–90; cinnamon 92–93, wine 91, 95; linen import 95; copper import 96; coast 100, 104; Incense Road 100–101
Aratta 38–39
archaeology 7–8, 12
archives *see* written sources
Argippaei 126
Arimaspians 126
Aristeas 126–27
Armenia 75; obsidian 20; metals source 68
aromatics 25, 90; China import 117; India export 106; nard 93; Somali coast source 103; woods 87
Artemidorus 10
Arthashastra 52, 95–96
Arctic 126
Asia 59, 78, 85, 99–100, 106, 121, 142
Assam 122–23
Assyria and Assyrians: Assur 30–31, Dilmun 36; Old Assyrian-Cappadocian system 29–31, 143; Phoenicians 64, 66; maritime trade 87
Athens 53, 74, 91; Black Sea trade 71; grain trade 72
Atlantic: Phoenicians and Carthaginians 65–66; Roman Empire 76; core of new system 141
Augustus 89, 97, 102
Awdaghust 138
axes 14–17, 54
Axum and Axumites 75, 99–100; *see also* Ethiopia
Azania 103–4

Bab el-Mandeb 46, 87, 99, 102, 107
Babylonia 31–32; Neo-Babylonian Empire 66–67, 87; royal exchange 48–49; textile production 30; tortoise shell imports 94
Bactria 123, 130–31, 134–35
Badakhshan 37, 39
Baghdad 138
Bahrain 20, 32
Bakare 107
balance of trade deficit 96–98, 136
Balearic Islands 65
Bali 110, 113
Baltic Sea and region 75; amber 21–22; Aegean link 58
Ban Gu 11–12, 136; Ferghana expedition 132; Han Wudi 124; Southeast Asian luxury goods 117; Xiongnu and Yuezhi 127; Zhang Qian's journey 130, 134
Banda Sea and Islands *see* Spice Islands
Barbaricum 105–6, 128
Bargysoi 108
barter 3, 60, 111, 137
Barygaza 94–95, 105–7, 128
bdellium 93, 106
beads *see* jewelry and personal decoration
beer 43, 119
Belgium 69
Bengal, Bay and region 85, 94, 107–8, 113, 118, 123
benzoin 115, 118
Berber merchants 138–39
Berenice Trogodytica 99, 104
bird feathers 111, 116–17 *see also* ostrich products
Black Death 139
Black Sea 75, 84, 111; grain export 72, 77; Greek settlement 71, 126; Roman Empire 76, 81; Troy 59–62
border markets 125, 128
Borneo 112, 118
Bosporus 61–62
Britain 16, 75; amber 21–23; Himilco's expedition 66; maritime route 69; Roman Empire 81
bronze 7, 17, 21; Dongson culture 112; Harappans 34; Phoenician-Assyrian 64; Roman Empire 78, 81; Troy 59–60
Bronze Age 6, 17–19, 57–58, 60, 79; amber trade 21, 23; end of 58–59, 62–63; palaces 21; ships 62
bulk and mass-produced or consumed goods 72, 77, 84, 94, 137, 140

Burma 92, 110, 113, 123
Burushanda 28
Buhen 43
Byblos 46–47, 63
Byzantine Empire 118, 138

Caesar, Julius 80–82
Cambodia 113–15, 120
camphor 110, 115–16, 118
camels 41, 140; China import 122, 134; Incense Road 101; on Nile to Red Sea track 99; Sahara 138
Canaanites 46–48, 54, 63; *see also* Phoenicians; Levant
Canary Islands 66
Canton (Guangzhou) 118
capitalism 5, 141–42
cardamom 110, 116
carnelian 34, 37, 116; Egypt export 57; Egypt import 40; India source 95, 106, 115; Nubia source 42; Sumer import 39
carpets and rugs 47; Carthage export 66; China import 134; nomadic pastoralists 125; Roman Empire 78
Carpathian Mountains 20, 61
Carthage 53; decline and destruction of 73–74; founding and rise of 65–67; rebuilt 76
Caspian Sea 111
cassia *see* cinnamon and cassia
caste system 85
Catal Huyuk 15
cattle and oxen 15, 43, 60, 78, 100, 122
Caucasus Mountains 25, 61
Central Asia 6, 28, 32, 75, 85, 125, 128–29; China 123, 125, 128–29, 131, 133, 138; decline 139; goods pass through 94, 134–35; medicines and drugs 90; Serica 111
central place trade 38
Ceylon (Sri Lanka) 75, 85–86, 92–94, 107–8
Chad, Lake 138
Champa and the Chams 113, 116–17, 120
cheese 47, 77
Chelonophagi 99
China 6, 75, 84, 90, 111, 119–20; cassia production 92; government attitude toward trade 124; India 116–17; image of merchants 51, 123–24; isolation 121; Ming and Qing periods 141–42; nomadic pastoralists 125, 127; opening

to west 130–34; 136; silk 94; Song, Yuan, and early Ming periods 140; Southeast Asia 113, 115, 117–18; Tang period 138; tribute system 117, 140; Zhou period 52, 123
Chryse 108–10; *see also* Southeast Asia
cinnabar 121
cinnamon and cassia 10, 92–93, 95, 111, 119; Champa export 116; Cinnamon Road 86, 93, 103; Somali coast 103; Punt 45
civet 139
Claudius 107
Claudius Ptolemy, 11; Issedones 127; monsoons 88; Rhapta and East African coast 103; Southeast Asia 110–11
clothing 78, 104, 125–26
cloves 85, 115, 117, 119
coins and currency: China 123; Greece 71; India 97; India import 106–8; Roman Empire 78, 81, 97–98; Southeast Asia import 115–16
Colaeus 65, 71
colonies and colonists 53; Chinese 133; on Dioscarides 104; Greek 68–69, 71, 79; Indian 90; Minoan 57; Phoenician 65; Sumerian 26, 41
Columbus, Christopher 140–41
commodities 1–3, 7, 26, 72, 90, 114, 124
Comorin, Cape 108
Confucianism and Confucianists 123, 140–41
Congo River 66
copper and copperware 3, 7, 17, 21, 25; Arabia import 104; Axum import 100; China 121–22; Cyprus source 47; Dilmun 32–33; Egypt 40, 43; Harappans 34; India import 106–7; Magan source 33, 35; Old Assyrian-Cappadocian system 29–30; Southeast Asia 111–12, 115; taxes on 36; Uluburun cargo 54–55
coral 95–96, 106, 111, 134, 136
core-periphery concept *see* World Systems
Corinth 71, 74, 76
Coromandel Coast 85, 107–8
cosmetics 8, 64, 71, 93–94, 96
costus 93, 96, 106
cotton 34, 90, 94, 100, 106–8, 115, 140
Crete 20–21, 55, 61; Minoan civilization 56–57
Cyprus 46–47, 55, 57, 61, 65, 67

Damascus 101
Danubian River and valley 61, 71, 75–76, 81
Darius I 50–51, 87
dates 4, 25, 33, 47, 78, 90–91, 104
Daxia *see* Bactria
Deccan 94–95, 106
Delos 22, 78–79
Denmark 18, 21–22, 69
Dilmun (Bahrain) and Dilmunites 32–33, 35–36, 39, 94, 143
Diodorus Siculus: British tin 69; wine for slaves trade 80
diorite 33, 42
Dioscarides (Socotra) 104
directional trade 15, 20, 22, 25, 38, 55, 58, 137
Dongson culture 112
donkeys 36, 38, 92, 140; China 122, 134; Egypt 40, 43, 45; India 106; lapis lazuli 37; Old Assyrian-Cappadocian system 30, 33
Dorians 58
down-the-line systems 15, 20–22, 38, 111
drugs *see* medicines and drugs
dyes 68, 95, 104, 122; *see also* murex

ebony 43, 45, 63, 95, 116
Egypt and Egyptians 6, 9, 19, 38, 40–46, 92; Axum 100; Babylon 48; decline 51; Greeks 71–72; Indian Ocean 84, 104; Levant 41, 46–48, 63–64; obsidian 20–21; Ptolemaic dynasty 10, 51, 73, 87–89, 95, 99; Red Sea 85; Roman Empire 77; Sea Peoples 58; Sumer 41–42; Twenty-sixth Dynasty 50, 71; Uluburun shipwreck 55
Elba 28, 41
elephants 33, 78, 117
Enlil 28
Enmerkar and the Lord of Aratta 38
Eratosthenes 107
Eritrea: obsidian 40; Punt 44
Erythreaean Sea *see Periplus*; Red Sea
Ethiopia: iron import 96; obsidian 19–20
Etruria and Etruscans 23, 68–69, 71, 79
Euboea 68, 71
Eudaimon Arabia (Aden) 100
Eudoxus of Cyzicus 87–88
Europe 6, 28, 59, 62, 85, 100; amber 22; Bronze Age 18; Central 21–22, 60, 71, 114; coasts 66; as manufacturing center

142; northern 16, 21, 69, 114, 120; obsidian 20–21;
exchange 1–3, 6, 137; Bronze Age 18; detecting the process of 9; Neolithic period 14–15; Paleolithic period 13–14; social act 4
Ezana 100
Ezekiel 63
Ezion-geber 49–50

faience 42–43, 54, 56, 61, 71
Far-Side Barbaria 102–4
Ferghana 130–34
Finland 21
fish 8, 48; Black Sea 71; Ichthyophagi 99, 104; Roman Empire 77–78; *see also* garum
flint 16, 19, 37
foods and foodstuffs 8, 47, 49, 63, 140; China 122; Indian Ocean 90, 103, 140; Roman Empire 77, 82; Sumer export 25
Formalism 4, 6
France 16, 66, 69, 78; *see also* Gaul
frankincense 45, 90, 93, 95–96, 101–4, 106, 117
Funan 114–15, 117–18, 120
furs 69, 71, 78, 106, 122, 126, 134
Fur Road 122

Gades (Cadiz) 65
Ganfu 130–31
Ganges River and delta 85, 94, 106–8, 116, 122–23
Gansu Corridor 122, 127–28, 130, 133
Gaozong 128
garum 76–77, 108
Gaul 69, 75, 77, 79–82
Gazirat Zabarjad 95
Gebbanites 101
gems, precious and semi-precious stones 29, 87; Ceylon source 107; China import 122; Egypt export 43, 71; Egypt import 41; India export 106; peridot 95, 106; Phoenician 47, 63; Sumer import 33; Southeast Asia 111, 115; *see also* lapis lazuli
Germany 75, 135; amber 22–23; Roman Empire 81–82
Gibraltar, Straits of 65–66, 69
gift giving and exchange 1–2, 26, 48, 50, 68, 137; China 117, 131; Homeric Greece 67; India 107; Mycenaeans 57–58; and political power 16–18, 81–82
glass and glassware 8, 47, 61; Alexandria export 95; Greece import 68; India import 106–7; inekku stones 55; Mediterranean export 78, 100; Rhapta import 103; Roman Empire export 81, 107, 115; Southeast Asia 111–12, 115
gold 8, 17; Arabia 100, 104; Axum export 100; Black Sea source 59, 71; China import 122, 132, 136; East Africa source 103; Egypt 41–42, 45, 48; Funan import 115; India 97; Old Assyrian-Cappadocian system 30–32; Ophir source 49; Phoenician-Assyrian system 64; Siberia source 126; Southeast Asia source 110–11, 113; Troy 59; Uluburun shipwreck 55; West Africa source 139
grain 8, 69, 73, 103; Arabia 104; Black Sea 59, 71; Carthage 65; China 124, 128; Egypt 42, 74; Greek colonies 68; nomadic pastoralists 125; Roman Empire 76–77, 83; Sumer 25, 32, 35, 38; wheat and barley 24
Great Wall of China 128
grave goods and tombs 7, 126, 134–35; amber 21; European Iron Age 69; Greek Dark Ages 67; lapis lazuli 37–38; Shang burials 122; Southeast Asia 111; weaponry 58
Greece and Greeks 20, 67; Classical period 72; Dark Ages 67; Egypt 50; Hellenistic period 73–74; Homeric period 52, 61, 67; Indian Ocean 84, 89; Mycenaean Period 21, 23, 49, 57–62, 67; olive oil export 71–72, 74; Roman Empire 78; Scythians 126; wine 95
Guardafui, Cape 46; *see also* Promontory of Spices
Gujarat peninsula 85

Habuba Kabira 26, 43
Hallstatt culture 135
Han dynasty 11, 117–18, 123–24, 128, 130–33, 135
Hanno 66
Han Shu chronicle *see* Ban Gu
Han Wudi 124, 130–35
Harappan civilization and Harappans 33–35, 39, 85, 86, 114; collapse of 36; *see also* Melukha
Harkhuf 43–44

Hatshepsut 45–46
Hector 62
Heger 1 type drums 112 *see also* Dongson culture
Hellespont (Dardanelles) 59, 61–62
hemp 122, 135
Herodotus 10, 22, 32, 50, 111; cinnamon 92; Colaeus 65; Eurasian steppe peoples 126–27, 135; frankincense 91; gold in India 97; gold in Siberia 126; silent trade for gold 66
hides and skins 4, 8, 16, 60; Africa export 139; Black Sea export 71, 126; China 121–22; Egypt import 43, 45; northern Europe export 69, 78, 82
Himalaya Mountains 92–93, 107, 122
Himilco 66
Himyarite kingdom 100
Hindu Kush Mountains 34, 38, 127
Hippalos 87
Hippocrates 91
hippopotamus teeth 54, 61
Hiram 49
Hittite Empire 31, 49, 58; Trojan War 60, 62
hoards 7, 37
Homer 60
honey: Black Sea export 71; Canaanite export 47; Egypt export 43; for medicinal purposes 91
horses 3, 17, 48; Arabia 104; Black Sea 71; China import 121–22, 124, 126, 134; Egypt 74; Han Wudi 131–33; India 90, 132; nomadic pastoralists 125; Roman Empire 78; Sumatra 116; Troy 61
Hungary 18, 20, 125
Huns 133
Hyperboreans 22, 127

Iathrib (Medina) 101
Iceland 69
Ichthyophagi 99, 104
Ili River and valley 127, 130–32
Iliad 59–61
imports and exports 3, 17, 24–25; Egypt 41; Greece 68, 72; India 35, 95; Roman Empire 77
Inanna 38
incense 43, 55, 90, 96, 115, 117
Incense Road 100–102, 138, 143
India 6, 9, 23, 28, 46, 58, 125; center of maritime zone 120, 140; China 116–17, 125; east coast rise 118; as economic powerhouse 85; gold production and import 97; Gupta Empire 138; horses import 132; India Beyond the Ganges 110–11; ivory export 93; as manufacturing center 142; between Mauryan and Gupta empires 52; Melukha 33, 36, 143; monsoons 88, 104; northern ports 105; pearls export 94; pepper export 91–92; Roman Empire 90; Southeast Asia 112–15; ship construction 85–86; silk 95; tin import 96; wine and aromatics imports 102
Indian Ocean 6, 9–10, 19, 32, 75, 84–85, 100; Chinese treasure fleets in 140; Dutch and English in 142; lapis exports from 38–39; Portuguese in 141–42; Ptolemy's map 110; Roman Empire 89, 93, 95; shells from 15; textiles 94
indigo 94, 106
Indonesia 85, 112, 114, 120
Indus River and delta 33–34, 85, 94, 106, 128, 134
industrialization 142
Iran 25–26, 30, 40, 71; bronze 34; lapis lazuli 38; obsidian 20; *see also* Persia and Persians
Ireland 16, 75; Himilco's expedition 66; maritime route 69
iron 21, 60; Axum import 100; China 122, 124; for gold 100; Greece 68, 71; India 95–96; Phoenician-Assyrian 64; Roman Empire 78, 96; Southeast Asia 111–12
Iron Age 58, 69, 111, 123
Irtjet 43
Isaiah 63
Israel: ancient 50; modern 14
Issedones 126–27, 131
Issyk Kul 127, 130
Italy 16, 18; amber 22; obsidian 20; Roman Empire 75, 78; wine 80, 95
ivory 48, 57, 63, 139; Axum export 100; Egypt 71; furniture inlaid 42, 69; India export 34, 106–7; Nubia export 40, 43; Punt export 45; Rhapta export 103; Southeast Asia 110–11, 116; Sumer import 33, 39; Syria export 47; Uluburun shipwreck 54; walrus 126

jade 34, 115, 121–22, 124, 134
Jade Gate 122, 132–33

Jade Road 122, 127, 134–35, 143
Java 110, 116–20
Jehosaphat 50
Jesus 91
jewelry and personal decoration 3; Axum import 100; Bronze Age 17, 21–22; Egypt export 47, 57; Greek and Etruscan 69; Harappans 34; lapis lazuli 37; Mesopotamia 25; Paleolithic period 14; Phoenician 64; Roman Empire 78, 81; Southeast Asia 113, 115–16; tortoise shell 94

Kane 104–5
Kanesh 29, 31, 143
Karum 31
Kashmir 93
Kattigata 111
Kazakhstan 127
Kerala 92, 95
Khuan Lukpad 116
Kingdom of Woman 121
Kirradai 108
kola nuts 139
Koptos 99
Kra, Isthmus of 114, 118–20, 143
Kunlun Mountains 122, 131
Kush 43, 71, 75
Kushan Empire and Kushans 94–95, 106, 116, 118, 128, 135
Kyrgyzstan 127

lacquer and lacquerware 116, 122, 124
Laodicea 95
lapis lazuli 37–39, 49, 134, 136; Egypt import 48; India re-export 34, 95, 106
latifundias 77, 79, 81
Latvia 21
lead 96, 106
leather products 25, 35, 82
Lebanon 41, 46; wood source 25, 28; *see also* Canaanite; Levant; Phoenician
Lemnos 60
letters of credit 73
Levant 57, 61, 63; Egypt 41, 46; Greece 67–68; Indian Ocean 84, 89
linen 94–95, 100, 106
Lipari 20
livestock 63, 122
Lixus 65
Loire River 69, 76
Lu Buwei 123

Luoyang 109–10

Maadi 40
mace 115, 119
Madagascar 86, 93, 103
Madeira 66
Magan (Oman) 33, 35–36, 96
Magellan, Ferdinand 141
Magnus Sinus 111
Malabar Coast 85, 107–8
malabathrum 92, 108, 122
Malacca Straits 84, 111, 118–19
Malay Peninsula and Malays 84, 110, 112, 116, 118; aloeswood source 115; cassia 93; gold source 113; Isthmus of Kra 114; monsoon sailors 86; tin source 96; tortoise shell source 122
Maldive Islands 93
Manchuria 111
Marcus Aurelius 109–10
marble: Greece 78; Southeast Asia 111; Troy 59
Mari 28, 41
maritime law 78
market and the market system 2, 4, 26, 69, 81; forces 67; price setting 142
Massilia (Marseilles) 68–69, 74, 79–80, 89
meats 69, 77–78, 80
medicine and drugs 3, 8, 56, 90; camphor used in 115; China import 117; cinnamon used in 92; Egypt export 87; Greeks sought 68, 71; nard used in 93; nomadic pastoralists import 125; storax used in 96; turtle egg shell used in 94
Mediterranean Sea and basin 6, 11, 32, 120, 125; amber 21, 63, 73, 84; eastern 10, 54, 59, 67, 69, 71, 88, 118; Egypt 40; India imports 95; Roman Empire 76, 79; shells 15; silk 135; western 64–65, 68
Mekong River and delta 115, 120
Melos 20–21
Melukha 33, 36, 143
Mentuhotep III 45
Mesopotamia 6–7, 19, 134; China 131; civilization in 24–26; copper import 33; decline 139; Egypt comparison 40; hub of trade system 28, 32
Messina, Straits of 68
metals 3, 8, 17–18, 57, 96, 137–38; Akkadian policy 29; China import 122; Egypt import 74; Greeks sought 68;

Indian Ocean 90; nomadic pastoralists 125; Phoenicians 63–64, 72; Roman Empire 78, 83; Sardinia source 59; Southeast Asia 114; Spain source 55; Sumer deficient in 25; Troy emporium for 61
metics 72
middlemen 25, 34, 84, 104, 107, 131; Arab 87, 92, 102; Dilmunites 32, 36; Greeks 69, 71; Indian 95; and misinformation 9; Nubians 44; Phoenicians 72; Roman Empire 77, 81
Minimalists 61–62
Minoans 56–57, 67; *see also* Crete
Mohenjo-Daro 33, 35
Moluccas Islands *see* Spice Islands
moneylending and banking: Greece 72–73; Old Assyrian-Cappadocian system 30–31; Roman Empire 79
Mongol Empire 139
Mongolia 6, 111, 125, 127, 130, 134
monsoons 86–88, 104, 107, 114–15
Morocco 14, 65–66, 138
Moses 91
Mozambique 103
Mu 121
murex 47, 65, 95
Musiris 107–8
musk 121
Muza 102, 104
Mycenaeans 57–62, 64–65, 67; *see also* Greece and Greeks
Myos Hormos 90, 99
myrrh 45, 90, 93, 95–96, 102–4, 115, 117

Nabataeans 101–2
Naples, Bay of 68, 76
Naran-Sin *see* Akkadian Empire
nard (spikenard) 93, 95–96, 106–8
Narmada River and valley 34, 85, 105–6
Natufians 19
Naucratis 71, 73 *see also* Egypt and Egyptians
Neanderthal 13
Nearchus 105
Necho II 50, 66
Nefertiti 55
Neleynda 107
Neolithic period 14–15, 19, 79, 85; amber 21; obsidian 20; Proto-Silk Road 134; societies 17
New Guinea 112

Niger River 75
Nile River and valley 6, 19, 40, 42, 99, 100
nomadic pastoralists 125–26, 135, 139
Norway 69
Nubia 38, 40, 42–44, 58, 75, 80
nutmeg 115, 117, 119

obsidian 15, 19–21, 37, 40, 56, 59, 143
Oc Eo 115, 120
ocher 14, 33, 45
Odyssey 60, 67
Olbia 71
olive oil 3, 11, 25, 40, 47,108; Greece 71–72, 74, Massilia 69; Minoan 56; Mycenaean 58; Phoenician 64; Pliny on 11; Roman Empire 76, 78–80, 83
Onesicritus 85, 107
Ophir 49–50
opium 56
Ordos region 134
orpiment 54
ostrich products: eggshell 54, 57, 61; feathers 139
Oxus River and valley 34, 39, 127

Pakistan 33
Palembang 119
Paleolithic period 13–14, 20
Palestine 40–41
Palmorala 20
Pamir Mountains 34, 132
papyrus 8, 47, 49, 57, 71, 85
Parthian Empire 75, 88, 118
partnerships 77
Pausanias 136
pearls: Ceylon source 94, 107; China import 136; India source 94, 107–8; Persian Gulf source 32, 94, 104
peddlers and peddling 15, 31, 77, 124
pentekontors 67
pepper and peppercorns 85, 95, 115, 140; black 107; Java export 119; long 106; Roman Empire import 91–92, 96; Southeast Asia export 117; West Africa malaguette export 139
perfume 36, 41, 43, 47, 56; Carthage export 66; China import 136; cinnamon 92; civet 139; Corinth 71; Egypt export 87; Funan 115; Indian Ocean 90; nard 93; Phoenician 64
peridot 95, 106

Periplus Maris Erythraei 9; Adulis 99; Arabian coast 100; Bay of Bengal 108; copper 96; East African coast 103; gold 97; Indian coast 105; Indian vessels 86; malabathrum 122; money 97; monsoon discovery 87; Muza 104; Seres 111; Somali coast 102; Southeast Asia 110; Thina 109
Persia and Persians 125, 135; China 131, 133; gold 97; Indian Ocean 90; Phoenicians 67; silk 138
Persian Gulf 6, 19; China 117, 140; copper source 25; corridor to Indian Ocean 84, 87; Red Sea competition 44, 104; Sumerians 32–34
Petra 101–2
Petronius 76
Philippines 112–13
Philistines 58
Phoenicians 46, 61, 63; Assyrian Empire 64, 66; circumnavigated Africa 50; decline 66, 71; Egypt 50, 66, 71; Neo-Babylonian Empire 67; Persian Empire 67; at Pithekoussai 68; in western Mediterranean 64–65; *see also* Canaanites
Pithekoussai Island 68
piracy and pirates 1, 78, 86, 141; Arab 85, 100; Bronze Age collapse 58; Cham 116; Delos slave market 79; Indian 107; Mycenaean 57; Red Sea 87; Sumatra 119; Vietnamese 117
Pliny the Elder 10–11, 19, 95; amber 23; balance of payments problem 97; cinnamon 93; cloves 119; frankincense 101; Hanno and Himilco 66; India 85–86; Indian Ocean 107; indigo 94; lapis lazuli 39; nard 93; monsoons 88; Nile-Suez Canal 50–51; olive oil 11; pearls 94; pepper 92; Persian Gulf 32; Phoenicians 63–65; Red Sea shipping 90; Seres 111, 136; wine 80
Poduca (Arikamedu) 108, 113, 116
Poland 16, 20, 22
Polanyi, Karl 4, 6–7
pomegranates 54
Pompey 79–80
porcelain 138, 140
porcellanite 16
Portugal: Himilco's expedition 66; in Indian Ocean 141–42
Poseidonius 87

pottery 3, 7–8; Chinese 117; Egyptian 40; Greek 71; Minoan 56; Mycenaean 57–58; Poduca 108, 113; Roman Empire 77, 79; Troy 59, 61
precious stones *see* gems
predatory activities 1, 60, 100, 116, 125, 141; *see also* piracy and pirates
prestige items or goods 17–18, 21, 24, 38, 106; chains of 69
price 3–4, 26, 31
profit and profit-making 2–5, 18–29, 69, 137; *Arthashastra* on 96; Canaanite 48; China 124; Classical Greece 72; Confucius on 123; Homeric Greece 67; Indians in Southeast Asia 113; obsidian 19; Roman Empire 77; Sumer 28
Promontory of Spices 102–4; *see also* Guardafui, Cape
Proto-Silk Road 134–35
Ptolemies *see* Egypt and Egyptians
Ptolemy (geographer) *see* Claudius Ptolemy
Punic Wars 74
Punt 44–46, 50
Purushapura 106
Pytheas 69

Qatar 20
Queen Mother of the West 121
Qin dynasty 123, 135
Qin Shihuangdi 123, 128

Ramses II 50, 85
Ramses III 46, 58
realgar 96, 106
reciprocity 1–2, 14–15, 18, 67, 111, 137
Red River 112
Red Sea 6, 9, 20, 140, 142; corridor to Indian Ocean 84, 87; Egypt 44, 46, 85; navigating 99; ports on 99, 102; Roman Empire 75–76, 89, 118; Solomon-Hiram expeditions 49
relay trade 25, 122, 126, 134, 138
resins 56, 106, 113, 117; bdellium 93; benzoin 115; frankincense and myrrh 90–91; storax 96; terebinth 54–55
Rhapta 103–4
Rhine River 76, 80
rhinoceros horn 93, 100, 103, 110–11, 116–17
Rhodes 73–74, 78
Rhone River 69, 76
rice 90, 103–4, 114, 119, 140

Richthofen, Baron Ferdinand von 135
robbery *see* predatory activities
Roman Empire and Romans 10, 74–83,
   118; Arabia 102; Ceylon 107; China
   109, 131, 136; Indian Ocean 88–90, 93,
   96–97, 99; Kushan Empire 128;
   Southeast Asia 111, 113, 119
rubies 95, 107, 115
Russia 71, 75, 80, 126

Saba and Sabaeans 100–101
Sahara Desert 75, 138–39
Sahura 45
salt 8, 16, 100, 116, 121, 124, 139
sandals 47, 57
sandalwood 95, 115
Sangara 86
Saone River 69
sapphires 37, 95
Sarane 100
Sardinia: metals 55, 66; Mycenaeans 58;
   obsidian 20; Phoenician inscriptions on
   65
Sargon *see* Akkadian Empire
Sassanian Empire 118
Sasu 100
scarabs 42, 57
Scotland 16
Scythia and Scythians 110, 126–27; *see also*
   Shakas
seals 7, 34–35, 37, 41, 54, 57, 115, 134
Seine River 69, 76
Seneca the Elder 136
Senegal River 66
Serica and the Seres 111, 121, 127, 136
sericulture *see* silk
Sesatai 122–23
Shahr-i-Sokhta 38–39, 134
Shakas 106, 128; *see also* Scythia and
   Scythians
Shang dynasty 122
Shanxi 134
Sheba (Saba), Queen of 49–50, 63
sheep 78, 80, 122, 133
shells 15, 17, 40, 85, 111, 117, 122, 143;
   see also tortoise shell
Shengdu 123, 131
Sheshonq 50
Shetland Islands 69
ship and boat construction 137; Chinese
   140; Egyptian 41, 47–48; European 69,
   141; Greek 67; Hellenistic period 73;
   Indian Ocean 85–86, 89; Mesopotamian
   32; Phoenician 63; Rhodes 78
shipwrecks 8, 75–76, 84, 87; *see also*
   Uluburun shipwreck
Shizi 121
Shortughai 39
Siberia 6, 75, 111, 126; fur source 106,
   122; gold source 97, 113, 122
Sichuan 122–23
Sicily 20–21, 68; Carthage wars 66; Greeks
   72, 74; Mycenaeans 58; Phoenicians 65;
   Roman Empire 77–78; wine 80
Sidon 46, 63–64
Sierra Leone 66
Silesia 20
silk 77, 94–95, 128, 131; Bactria 134; as
   China's most important export 122, 124;
   India 106–8; Roman Empire 136;
   sericulture 135, 138; Southeast Asia 113,
   115, 117
Silk Road 118, 120, 129, 136, 143; and
   Incense Road 101; maritime version 113,
   115, 118, 139; under Mongol Empire
   139; name 135; opening of 134–35
silver 8, 25, 35, 41, 46, 49, 71; Americas
   141; Arabian coast 104; China 122, 136,
   141; Funan 115; Old Assyrian-
   Cappadocian system 29–31; Phoenicians
   64–65; Roman Empire 78, 81, 98; Troy
   59–60; Uluburun shipwreck 55
Sima Qian 11–12, 124, 135; frontier trade
   122; Great Wall 128; Lu Buwei 123;
   Xiongnu and Yuezhi 127, 130–31
Sinae 110–11
Sinai 40
skins *see* hides
slaves 8, 47, 60–61, 69; Arabia 91; Black
   Sea export 59, 71; Champa source 116;
   Dioscarides import 104; India import 106;
   Phoenicians 63, 65; Roman Empire 79–82;
   Scythians export 126; Somali coast export
   103; West Africa export 139
Slovakia 20
Sogdiana 134
Solomon 49–50
Song dynasty 117
Somalia 44, 90–91, 93, 96, 102
South Africa 14
South China Sea 84–85, 111–12, 114, 116,
   121
Southeast Asia 6, 11, 46, 75, 118, 140;
   Africa 84; China 113, 115, 117–18;

Chryse 108, 110; Cinnamon Road 103; early commerce 111–12; India 112–13; ivory and rhinoceros horn source93; Malays 86; Roman Empire 113; sandalwood source 95; Srivijaya dominated 120; state building 114
Southwest Asia 14; under Abbasids 138; Black Death 139; Bronze Age collapse 59; interior of 64, 68; obsidian 20; trade network spanning 42
Spain 16, 55, 63, 65–66, 69; Roman Empire 75–77
Spice Islands 85, 119
spices 8, 36, 56, 63, 87, 140, 142; China import 117; India export 106; Roman Empire import 77, 89–90, 91–92; Southeast Asia export 113
Srivijaya 53, 119–20
Strabo 10–11; Arabia 102; Ceylon 107; East Africa 103; Egyptian desert crossing 99; Gaul 80; India 85, 108; Indian gold and silver mines 97; Laodicean wine 95; Nile-Suez Canal 50; peridot 95; Petra 101–2; Phoenicians 65; realgar 96; Red Sea ships 89–90; Scythians 126
storax 91, 96, 106
Substantivism 4, 6
Sudan 44, 71
Suebi 80, 82
Suez, Gulf of 45; canal connecting with Nile 50–51
Sulawesi 113
sulfide of antimony 96, 106
Sumatra 90, 110, 112–13, 115–19
Sumer and Sumerians 19, 24–25; lapis lazuli 38–39; Persian Gulf-Indian Ocean 32–33, 35–36, 85
Sunda: chain of islands 110, 112; Straits 116, 118
supply and demand 2–5, 17, 26, 28, 31, 93
Sweden 16, 18
Syria 7, 15, 25, 38, 40, 71, 75; Al Mina 68; Egypt 41; Habula Kabira 26; Laodicean wine 95; Sumer 25

Tacitus 22
Tadmekka 138
Taklamakan Desert 132–33
Talaud Islands 113
Tana Tradition 103
Tamils 107
Tamralipti (Tamluk) 108, 116

Tang dynasty 138–39
Tanzania 103
Tarim Basin 122, 133
Tarshish *see* Tartessia
Tartessia 65–66, 69, 71
taxes, tariffs, customs, duties 51–52, 84; *Arthashastra* on 96; China 124, 135, 140; Egypt 71, 74, 87; frankincense 101; Funan 115; India 106; Mesopotamia 28; nomadic pastoralists 126; Nubian states 44; Old Assyrian-Cappadocian system 31; Persian Gulf 36; Roman Empire 76, 82, 89, 92, 98; Srivijaya 119
teak 86, 95
Tepe Hissar 38–39
textiles 4, 8, 137; Arabia import 95; Axum import 100; Bronze Age wool 17; Canaanite 47; Egypt export 43, 48, 71; India 34, 94, 106, 142; Indian Ocean 90, 140; Mesopotamia export 25, 29–30, 35; Minoan export 56; Phoenician 65; Roman Empire 77–78, 83; Troy export 61; West Africa import 138
Thailand 96, 111, 113, 116–17
Thina 109, 123
Thrace 59
Thule 69
Tiberius 98
Tibet 34, 122
timber 8, 41, 78, 140; Black Sea export 71; Canaanite-Phoenician export 47, 49; Egypt import 74; Minoan export 56
Timbuktu 138
Timor 110, 115
tin 4, 7, 25, 34; Afghan-Troy 60; Britain and Brittany export 69; China import 122; Old Assyrian-Cappadocian system 29–30; Roman export 96, 106–7; Southeast Asia 111, 114–16; Tin Islands 66; Uluburun shipwreck 54
tombs *see* grave goods
tortoise shell 94, 122; Axum export 100; Ceylon export 107; Dioscarides export 104; Rhapta export 103; Southeast Asia export 110, 116; on Uluburun shipwreck 54
trade: commercial based on market principles 2–4, 15; Canaanites 48; Egypt 41, 48; obsidian 19; rise of political power 17, 81; Sumer 26
traders, professional 16, 19, 26–27, 48, 58, 72, 137; China 51–52, 124; India 106;

relationship with authorities 51; Roman Empire 76; Scythian gold 126; Southeast Asia 111, 113
trade states 53, 119, 140
tramping 55, 67, 103
Trans-Saharan 138–39, 143
Trans-Sudanic 138
trickle trade 15, 38, 40–41, 137–38
Tripoli 138
Troy and Trojan War 59–62
Turkmenistan 34
turquoise 37, 40, 95, 106
Turret-Grave people 101
Tyre 46, 63–64, 66–67

Ubaid culture 7
Ugarit 46–47, 57–58, 63, 68
Ukraine 21
Uluburun shipwreck 8, 22, 54–55, 61
unguents 8, 56, 64, 71, 90, 92, 106
Ur 29, 32, 35
Ural Mountains 61, 126
Uruk 24, 26, 38
Uzbekistan 34, 127, 133–34

Vasco da Gama 141
Veneti 69
Vespasian 98
Vietnam and Vietnamese 112, 114–17
Visigoths 92
votive offerings 8, 15, 69

Wadi Hammamat 42, 45
Wallerstein, Immanuel 5, 7
Wangara 138–39
war: impact on trade 52–53; 74, 106
weapons and weaponry 25, 47, 60, 69, 126, 128; Bronze Age 17; Egypt export 45; India export 95; Minoan export 57; Mycenaean export 58; Neolithic period 16; Rhapta import 103
Wen-Amun 48
wild animals 78
Wilusa *see* Troy and Trojan War
wine 3, 25, 60; Arabia export 91, 95, 102; Arabia import 104; Carthage export 66; East Africa import 103; Egypt export 43; Egypt import 40; Greece export 71–72, 74, 126; India import 95–96, 106–7; Massilia export 69; Minoan export 56; Mycenaean export 58; Phoenician export 47, 64; Roman Empire 76–80, 83
women in trade 112
wood 8, 90, 95, 113; African blackwood 54; Canaanite-Phoenician 46–47; China 122; Egypt 40, 45; Harappans 34; Persian Gulf 32, 36, 87; Sumer 25; *see also* timber
wool 29, 63–64, 94, 122
World Systems 5–6, 137, 142
written sources 8–12
Wusun 127, 130–32

Xinjiang 111, 122, 127, 134
Xiongnu 127–29,130–31, 133–35

yaks 121
Yam 43–44
Yavanas 86, 89, 107–8
Yemen 40, 49, 87, 100
Yuezhi 127–28,130–31
Yunnan 112, 123

Zakarbaal 48
Zambezi River and valley 103
Zhang Qian 130–32, 134–35
Zheng He 140
Zhiayang 116
Zhou dynasty 122–23

eBooks – at www.eBookstore.tandf.co.uk

A library at your fingertips!

eBooks are electronic versions of printed books. You can store them on your PC/laptop or browse them online.

They have advantages for anyone needing rapid access to a wide variety of published, copyright information.

eBooks can help your research by enabling you to bookmark chapters, annotate text and use instant searches to find specific words or phrases. Several eBook files would fit on even a small laptop or PDA.

NEW: Save money by eSubscribing: cheap, online access to any eBook for as long as you need it.

Annual subscription packages

We now offer special low-cost bulk subscriptions to packages of eBooks in certain subject areas. These are available to libraries or to individuals.

For more information please contact webmaster.ebooks@tandf.co.uk

We're continually developing the eBook concept, so keep up to date by visiting the website.

www.eBookstore.tandf.co.uk